THE CHRISTIAN PHILOSOPHY
OF HERMAN DOOYEWEERD

VOLUME I

The Transcendental Critique
of Theoretical Thought

© Dr David Hansen

Pierre Charles Marcel (1910-1992)

The Christian Philosophy
of Herman Dooyeweerd

Volume I

THE TRANSCENDENTAL CRITIQUE
OF THEORETICAL THOUGHT

Prolegomena to the
Philosophy of the Law-Idea
of Herman Dooyeweerd

*Thesis presented to the Faculté libre
de Théologie protestante at Montpellier
23 June 1956*

PIERRE MARCEL

Translated and edited by Colin Wright

WordBridge
PUBLISHING
εν αρχη ην ο λογος
AALTEN, THE NETHERLANDS

This book has been typeset exclusively in Monotype Bembo® Book, the main body of the text being set in 12pt, apart from Hebrew and Greek text which is typeset in Antioch Vusillus®.

"The origins of Bembo® go back to one of the most famous printers of the Italian Renaissance, Aldus Manutius. In 1496, he used a new roman typeface to print the book *de Aetna*, a travelogue by the popular writer Pietro Bembo. This type was designed by Francesco Griffo, a prolific punchcutter who was one of the first to depart from the heavier pen-drawn look of humanist calligraphy to develop the more stylized look we associate with roman types today. In 1929, Stanley Morison and the design staff at the Monotype Corporation used Griffo's roman as the model for a revival type design named Bembo. They made a number of changes to the fifteenth-century letters to make the font more adaptable to machine composition. The italic is based on letters cut by the Renaissance scribe Giovanni Tagliente."
    – quoted with kind permission, from Linotype's website.

First printed edition   2013

French original: ©2013, Editions Kerygma, Aix-en-Provence, France.
English translation: ©2013, Colin Wright, Cwmafan, Wales.

ISBN-13 : 978-90-76660-32-5

Editor's Preface
to the English edition

The publication of Pierre Marcel's theses on the Christian philosophy of Herman Dooyeweerd is long overdue.

Marcel's original theses were typewritten, and I have had access only to poorly photocopied versions. For this reason it was impossible to scan them on a computer, and they have had to be completely re-typed. However, in the process a number of grammatical as well as typing errors have been corrected. No changes have been made to the text itself other than those listed below:

a. Marcel used various methods for emphasising his point. Sometimes he put a word in capitals; at other times he used underlining; occasionally he used letter-spacing. Why Marcel should have used the latter is a mystery: it is not French, and only really works with the now-defunct *Fraktur* or *Gothic* text of Germany. In a typewritten document it is very difficult to make out, and I was often unsure whether the text had been emphasised this way. In one or two places I have left words in capitals as I found them, but everything I felt was letter-spaced or underlined is now set in italics.

b. Marcel supplied very limited indexes to his theses, no more than a list of authors quoted. I have attempted to add something a little more substantial but, as this work will also be published in digital form, a comprehensive index would be unnecessary. I have also added separate indices for words and phrases in the text that were in Greek, German, Latin or Dutch.

c. Because the originals were typewritten, Marcel was unable to print Greek words in the Greek alphabet. There are about thirty instances in the first thesis and Marcel trans-literated all of them into roman text. Although I have not removed every instance of transliteration – popular today but mystifying to me – I have added the Greek word in each case.

d. Marcel cites a number of Dutch works and lists them in a bibliography at the end of this thesis. Most, if not all, were written before 1948. In that year a major revision of Dutch spelling was undertaken and many of the titles listed would be spelt quite differently now. However, I decided to preserve the older spelling so that the reader would the more readily be able to find the books if he so chose. Apart from the original material, I have added an English translation to most of the contents of the bibliography. I have not attempted to bring it up-to-date. There is now a much larger literature on the subjects discussed in this thesis, especially from the reformational school that is sympathetic to Dooyeweerd, and it would be impractical to include it all. Besides it would no longer indicate what Marcel was working with when he undertook this project.

e. In a *very* small number of places I have made a silent "correction" to Marcel's text, but only where it was patently obvious that this was required. A great man deserves no less. As the proverb says: *Even Atlas slept*.

Footnotes and References.

I have sought to correct and enlarge these where possible. Many lack sufficient information to determine the publisher, edition, year of publication, etc., without a great deal of labour on the reader's part. All my own comments are placed within square brackets. Direct quotes, where possible, have been verified against the editions Marcel used. I have made no attempt to relate them to later editions. Where possible I have given the quotation in its original language in the footnotes in square brackets. I have also drawn attention in a number places where an English translation is now available.

Terminological Issues.

In the *De Wijsbegeerte der Wetsidee* Dooyeweerd used the German word *Gegenstand* as a technical term, having a special meaning in his philosophy. It was used in the same way in the

English translation: *A New Critique of Theoretical Thought*. However, in note 7, chapter 2, of this edition, Marcel explains why he does not use this term but prefers the word "object" in double-quotes. Even though I believe that this was a bad decision on Marcel's part, I have retained what he wrote. To remind the reader of this usage, I have often put the word *Gegenstand* in brackets or in a footnote.

However, for all that, Marcel never refers to the Gegenstand-relation as the *"object"-relation*, except in three instances (§6, §93, §166) in the second (1960) thesis (second volume of this edition. Generally Marcel uses the expression *antithetic relation* or *theoretical antithetic relation*. This finds some support in Dooyeweerd, who does use the expression *antithetic Gegenstand-relation* at times.

Acknowledgements.

I could not have undertaken this task without the support and help of numerous friends and scholars. Perhaps I should acknowledge here also that without Google and the vast array of literature to which its search engine has access the task would have been impossible. To my good friend Jean-Marc Berthoud of Lausanne I owe a special debt of thanks for introducing me to Marcel in the first place, for providing me with copies of Marcel's theses, and for generous encouragement at all stages of the project. No less gratitude is due to Professor Paul Wells, Dean of Faculté Jean Calvin (formerly La Faculté Libre de Théologie Réformée) at Aix-en-Provence, whom I have plagued with emails about various questions on the text of Marcel's theses, and to which he responded with patience, grace and invaluable information; without his input this project would probably not have seen the light of day. The internet also enabled me to benefit from the scholarship and advice of Dr Glenn Friesen of Calgary, Canada. Dr Friesen graciously, promptly and helpfully answered all my emails on issues with the German language on questions of law and problems with Dooyeweerd's footnotes. The standards he sets for Christian scholarship I find truly inspiring and have endeavoured to emulate. Ruben Alvarado, whose *Friedrich*

Julius Stahl translation project sets the standard for all of us, kindly provided unstinting and invaluable help with questions relating to the Dutch and German languages. To Cosette Benoit, graduate of Lausanne University, I owe a debt of gratitude for hours of work trawling Lausanne and Geneva university libraries for important material. I am also hugely indebted to Bernadine McGuire of Neath College for carefully checking and improving whatever I had to write in French, including this preface, numerous footnotes and the glossary. Her advice on this matter has saved me from many an embarrassment, and the book is much the better for it. Needless to say any faults that remain are wholly my own. I must not forget the helpful advice of Dr Henk Geertsema, especially on one very strange word, and thanks go to Prof. Danie Strauss who generously gave me permission to include the Glossary of Terms found among the appendices. Finally, my thanks go to Mieke Powell, a good friend for many years, for giving her time to check and improve my translation from Dutch of all the items in the Bibliography.

Finally, reader, you have before you the fruit of Pierre Marcel's vision of introducing French-speaking Christians to a truly Christian and Reformed philosophy. A busy pastoral ministry and the intervention of a World War could not break his resolve to carry out the commission bestowed upon him by his beloved teacher, Auguste Lecerf. The work was never completed – Marcel had projected other volumes on epistemology and the structures of individuality – but what you do have is a faithful exposition of the *Philosophy of the Law-Idea* from one of France's finest Christian scholars.

Colin Wright
Cwmafan, South Wales
May 2013

Contents

CHAPTER 1 – The Problem of Time.

CHAPTER 2 – The Second Way of a Transcendental Critique of Philosophy.

Part 1. – The dogma of the autonomy of theoretical thought.

Part 2. – The first transcendental problem of theoretical thought. The antithetic relation of theoretical thought and the subject–object relation in naive experience.

Part 3. – The second transcendental problem of theoretical thought. The starting point of the theoretical synthesis.

CHAPTER 3 – The Central Significance of the Transcendental Basic-Idea of Philosophy

CHAPTER 4 – Philosophy and Worldviews

Part 1. — The place of the Philosophy of the Law-Idea in the historical development of philosophy.

Part 2. — The distinction between philosophy and a worldview. The criterion.

Part 3. — The postulate of neutrality and the "theory of worldviews".

CHAPTER 5 – The Antithetic and Synthetic Viewpoints in Christian Philosophical Thought

CHAPTER 6 – General Outline of the Philosophy of the Law-Idea. The Relation between Our Philosophy and the Special Sciences.

Foreword

"He's amazing!" exclaimed Auguste Lecerf. It was March 1934, and we were in the library at his apartment on the rue des Saints-Peres, Paris.

He picked up the first of three enormous volumes bound in green cloth. I couldn't make sense of the title in gold lettering: *Dr H. Dooyeweerd, De Wijsbegeerte der Wetsidee*.[1] Lecerf began to speak enthusiastically of this Professor of Philosophy and History of Law at the Reformed Free University of Amsterdam. He had already persuaded me that as soon as I had completed my degree in theology, I should learn Dutch. This would give me direct access to important Reformed sources that had been published in the Calvinist revival in Holland in the 19th century. These, he claimed, were indispensable for a dogmatic theologian. But now he was developing a new argument and imposing a new obligation on me. I had to go to Holland to get to know the thought of Herman Dooyeweerd. His importance for the future of Calvinistic thought in the world as well as France was impressed upon me.

I must confess that Lecerf's account – even before I knew a single word of Dutch or had read a single page of Dooyeweerd's work – had already filled me with respect and admiration for the author of the *De Wijsbegeerte der Wetsidee*. It filled me with fear too, for Lecerf added with his usual modesty: "I'm too old now (he was 60 at the time) to assimilate Dooye-

---

[1] [Ed.: The Dutch title of Dooyeweerd's magnum opus. The English translation was entitled *A New Critique of Theoretical Thought* (abbrev. to NC), but a more exact translation would be *The Philosophy of the Law-Idea*. Dooyeweerd himself coined the phrase *Philosophy of the Cosmonomic Idea*. Where the original work is referred in this thesis the Dutch title will be used (sometimes abbreviated to WdW), though Marcel often used the French equivalent.]

weerd's thought. It needs a young mind and youthful strength to undertake this work and to draw out the consequences for Calvinist theology. I'm giving you the job."

In vain did I object that I did not at all feel like a philosopher and that it would be risky for me to work on dogmatics and philosophy at the same time. He smiled, but he wouldn't budge. All I could do was obey.

So it was that the *Académie de Paris*, on the recommendation of the *Faculté Libre de Théologie* (Free Faculty of Theology) in Paris, granted me a scholarship to study at the *Institut Français* in Amsterdam, with a view to familiarising myself with the thought of Herman Dooyeweerd and his brother-in-law, D. H. Th. Vollenhoven, Professor of Philosophy at the same university.

Herman Dooyeweerd was born in 1894. His secondary education was at the Amsterdam Reformed School. His higher education was in the Faculty of Law at the Reformed Free University of Amsterdam under the direction of Professors Fabius, A. Anema, and P. A. Diepenhorst. In 1917, at the age of 22, he was granted the degree of Doctor of Law for a thesis on "The Cabinet in Dutch Constitutional Law" *(De Ministerraad in het Nederlandsche Staatsrecht)*[2]. He held various public offices in the government until in 1923 he accepted the post of Assistant-Director at the Abraham Kuyper Institute in The Hague, and started the political review *Antirevolutionaire Staatkunde (Antirevolutionary Politics)*.

On the 15th October, 1926, at 32 years of age, Dooyeweerd was appointed Professor of Philosophy and History of Law at the Reformed Free University of Amsterdam. His inaugural lecture was *The Significance of the Law-Idea for Jurisprudence and the Philosophy of Law*. It marked an important date in the development of Christian philosophy. He was looking for a genuinely Christian foundation in the field of law. He was already tackling very broad philosophical questions, which

---

[2] All untranslated Dutch words are given in their original spelling. In 1948, after much of the literature discussed in this thesis was completed, a major revision of spelling and grammar was instituted. E.g. *Nederlandsche* became *Nederlandse*.

were soon to take shape in the original development of a new philosophy.

To begin with, Dooyeweerd had come under the influence of neo-Kantian philosophy, and later of Husserl's phenomenology. As a committed Christian and Calvinist he sought to develop a synthesis between the Christian faith and philosophy. It was not long however before he made an important discovery that completely changed the whole direction of his thinking and furnished him with the opportunity to write a number of original works. This discovery was that all thought, of whatever kind, took its origin in the religious root of personality. No doubt others before him had had this conviction. But it is to Dooyeweerd that the credit is due for having drawn out all the consequences and for having given them a systematic exposition. His prodigious analytical and systematising spirit, wedded to the service of his intuition, gave birth to a new philosophy, and placed him at once in the front rank of contemporary thinkers.

Immediately, Dooyeweerd understood why every attempt at synthesis between the Christian faith and philosophy, including the one he had tried so hard to develop, had been doomed to failure. Philosophy, in fact, had been founded on faith in the autonomy of human reason and that reason, drawing its inspiration from the religious root of personality, was not in reality autonomous at all. He came to understand the central significance of the "heart", which Scripture affirmed so often to be the religious root of human existence. And from this Christian standpoint, he came to see the necessity of a revolution in philosophical thought.

Both the *natural* and *spiritual* aspects of the temporal cosmos ought of necessity to be referred, conjointly, to the religious root of creation. However, the *natural* aspects of temporal reality had been reduced in Kantian philosophy to mere dependants of the "transcendental subject". At the end of the day, this turned out to be nothing but a theoretical abstraction.

Moreover, judged from a Christian standpoint, the whole approach of any form of philosophical thinking that proclaims the autonomy of its thinking is unacceptable because it withdraws human thinking from the divine revelation in Jesus Christ.

If we take seriously the biblical point of view regarding the root of temporal reality, we have to break *absolutely* with the philosophical conception of reality that is rooted in what Dooyeweerd calls the "immanence standpoint".

The discovery of the *transcendental basic-Idea,* which is found at the root of all philosophical thought, allowed him to demonstrate that the various theoretical views of the structure of reality developed by immanence-philosophy all depended in fact on supra-theoretical aprioris. In this way it was possible to develop a critique of philosophical thought that penetrated to a much deeper level than any supposedly pure theoretical critique could. If even temporal reality is not neutral with respect to its religious root, if in other words, every notion of a static temporal cosmos "in itself" and so independent of the religious root of humanity, rests on a fundamental mistake, how is it possible to believe any longer and with any seriousness in the religious neutrality of theoretical thought?

One of the fundamental principles of the new philosophy, the cosmological principle of *sphere sovereignty,* was suggested to Dooyeweerd by Abraham Kuyper, the famous Dutch thinker and statesman. But this principle could not come to full fruition until the introduction into philosophy of a Christian religious foundation. It is on this principle that the whole *General Theory of the Law Spheres* is founded. It is expounded in Volume II of the *De Wijsbegeerte der Wetsidee.* And it was developed after the discovery of the internal structure of the modal aspects of human experience, already expounded in the inaugural lecture of 1926, as mentioned above.

In the development of his theory Dooyeweerd had to overcome numerous difficulties, not only because it was impossible to find any point of contact with immanence-philosophy, but because his theory could only become fruitful within the cadre of the *special* theory of the law spheres. And this, in the light of the Christian transcendental basic-Idea, studies the fundamental problems of the various special sciences.

In his early publications Dooyeweerd always studied the theory of the law-spheres in relation to his own speciality: law. Above all, he wanted to be sure that this philosophical theory had real value, better yet, a value *in terms of principle*, for special scientific thought, before enlarging on his provisional systematic conclusions.

The theory of the structures of individuality itself, developed in Volume III of the *De Wijsbegeerte der Wetsidee*, had given rise to numerous systematic problems. In his book *The Crisis in the Humanistic Theory of the State* (*De Crisis in de humanistische Staatsleer*) in 1932, Dooyeweerd had not only stressed the importance of this theory for the conception of the structure of naive experience, but had also demonstrated its significance for psychology and law. However, the scope of this theory takes in every science and all the fundamental structures of empirical reality.

In the three volumes of the *De Wijsbegeerte der Wetsidee* (1933 and 1934) we have the first systematic and comprehensive development of the issues at stake.

Even though Dooyeweerd has laid the foundations of this new philosophy and continues to deepen his thought and publish respectable works exploiting his astonishing profundity, he is perfectly aware that the elaboration of this philosophy is only at its beginning. If it is to be developed in a truly scientific manner, it requires the collaboration of scientists and Christian scholars in every area of scientific thought. It must be the business of each of them to draw out the consequences, in their own speciality, of the fundamental ideas of this philosophy. It is, he says, a matter of life and death for this young philosophy.

Herman Dooyeweerd has been particularly grateful for the assistance of his brother-in-law and colleague, D. H. Th. Vollenhoven, whose name – associated with important works he has himself written – is henceforth inextricably linked to his own. In like manner he has recognised the assistance of the

South African psychologist H. J. Stoker, whose publications have made known the movement for Reformed philosophy in a quite independent way in South Africa. Stoker's extremely constructive comments have drawn Dooyeweerd's attention to various points that needed to be addressed.

A quarterly publication (*Philosophia Reformata*) and a Philosophical Society (*Vereniging voor Calvinistische Wijsbegeerte*) now bring together hundreds of teachers, professors and scholars from every scientific discipline. The recent American translation of the *De Wijsbegeerte der Wetsidee* (4 volumes are planned) – *A New Critique of Theoretical Thought* (1953ff) – allows specialists who do not have access to the Dutch text to become acquainted with the essentials of this philosophy and it engages on the international scene an ever-growing audience, even Catholics.

What is even more unusual is that special chairs devoted to the study of Herman Dooyeweerd's philosophy have been created in the universities of Utrecht, Leiden, and Groningen, in the School for Economic Science at Rotterdam and in the Technical School of Delft.

It is by now, then, a very broad movement, and it is high time that we in France began to study this thought. It is fundamental for a genuine reformation of philosophy. Its importance in the development of the various sciences as well as in the philosophy of science must no longer be neglected. I think in particular of my own field – theology – where there is, as far as I know, no task more urgent than that of reforming once more the various *theological* disciplines. Using a radical reflexive critique, we also need to excise from them a raft of pseudo-problems and themes that stem from unbiblical philosophical thought and assumptions that are irreconcilable with a truly biblical and Christian viewpoint, and that have all too often had a pernicious influence on Christian thinking as well as on a general world- and life-view.

This has nothing to do with setting up of a new "system", which would only be subject to all the faults and errors of human thinking. Rather, what is at issue is the *foundation* and the *root* of all scientific thought *as such,* and their relation to a general world-view. This matter concerns not just scientists and scholars, but *all* believers, whatever their level of culture.

Having thus submitted to the discipline imposed on me by August Lecerf's directives, I now set myself the task of making known the essentials of Herman Dooyeweerd's thought to those who know only the French language. I do it with the most profound regard for, and a real fellowship of thought with, my Amsterdam Master. For, insofar as I understand it, I am personally committed to the *Philosophy of the Law-Idea*. For God's glory, I think we must initiate in our Christian circles a battle for the reform of philosophy and science, and that includes some aspects of theology.

I have nevertheless the feeling that the task is beyond the modest talents that God has given me. I am not in the least sensible of either the abilities or the erudition of the leader of a school, let alone those of a philosopher. The War, a pastoral ministry, and various other occupations have not allowed me to devote the necessary time to acquiring either the culture or the style of a philosopher. And more than ever I consider as valid those reservations regarding my competence, which in vain I impressed upon my venerable teachers, August Lecerf and Henri Monnier. My sole ambition is to try and draw the attention of Christian scholars and philosophers to the considerable interest in this new philosophy that is now accessible in all its essentials in an English translation. If God gives me time and strength I want to adapt and publish *De Wijsbegeerte der Wetsidee* in French and, if possible, popularise it with some items accessible to the general public.

It would be a signal mercy if I could be discharged of this burden at the earliest opportunity, and confide it to specialists who – as I have done and in light of the importance of the issue – would engage to learn the Dutch language so that they could gain direct access to sources that are far larger than could ever be translated into French or English. If only a small group of philosophers and scientists would get to work and discover the wonderful horizons that the *De Wijsbegeerte der Wetsidee* opens up to them!

What method should I adopt in my exposition of this new philosophy? More especially, how should I choose the subject of the present thesis? Given the wealth of publications put out by Dooyeweerd and Vollenhoven and, for some years now, by their disciples[3], should I perhaps choose just one subject, one theme, from this philosophy, and develop it in the context of our contemporary French literature? Or should I look into its consequences for the field of theology or dogmatics? However, with the sources virtually unknown due to the absence of any comprehensive exposition even for specialists, such a study would surely have given the impression of an *ex cathedra* statement. In addition, its practical usefulness would be virtually nil. On the other hand, one cannot really isolate a particular theme from this philosophy without already having of a general view of it. So any studies along these lines need to be undertaken at a later date.

Clearly, then, a start needs to be made with a general overview of the *De Wijsbegeerte der Wetsidee*. So initially I conceived the plan of presenting a positive synthesis of the significance of the *transcendental basic-Idea* for philosophy and an overview of the *General Theory of the Law-Spheres*. I planned to omit a large part of the comprehensive investigations Dooyeweerd devoted at each step to exposing the inadequacies and failings of immanence-philosophy, as well as all that is original in his thought as far as the *history* of philosophy is concerned. This was the original plan of the present thesis, as I submitted it in 1953.

However, a new fact arose which forced me to change my plans. The English translation, the first of whose four volumes appeared in 1954, was not a straightforward translation of the original Dutch. Since 1934, Dooyeweerd's thought had not remained static, but had significantly deepened. The English edition contains numerous additions, in particular one of about fifty pages of cardinal importance devoted to *the transcendental critique of theoretical thought*. In the first (Dutch) edition this had not been dealt with in a systematic fashion, but only in relation

---

[3] A bibliography will be found at the end of this volume.

to the Archimedean point of philosophical thought. The presence of this systematic critique had considerably added to the importance of the chapter devoted to "Philosophy and General World-View" to which, in my original plan, I had no intention of making any allusion. The fundamental interest of this critique could not be neglected. This is why I have now had to abandon the exposition of the *General Theory of the Law-Spheres* and devote the whole thesis to what in the original plan was intended to make up only the Introduction and the first three chapters.

Nevertheless, one advantage of this was that the present thesis is now devoted entirely to a single subject, which allowed me to enter into the heart of Herman Dooyeweerd's thinking, and to savour the acuteness of his judgement and the power of his penetration. Leaving aside the second part of Volume I, devoted to "The Development of the Fundamental Antinomy in the Cosmonomic Idea of the Humanist Immanence Philosophy" (which I do not tackle in the present work), we are left with the necessary introduction to the positive exposition of the philosophy of the Law-Idea, which I expect to tackle later. The current thesis is thus conceived as the first volume of a series. That is why I often allude to the sequel as if it were included here.

It remains to determine the form of this work. Herman Dooyeweerd expressed himself in extremely compact Dutch. It is often very difficult and, in keeping with the spirit of the Dutch language, makes excessive use of compounded words. "Who will translate Dooyeweerd for us?" the Dutch themselves often ask wearily. Indeed, though one might say that it's the Dutch that sets the tone, the Amsterdam Master employs Greek terms, Latin terms and German terms (sometimes even French terms) on every page. He never translates them as they act as a means of expression for him. Also, he generally cites his references in foreign languages, especially German – which every educated Dutchman is expected to understand.

By taking the Dutch edition as my text, while taking account of all the additions and changes in the new English edition, I have striven to eliminate all these obstacles and to use the most elegant French possible to express and evaluate his grand thought. It was quite difficult work and not without its risks. I do not think I have been completely successful, and I certainly had many recommendations from a host of specialists for improving the vocabulary. I kept as close as I possibly could to the method of exposition that is common to our French way of thinking. When necessary, I took care to make the reader's task easier by making additions or simplifications. On the other hand, I was anxious to assert Dooyeweerd's own authority as far as possible, and to project my own interpretation a little as possible. These factors determined the style of this Prolegomenon. So, this thesis is not really a translation in the classical sense of the term. Neither is it an "original" work properly speaking – such could only be based on a preliminary exposition of this philosophy.

Two further comments before concluding this prologue. Firstly, I am perfectly aware, as Dooyeweerd was, that because the proposed transcendental critique of theoretical thought seeks to penetrate to the religious ground-motives that decisively influence the thought processes of every thinker, it runs the risk of arousing among our opponents, in particular those with a French background, an emotional reaction. It will be taken by some as a personal insult. I recognise that such expressions may be taken amiss. We should be grateful that Dooyeweerd was aware of this and in the English edition he removed or attenuated the form of some statements and expressions which, in the Dutch edition, at times assumed an unpleasant character, at times even an irritating one, despite the fact he had tried to avoid this danger:

In tracking down a philosophical train of thought to its deepest religious foundations I am in no way attacking my adversaries personally, nor am I exalting myself in an *ex cathedra* style. Such misunderstanding of my intention is very distressing to me. An act of passing judgment on the personal religious condition of an adversary would be a kind of human pride which supposes it can exalt itself to God's judgment seat. I have continually laid emphasis on the fact that the philosophy which I have developed, even in the sharp penetrating criticism which it exercises against non-Christian immanence-philosophy, constantly remains within the domain of principles. I wish to repudiate any self-satisfied scientific attitude in confronting immanence-philosophy. The detailed criticism of the Humanistic immanence-philosophy in the second part of the first volume, must be understood as self-criticism, as a case which the Christian thinker pleads with himself. Unless this fact is understood, the intention of this philosophy has not been comprehended. I should not judge immanence-philosophy so sharply were it not that I myself have gone through it, and have personally experienced its problems. I should not pass such a sharp judgment on the attempts at synthesis between non-Christian philosophy and the Christian truths of faith, had I not lived through the inner tension between the two and personally wrestled through the attempts at synthesis (*A New Critique of Theoretical Thought*, I, p.viii.).

My second comment is of a more formal character. Some readers may be put off by the seemingly complex terminology of this new philosophy. But this first impression should not be allowed to deter the reader from a more profound and fruitful study of this remarkable thought. A popular exposition, which demands only a limited effort, would never lead anyone to a truly philosophical reflection. It could, moreover, only follow, and not precede, the publication of a genuinely scientific work. So, for those who are not specialists in philosophy, I intend to publish as soon as possible a popular introduction, on the lines of J. M. Spier's *Inleiding in de Wijsbegeerte der Wetsidee* published in Holland in 1938. It was recently translated into English as *An Introduction to Christian Philosophy*.

In my opinion, the vocabulary of the *De Wijsbegeerte der Wetsidee* is neither difficult nor complex, and is much clearer it seems to me in its French form. Reading it is no more difficult than reading the various "Critiques" of Kant, no more difficult than the Calvinist reading of Thomist works or vice versa. The difficulty arises from a "way of thinking" quite unlike the one that most traditional philosophical viewpoints have accustomed us to. It arises also from its matchless profundity, for nothing is merely what it appears on the surface. At first glance, it is true, one feels somewhat baffled. But the Christian reader, especially if he is of the Reformed persuasion, who engages with it and increasingly grasps what it is about, soon finds himself much more comfortable than in any system of immanence-philosophy. Not without pain, for sure, for it is also involves *the reform of his own thinking* in the fields of philosophy and science, and he has to continually free himself from the traditional views of reality and epistemology drummed into him throughout his secondary and higher education. Hence, is it not incumbent upon us to think and act christianly in every area of life, life over which Christ himself exercises his Lordship?

There is only one way to become familiar with Herman Dooyeweerd's thought: begin at the beginning, and follow him step by step, straining at every turn to penetrate to the fundamental religious attitude of this whole way of philosophising. Neither time nor pains will be wasted. It is futile to try and glean bits by referring to various parts of it "to see what he says".

However, just as Christian thought cannot isolate itself in a negative attitude towards non-Christian philosophy (and Herman Dooyeweerd is an edifying example) so non-Christian philosophy cannot isolate itself by adopting a contemptuous attitude towards Reformed philosophy.

We are not looking for a rapid and easy victory for this new philosophy. We hope that all the problems which it raises might be taken into account by Christian thinkers especially, and that non-Christian thinkers will understand the importance of the new questions and problems that it poses for them.

As for me, whatever pain and labour it has cost, there is the joy of relishing the happiness and inner peace that accompanies scientific work when it is founded on Christ, the Way, the Truth and the Life.

Pierre Marcel
Saint-Germain-en-Laye
April 1956

Introduction

The First Way of a Transcendental Critique of Theoretical Thought. The Archimedean Point.

1. Philosophical activity.

The word *philosophy* has two distinct meanings. It can signify the *result* of philosophical activity: in this sense, we speak of the philosophy of Plato or Kant. It can also signify *philosophical activity itself,* and it is in this sense that we understand it.

To philosophise is to think *actively* and *scientifically*. When thinking is undertaken in a scientific manner it is *discriminating* and *antithetic*. That is to say, it is set over against its object and, in a sense, *opposed* to it. Scientific thought is thus different from naive thought. The latter is our everyday thought in practical life, and it results in *naive experience.*

When I consider an object, an apple-tree for instance, I can view it in two ways. Firstly, I examine it as a whole, engaging with the object under consideration and fitting myself into the concrete reality that it represents. My thought wanders: I try to estimate its age, to imagine the taste of its fruit, to guess its value or aesthetic quality, etc... My thought runs and flits around uncontrollably from one thing to another. Such is the nature of naive thought in naive experience. However if I want to examine this object in a scientific way I am obliged to make very precise distinctions. In the apple tree I distinguish the various aspects that it presents *by separating them out*. I *isolate* and *disassociate* each of them from the whole that forms the tree. Every science settles on one aspect of reality as its object of study. Scientific thought is thus *discriminating* and *analytical*.

In the apple tree, the mathematician only considers the aspects of number and space; the physicist, that of movement; the biologist, that of organic life. The psychologist studies its sensory objective appearance as it is ordered in our sensory subjective perception. The logician on the other hand regards this tree in terms of an objective relation of logical characteristics that we assemble together subjectively into the concept of a tree. The historian examines it under the aspect of the civilising work of humanity or in relation to some particular event. For the linguist it is an object of designation. To the economist it represents a certain value. The sociologist only studies it as an object that has entered into the social life of mankind. Its beauty and harmony attracts the attention of the aesthetician. The jurist looks on it as an object of law and the moralist as an object of love or hate. Finally, the theologian regards it as an object of faith, believing that this tree is God's creation and that it is not the arbitrary product of blind natural forces.

In the second place, scientific thought is *antithetic* thought. The close relationship that naive experience maintains with life in its totality here gives way to a type of thinking that is located *at a distance* from its object and *opposed* to it. The scientist does not let his thought wander about. He makes sure that he does not unwittingly abandon that aspect of the object he is thinking about in favour of others; it is exclusively to this aspect that he directs his attention. He carries out his examination in a logical and systematic order until he has exhausted his field of study.

2. The internal coherence of the
various aspects of reality.

When we try to give an account of reality in the way it presents itself to pre-theoretical naive experience and as it confronts us in the theoretical *breaking-up* of its various aspects in the sciences, what strikes us is the *indissoluble coherence* of all these aspects, not one of which exists in itself or by itself. What we mean is: this apple tree is not just a quantity of moving stuff. This would be *meaningless*. In some way, each aspect of this tree is related to all the other aspects and maintains an indissoluble coherence with them. The numerical aspect, the spatial aspect, the aspect of physical energy, the organic aspect, the psychical, logical-analytical, historical, social, economic, aesthetic, juridical, moral and faith aspects, all aspects of created reality[1] – whose number and arrangement we will have to justify later – are interdependent, as reliant on each other as the links in a chain. It is as plain as a pikestaff that though the different aspects of this apple tree are not reducible to any of the others, they nevertheless have some sort of correlation among them, since they form a genuine *unity* which presents itself – in the case in question – in the individual form of an apple tree. This is true of all temporal reality, which is composed of numerous aspects and which cannot be enclosed in any particular aspect.

So an *internal coherence*, which we call a *universal coherence*, unites all the various aspects or modalities of reality. None of these aspects exists by itself or for itself; each of them is interwoven in this mutual relation; each of them, within itself and without itself, *points towards* all the others, without which it would be impossible for it to exist. It is only in scientific thought that these various aspects can be separated one from the other and considered as bound to each other.[2]

3. A "totality" is expressed in the universal coherence.

Besides, this *universal coherence* comes to expression in each aspect of our cosmos[3]; it points beyond itself to an extremely profound *totality* that *is expressed* in this coherence. An illustration will help us to clarify this fundamental statement.

The sun's light is refracted through a prism into a spectrum made up of seven bands of colour. Each band is in itself a dependent refraction of white light. None of them can be regarded as the sum of the various colours and none of them exists apart from its coherence with all the others. If the white light is

---

[1] Professor Dooyeweerd is in the habit of prefixing *created, creaturely, temporal* to the word *reality*. This will be the meaning of *reality* when we use it without an adjective, to avoid being cumbersome.

[2] We refrain from any justification of these preliminary statements in this *Introduction*.

[3] *Cosmos*, which we distinguish here from *world*, designates the universe as a well ordered system and, consequently, as a *creation*.

intercepted before being refracted the whole play of colours vanishes into nothing.

In this illustration the non-refracted light represents the *totality* we are considering. Each aspect of reality points towards this totality, since *it is expressed* in the universal coherence of its various aspects and confers *a meaning* on each of them. Just as this light takes its rise from the light source, so the totality of our cosmos takes its rise from an *Origin*, an *Arche* (Ἀρχή), by whom and for whom it was created.

4. Meaning as the mode of being of all creaturely existence.

This simultaneous *expressing* and *pointing* character of reality is universal. It characterises the whole cosmos and the *mode of being* of all reality: it is dependent and non-self-sufficient. In a word, all reality is *meaning*. *Meaning is the being of all created existence, its mode of existence. The root of meaning is religious, and its Origin is divine.*

This idea of *meaning* is absolutely fundamental. It is important that from now on we make its definition clear in Reformed philosophy.

When we say that all that is created *has a meaning*, or rather *is meaning*, we are trying to emphasise the *heteronomy* of all creation. The Scriptures declare: "If God only thought of Himself, if he were to withdraw his Spirit and his breath, every creature would die together and man would return to the dust" (Job 34:14-15)[4]. It is because God is the Author of all things that nothing exists of itself or for itself. *Everything exists in relation to everything else.* Each aspect of cosmic[5] reality points towards the other aspects of this reality, that itself forms a coherent whole. What is created never finds any resting place within itself. The entire cosmos thus points beyond itself, towards its Creator, for God has created everything in relation to Himself. His

---

[4] [It is not clear which French version Marcel is using. The AV (KJV) reads: "If he set his heart upon man, if he gather unto himself his spirit and his breath; all flesh shall perish together, and man shall turn again unto dust."]

[5] The adjective *cosmic* is related to *cosmos* in the sense defined above. It should not be understood in the way it is employed in the natural sciences.

intention was that all his creatures – things, men, social groups – should exist in relation to each other. It is He alone who has conferred *meaning* on all creation. However God, who gives *meaning* to all things, is not himself *meaning*. He is elevated beyond all *meaning*; he alone is *self-sufficient, autonomous,* and exists by and for himself. He alone is God. All that is meaning finds its origin, its purpose, and its end in Him. "I am the First and the Last," says the Lord Jesus Christ, "the Alpha and the Omega, the Beginning and the End" (Revelation 1:8; 21:6; 22:13). God alone is absolute. *The meaning of reality thus presupposes its heteronomy, its relativity. Everything exists in strict relation to everything else, and all things together exist in relation to the Creator and in dependence on him.*

And so each aspect of reality is an *aspect of meaning*[6] of reality. It points towards the other aspects of reality. It is intimately *linked* to reality and *refers* to it. No *aspect* of reality can be grasped by itself without destroying the *very coherence of meaning* of reality and setting up a mere abstraction. It would be to lose sight of the fact that God alone gives things their *meaning* and that he alone is their Origin and End.

Each thing or part of the cosmos *is meaning*, because it is related to the others, because it was created in strict coherence with them, and because it is upheld in its mode of existence by God. Hence it transpires that *the whole cosmos points beyond itself towards the fullness, the totality, of meaning.* And so the quality of *existence* can be attributed only to God, while creation, having only a dependent mode of reality or existence, is only *meaning.* Earlier, when we called meaning the "being" of all that is created, the word "being" designates only the *essence,* which never transcends the limits of meaning.

But now, this human person, this ego, also belongs to this created reality. God created this ego as an expression of his image. As such it participates in every aspect of this reality. It is

---

[6] The author [i.e., Dooyeweerd] indulges in the use of compound words in keeping with the spirit of his language. From here on we will, on the whole, speak of *aspects* of reality, assuming that it is understood that these are aspects of *meaning*. The same applies to a host of other compound words like *coherence of meaning, totality of meaning,* etc.

embedded in it with all its functions, both natural and noetic.[7] In the coherence of all its functions the ego *expresses itself* as a totality in all the aspects of cosmic reality. Man himself is *meaning*. Thus *meaning is also the mode of being of our own personality*.

> 5. The scope, task and definition of philosophy.

Given the above, what is the field of investigation of philosophy, and what is its task? Its field of investigation is *the totality of created reality*, encompassing all its aspects in such a way as to present them as in a strict coherence among themselves. That is, it is the cosmos itself, the fullness of the works of God.

Its task is to provide us with a theoretical vision of a universal coherence, envisaged as a coherence of meaning *pointing towards a totality*. Philosophy seeks to elaborate *a view of totality*. It also tries to project this theoretical view of totality onto our universe and, while never overstepping its limits, attempt to determine how everything is related to the whole.

Philosophical thought is theoretical thought applied to the totality of meaning of our cosmos.[8]

---

[7] By *natural* we mean the numerical, spatial, physical and biotic functions. By *noetic* [Fr. *noologique*] we mean all other functions.

[8] The limits of philosophy can be seen immediately from this definition. Its subject is the totality of meaning of the cosmos. God, celestial matters, the mysteries of the Kingdom are excluded from it. Such a definition sheds new light on the debate that separates Thomists and the Reformed on the question of the legitimacy of philosophy. The terms of the debate are profoundly simplified. Cf E. Gilson, *Christianisme et Philosophie*, J. Vrin, Paris, 1936. [English translation: *Christianity and Philosophy*, trans. Ralph MacDonald, New York, Sheed & Ward, 1939.]
In Calvin's terminology, philosophy concerns "earthly things" and is enclosed in "the limits of the present life". "I call 'earthly things' those which do not pertain to God or his Kingdom, to true justice, or to the blessedness of the future life; but which have their significance and relationship with regard to the present life and are, in a sense, confined within its bounds. I call 'heavenly things' the pure knowledge of God, the nature of true righteousness, and the mysteries of the Heavenly Kingdom. The first class includes government, household management, all mechanical skills and the liberal arts. In the second are the knowledge of God and of his will, and the rule by which we conform our lives to it" (*Institutes*, II, ii, 13). "This spiritual insight consists chiefly in three things: (1) knowing God; (2) knowing his fatherly favour in our behalf, in which our salvation consists; (3) knowing how to frame our life according to the rule of his law (*Institutes*, II, ii, 18)."

This cosmic character of philosophy cannot be misconstrued with impunity. Every question regarding the possibility of a genuine philosophical thought is expressed in these introductory theses.

We shall presently examine certain essential conditions for the existence of true philosophy.

6. The thinking ego and philosophical thought.

Philosophical thought is an actual activity.[9] When I think, it is I who am thinking. This activity of the ego expresses itself not just in my thinking, but in every function through which it expresses itself in our temporal cosmic coherence. My ego functions actually and simultaneously in every aspect of our universe. I myself have an actual function in the numerical sense as being a unity. I have an actual function in space, in the realms of physical energy, organic life, psychic feeling, logical thought, historical development, and language; in my relations with my fellowman, in my economical evaluations, in aesthetic activity or contemplation, in the realms of morals, justice and faith. It is in this whole system of cosmic functions and in relation with other egos that I myself actually exist.

When I think philosophically my entire ego is actually active in this thought. Thought, as such, can only be isolated from this self in an abstract concept and, at the same time, at the cost of its actuality. An actual and total abstraction of the ego that thinks is necessary if we are to form concepts in philosophical *thought*. But that does not prevent this ego from continuing to be actually active in the construction of these concepts.

Calvin's attitude to true philosophy is that "it makes man truly human" and he condemns false philosophy for "contradicting, neglecting or replacing revelation in its claim to reach up to heaven and judge the secret mysteries of the kingdom of God and to steal the knowledge of them by force." Cf. Comm. On I Cor. 1:20; Col. 2:8; Titus 1:2; Mark 1:22; Sermons on Job, Opera Calvini XXXIII, 709-710, etc.

[9] This word and all its derivatives are naturally taken in their primary sense: *that which acts*. Cf. Lalande, *Vocabulaire de la Philosophie*, Meaning A.

So while philosophy has to be directed in its theoretical activity by an *Idea*[10] *of the totality of meaning* in order to correspond to its definition, it is nevertheless impossible without a philosophical reflection on the ego, the human person. Otherwise it would have to abandon from the outset any possibility of taking for its subject the totality of meaning of the universe, *to which our personality belongs*, and which is its true subject.

The philosophical *knowledge* of the self – this *Know thyself* (Γνῶϑι σεαυτόν) – is precisely the *great* problem of philosophy. For in just that instant when it thinks philosophically, the ego transcends necessarily every philosophical concept. The self, as we shall see, is in fact the *concentration point* of all the cosmic functions of my person. It is a subjective *totality* that cannot be reduced to philosophical thought or any other function whatever, or to a group of functions. It is presupposed by them.

7. The reflection of the ego on itself.
The starting point of philosophy.

The fundamental problem of philosophy is thus to discover how a philosophical knowledge of the *self* is possible, since such knowledge must transcend the domain of concepts. It will only be so if our ego – which even in its actual thinking activity transcends the limits of thought – takes back *to itself* its activity of thought. It is not philosophical thought that, in self-reflection, reflects on the self; rather it is the *ego* that, in philosophical thought, reflects on *itself*. This reflecting movement of the activity of thinking necessarily transcends the limits of theoretical thought that, in its subjective actuality, cannot withdraw into itself. Its actualisation springs from the self that transcends it. Apart from the self it can neither be actual nor exist. Hence philosophy must have a fixed point, *a concentration point situated beyond thought*, and from which it is possible when philosophising to scan the totality of meaning and so to arrive at a genuine knowledge of the self.

---

[10] *Idea* is used in a technical sense. It denotes a *limiting-concept* which refers to a totality and which cannot itself be grasped in a concept.

The same conclusion would be reached if we started with the definition of philosophy, namely, *theoretical thought directed to the totality of meaning*. It is impossible for me to *begin* philosophising before having impressed on my thought a particular direction with respect to the *Idea* I have of the totality of meaning of the cosmos. I have to position myself somewhere *in this totality* so that it doesn't remain foreign to me. In order to conceive the Idea of the totality of meaning I myself, as a person, have to participate in it. In directing my thought to the Idea of the totality of meaning I have to be able to reach a point *beyond* all the aspects of reality, of which I myself am an integral part, and beyond their cosmic coherence. This point must be a peak from the top of which I will be able to encompass this cosmic coherence as well as the diversity it contains. It must be a point that overarches every individual function within the cosmic coherence in which I myself am active.

The surest way of going astray would be to take as a starting point that single aspect of meaning of reality which it had come to be believed could legitimately be used to account for all the aspects of reality; as if white light could be accounted for by a single colour of the spectrum. *It is only by transcending the speciality*[11] *of meaning, and its coherence, that I can arrive at an actual view of the totality of meaning* and, hence, find the starting point for philosophy, which is beyond philosophy itself.

> 8. The Archimedean point of philosophy and the concentric direction of philosophic thought.

This fixed point – suggested by the two parallel methods of investigation, and without which we cannot have any Idea

---

[11] We have used the word *speciality* to translate the term *zinbijzonderheid* in order to indicate the special and specific meaning of the aspects of reality. Speciality, taken as a whole, leads to the diversity of meaning (*zinverscheidenheid*). [Marcel used the word *specification* rather than *speciality*, though the latter was used in the English translation of the *New Critique*. He added here: "The term *speciality* adopted in the English translation does not sit well in French."]

of totality – we call the *Archimedean Point of philosophy*.[12] When it stands here, our ego discovers that the view of totality is only possible if it also has *a view of the Origin of beings and things*, that is, of both the totality and speciality of meaning. We have seen that the totality of *meaning*, because it exists as and remains *meaning*, cannot exist in itself. It presupposes an *Origin* that provides meaning. All meaning is of, by and for an Origin that cannot itself be meaning.

The impulse that is found at the root of all philosophical thought has its beginnings in a profound human restlessness, namely, the search for the Origin of all that exists. *Inquietum est cor nostrum et mundus in corde nostro*. This direction towards the supreme Origin, which we call the *concentric* direction of philosophical thought, arises out of the restlessness of our personality that is actually active in philosophical thinking. It arises out of our own self, out of the deep roots of our being. It is located in our personality in all the temporal functions where my ego actually exists. Philosophical thought cannot escape the question of the Origin of our personality or of the totality of meaning in which it participates. Philosophical thought *as such* extracts the actuality of this meaning from the very personality which restlessly seeks its Origin in order to comprehend its own meaning and, by that means, the meaning of our whole universe. This concentric direction demonstrates that our ego depends subjectively on a *Law* that derives its fullness of meaning from the Origin of all things, which also *sets its limits* and *determines* it.

All meaning is heteronomous[13] and dependent. If philosophical thought is nothing else than thought directed to the totality of meaning of the universe, it cannot avoid an appeal to the ultimate Origin. *The fundamental and genetic tendency of philosophy is to be thought which emerges out of this Origin and returns to it.*

---

[12] Archimedes said: "Give me somewhere to stand outside the earth and I will lift the world."

[13] [i.e., Subject to a law or standard external to itself, not autonomous.]

In the preliminary questions of philosophy thought will never come to rest until it discovers this Origin, which alone gives it *meaning*. It is impossible to escape this concentric direction. The immanent laws of philosophical thought prevent it from finding any rest in creaturely meaning.[14] It has to think by and for this Origin that underpins the existence of all meaning. *It is only here, where the meaning of every question vanishes, that the Origin is reached and where philosophical thought finds rest.*

This brings into consideration the following brace of presuppositions:

1.– An *Archimedean point* for the thinker by means of which our selfhood, in its philosophising[15], can project a totality-view onto the cosmos.

2.– Within the Archimedean point itself, the *choice*[16] of a position with respect to the Origin, w*hich itself transcends all meaning* and in which the philosophising self comes to rest. For if it attempts to go beyond this Origin its questions can no longer have any *meaning*.

9. The three conditions required by the Archimedean point.

This Archimedean point ought to be subject to the following three conditions:

a. It cannot be independent of my *subjective self*. It is this which actually acts in philosophical thought, and in which alone, as the centre of my existence, I am able to transcend the diversity of meaning.

b. It cannot be independent of the law, which is the condition of the ego's existence. Without this law the subject sinks into chaos or, worse, into nothing. My ego only exists to the extent that it is circumscribed and delimited by this law.

---

[14] Translating the Dutch phrase *creatuurlijk* by *created* is inadequate. Many of us have in our turn used this phrase to evoke the *mode of being* of all *meaning* insofar as it relates to creation. This meaning is and remains heteronomous, always dependent on the creating Origin.

[15] The term 'philosophising' is used in the sense of the *philosophical activity of thought*.

[16] The [Dutch] term *stellingkeuze* has been translated as *choice*, that is, a principled position anterior to every step in philosophical thinking.

c. It must transcend all diversity of meaning and be found in the totality and unity of meaning of the cosmos, in which my ego participates, if it is to have an Idea of it in philosophical thought. In fact if the Archimedean point were immersed in the diversity of meaning it would not be capable of acting as the concentration point from where a totality-view could be applied to the diversity of meaning. Besides, it has been mentioned in passing that it has to be *beyond* the coherence of meaning of the various aspects of reality.

10. The totality of meaning cannot be found in the diversity of meaning.

Just as white light does not exist in the separate rays of the spectrum, so the totality of meaning cannot exist in the *immanent coherence* that underpins the various aspects of reality. This coherence lacks any *internal concentration point* that can unite the various functions as *fullness of meaning*. Self-reflection offers us a tangible example of the truth of this.

We have already seen that:

a. Our personality expresses itself in every aspect of our being;

b. This expression is only possible if every function finds its *concentration point* in the *personality* or *self*, beyond the diversity of meaning and hence *transcendent;*

c. Our personality cannot be reduced to a correlative coherence of the complex[17] of functions by which we function in the cosmos;

d. Finally, the diversity of meaning only exists in the correlative coherence of all the meaning-types, as the *expression* of a fullness that is characterised by diversity.

That is why the totality of meaning, as the fullness of meaning, is demanded as the transcendent centre in which all the functions are united together – on account of their mutual coherence – *to being directed in a single direction towards the Origin of all meaning.*

---

[17] Taken in sense A of Lalande's *Vocabulaire de la Philosophie.*

11. The choice of Archimedean point
is not an act of theoretical thought.

Thus the Archimedean point must, unconditionally, be *the concentration point of philosophical thought*. As such, it must be beyond the diversity of meaning and even of its coherence. It is not possible for it to be immanent in philosophical thought itself. In fact, we cannot find any point anywhere in thought itself that actually transcends the diversity of meaning. In its subjective actuality the thought-function can never be the object of thought. Is it possible then to substitute "credo" for "cogito"? For sure, I can apply my faith to the coherence of the different aspects of the cosmos. But faith, as an immanent function, does not allow me even to transcend the coherence of my own functions. In faith no actual immanent pole exists from where I can transcend the diversity of meaning in its coherence. In fact believing and thinking only differ in a *functional* sense. I cannot transcend this cosmic difference of meaning between believing and thinking by my thought or by my faith, both of which are immanent functions.

Now, we observe that, whichever way we turn, it is impossible for the choice of the Archimedean point to be a *purely theoretical act*. Rather, *it is the personality — the religious root of existence — that plays upon the instrument of philosophical thought*. In thinking about things as they are, philosophical thought is, in and of itself, incapable of supplying the Archimedean point. It only exists in the cosmic coherence of meaning and never transcends it. The immanent ideas that we have of the coherence of meaning and of totality are *limiting concepts* that reveal the heteronomy of theoretical thought even in the field of philosophy. Thus there is no possible way of transcending the coherence of the cosmic diversity of meaning, *other than the religious root of existence, from which all philosophical thought takes its rise*.

Determining the Archimedean point of philosophy will thus always be an *apriori choice*, of an essentially *religious* nature. It is an extremely serious act of choosing, for it affects all theoretical thinking, its Idea of the cosmic coherence of meaning, its conception of law, subject, truth, and the conditions of knowledge, etc.

12. The heart as the religious concentration point of human existence.

What is this transcendent religious root of human existence? It is the *heart*. The heart is the only point from where we can transcend the temporal diversity of meaning in a coherence of *time*. According to Scripture: "God has placed eternity in the heart of man" (Ecclesiastes 3:11). The heart is the fullness of our personality, the truly transcendent focal point of our existence, bringing together all our temporal functions. As such, the heart is also the necessary starting point of philosophical thought. Out of the heart, Scripture says, "spring the issues of life" (Prov. 4:23). And Christ says: "Where your treasure is, there also will your heart be also" (Matt. 6:21).[18]

So it is absolutely impossible to eliminate the heart from philosophical thought. For in any theoretical abstraction of thought, it is precisely our whole personality that acts. The fullness of our personality can only be found at the religious centre of our creaturely existence, where the direction of our life is determined in relation to God, the Absolute and Ultimate Origin of all things. It is in man's heart that answers to the most serious and profound questions take shape.

Accordingly, for us the *heart* should never be identified with *faith* or *feeling*. Neither should it be identified with any complex of functions. It is not a blind or deaf witness. It is the authentic fullness of our selfhood, in which all our temporal functions find their *religious concentration*, the religious fulfilment of their true meaning.

Unfortunately, in its rebellion against God, as also against the totality of meaning and against itself, humanity has lost

---

[18] Note. The word *heart* in Scripture has various complementary meanings: 1) The literal meaning of a bodily organ, and a figurative meaning such as "in the heart of the forest". 2) The heart constitutes the inmost depths of a man, as opposed to his outer clothing and the words from his lips. 3) At the same time, the heart is considered to be a) the source of all a man's vital forces, b) the foundation of our emotional life and our thoughts, as well as all wisdom, understanding and intelligence and c) the origin of both our words and our actions. 4) The heart is understood as the origin of every sinful action. 5) Finally, the heart is seen as the very core of our temporal existence, the target of the regenerating work of the Holy Spirit in believers.

sight of this fundamental truth, a truth that can never be the object of any purely theoretical discussion for, in the fullness of its meaning, it *transcends* theoretical thought. *It embodies the necessary condition of every philosophy, whichever path it follows.* We will return to this point later.

This fundamental truth – that the transcendental root of our creaturely existence is found in the heart, the religious concentration point, and not in theoretical thought or in our sensory, aesthetic, rational or moral functions – only assumes its full significance in the light of the revelation of the original fall of the human race (considered as an *abandoning of the religious root of the cosmos,* an *apostasy*), and of the revelation of salvation as possible only in Jesus Christ, the new Root of the regenerated cosmos. *No genuine knowledge of the selfhood is therefore possible without the heart being enlightened by Divine Revelation.*

The formulation of these first principles for the definition and the possibility of any genuine philosophical thought puts us in possession of the first way of a transcendental critique of philosophical thought. We will apply this method immediately to *immanence-philosophy*[19] and highlight some profound differences which, from the outset, put it in opposition to a Reformed philosophy.

> 13. In immanence-philosophy the transcendental subject of philosophical thought is only an abstraction of the thinking ego.

Our first comment is the observation that all immanence-philosophy refuses to consider the possibility that philosophical thought goes beyond its immanent limits in order to attain self-knowledge. *Only insofar as* the ego actually appears *in philosophical thought* can it become an object of knowledge. The "object" of thought is no longer the concrete individual self, existing in time, but simply a "residue" resulting from a methodical elimination of all its moments of meaning that cannot be grasped by pure thought. In immanence-philosophy,

---

[19] For the definition meaning of this term see below, §15.

the so-called "transcendental-subject" possesses no individuality whatsoever; it does not transcend thought, but only appears as the immanent subjective pole of thought. *It is no longer I who reflect on my self, but philosophical thought which reflects on its own activity.*

However, this reduction of the thinking ego to a supposed "transcendental-subject" can only be achieved by the ego that thinks, *and this ego cannot in its turn be the product of an abstraction.* What's more, it is impossible for philosophical thought to isolate itself from its subjective actuality precisely because, being "pure thought", it has no *personality*. This "transcendental-subject of thought" is only an abstraction of the thinking *self*, and hence an abstraction without meaning, and inherently contradictory. For the thought-function[20] can never exist "in itself"; it cannot be actual or have the least existence *apart from the transcending ego*.

14. The postulate of the autonomy of thought.

It is quite wrong for immanence-philosophy to lay claim to being "critical". Indeed, it considers as an apriori condition of philosophical thought (so this is a *religious* choice of position) that the apriori Origin of our intelligible world resides in our cognitive functions, which are from the beginning theoretically regarded as *independent*, that is, *as being free from any further extraneous determination*. Here, the *intelligible world* draws its meaning from the apriori structure of the cognitive functions, which are declared to be autonomous, and its origin is taken to be of a logical-transcendental character. Therefore, in immanence-philosophy, the question of the *meaning of our knowledge* is precluded, because the Origin *transcends* all meaning. Moreover, thought holds that it can find "rest" in a function that is immanent. We shall return to the tragic consequences that flow from these *un-critical* premises.

---

[20] [Fr. *fonction-pensant*. Marcel uses this to mean what Dooyeweerd expressed as *subjective logical function* or *logical function of thought*, NC. I. p.7]

15. Deified thought as the Archimedean point of immanence philosophy.
Immanence-philosophy defined.

While regarding the *autonomy of thought* with respect to any
divine revelation as the alpha and omega of every philosophical
idea, the prevailing philosophy cannot challenge the need for
an Archimedean point. In his *Cogito ergo sum*, Descartes
thought he had found the only fixed point against the methodical universal scepticism regarding reality as it is presented to
experience. But the prevailing philosophy will not accept that
this Archimedean point can be found outside of philosophical
thought itself. It is forced to cling *to the immanence standpoint*,
and reject for its thought every support which transcends, in
any way, the immanent limits of cognitive functions as such.
As far as it is concerned, this alone guarantees the scientific
character of philosophy.

Nevertheless, immanence-philosophy does not reject the
possibility of understanding the totality of meaning and of the
Origin *metaphysically*. Classical immanence-philosophy was
wholly based on a metaphysical *prima philosophia*. But then, it
has to overstep the creational limits of thought with the idea of
an *absolute* thought that contains within itself the fullness of
being, that is, deified thought (νόησις νοησέως, *intellectus arche-
typus*). Thought, as such, is absolutised and, being assumed to
participate in divine reason, becomes itself the Archimedean
point. *The totality of meaning is sought in a system of ideas immanent
in thought.*

The immanence-standpoint, however, does not necessarily
require belief in the autonomy of human thought as regards
the other immanent functions of consciousness. History proves
that this view has spawned a large number of trends, from
metaphysical rationalism to the modern irrationalist philosophy of life, and even existentialist philosophy which, having
broken from the rationalist Cartesian *cogito*, believes with
Dilthey that it has discovered its Archimedean point in the
vivo.

Accordingly, we do not take the expression "immanence-
philosophy" in the narrow sense of a philosophy that sees all
reality as immanent in consciousness and that has broken every

bridge between the functions of human consciousness and "extra-mental reality", but in the general sense of any philosophy which seeks its Archimedean point in philosophical thought itself, whether this thought is viewed in a rationalist, irrationalist, metaphysical, psychological, historical or, transcendental-logical sense.

16. The theoretical character of philosophical enquiry.

Indeed, there exists in modern immanence-philosophy a strong current that stresses the theoretical nature of philosophical enquiry, and maintains that the theoretical is the only viewpoint from which we can grasp the universe with an Idea of totality, while at the same time expressly denying the right to philosophy of claiming the monopoly of value for its theoretical universe. It recognises, in fact, there are other viewpoints from which we can view the universe and other "worlds" – the religious, aesthetic, moral, etc., which are "a-theoretical". But this current of thought asserts nonetheless the autonomy of "transcendental" theoretical thought, on the one hand as *Archimedean point*, and on the other as *Origin of the theoretical universe*.

The theoretical universe, indeed, becomes the "creation" of philosophical thought, whose task is to first demolish all the chaotic a-theoretical material and then re-order it by means of its creative activity into a structured universe. Reality is reason.

17. The postulates of objectivity and neutrality.

Immanence-philosophy insists that this is the only way the *scientific* character of philosophical thought can be maintained. If philosophy were to bind itself to presuppositions beyond its immanent limits, what would become of its "objectivity", its "universal validity", and the "controllability" of its assertions? Religious beliefs that imply an "intuition" of the world are certainly respectable; a philosophy that knows its limits will be careful not to undermine them, but in any case the claims of these convictions cannot be recognised within the domain of philosophy itself. Truth must be theoretical, objective, and equally valid for all who desire to think theoretically.

Whenever philosophy ceases to have any power over personal life, the famous "neutrality-postulate" of immanence-philosophy is brought forward, is believed. "Is believed", we say, because exactly at that point an apriori choice is made. To establish theoretical thought as such, to set it up as Archimedean point or as Origin (or both at once) cannot be the act of a "transcendental subject of thought", a mere abstract concept. It can only be the act *of the whole ego,* which transcends thought. In immanence-philosophy the ego itself sets up philosophical thought as the Origin of the cosmos. However this Origin – beyond which questions cannot be asked that have any meaning – does not exist, as we are well aware, as a heteronomous being of meaning. It exists by itself and for itself. As a result this choice implies the activity of the *whole person*, consequently of the heart. The initial concentration of philosophical thought in the unity of direction implies that this choice is a religious act. But it is an act that is developed in an idolatrous way that adulterates meaning. It steers all philosophical thinking away from the fullness of Truth.

> 18. The choice of an Archimedean point is a religious, not a theoretical, act.

So, the proclamation of the autonomy of philosophical thought, even with the restriction "in its own domain", is an *absolutisation of meaning*. It is the deification of a single aspect of reality. The fact that philosophers are prepared to recognise that this absolutisation in the *theoretical* domain is not the only legitimate one – since philosophy leaves the religious man, the aesthetic, or the moralist the choice of other gods – does not detract from the idolatrous character of their claim. A philosopher who accords this liberty to the non-theoretical is, so to speak, theoretically polytheistic. He refrains from proclaiming that his theoretical god is the only true god, but in the temple of this god no others are to be worshipped. The choice of the Archimedean point in immanence-philosophy can never be a purely *theoretical* act that has no religious presuppositions. It the personality itself, the religious root of being, that plays on the instrument of philosophical thought. And from the immanence standpoint this must remain *invisible*.

We shall have occasion to return to this issue: for the "neutrality-postulate" of immanence-philosophy is a fiction.

19. The absolutisation of meaning and the origin of all "-isms".

In order to clarify the general framework of our thought we shall look ahead a little in this Introduction to the final results of our enquiries, while reserving a detailed study of them till later.

The fundamental feature of the Fall and of sin is that man is now in revolt against God, the Origin of our universe, and thus in revolt against the totality of its meaning. Left to himself, he can no longer occupy the only genuine Archimedean point from which it would be possible for him to attain genuine self-knowledge. Neither is he able to attain an accurate idea of the totality of meaning or of its Origin. By refusing to serve the true God, rebellious mankind has lost any possibility of *orienting himself*. In total revolt against God, his self-consciousness is of necessity *dispersed* through the diversity of meaning of our temporal universe.

The concentration of being in the personality thus becomes a concentration in the absolutisation of creaturely meaning. In the very confused variety of its currents of thought, immanence-philosophy is merely a residue of the rebellious attitude against the religious root of humanity. Dispersed in the diversity of meaning, consciousness can only find a concentration point by means of an absolutisation of meaning. This fact gives us the key to the origin of the endless "-isms" in immanence-philosophy.

When man no longer knows *himself*, how can he direct his attention philosophically to the totality of meaning of the universe? For the synthesis of meaning, without which theoretical thought is impossible, can only be carried out by a self that transcends the diversity of meaning. Since this self cannot do this, and because it is completely immersed in this diversity, it has to make do with one or other of the particular aspects of reality in its attempt at synthesis, as if it could construct white light out of a single ray of its spectrum. This is why immanence philosophy will contain countless "-isms" until by critical self-reflection it becomes aware that its Archimedean point is no more than an *apriori* choice in which one or other of the meaning-aspects of reality is elevated to the rank of Absolute.

However immanence-philosophy will always be of the opinion that in regard to its own affairs it has avoided the pitfalls of these "-isms". The idealist, who (with the help of synthetic thought of meaning) absolutises the normative aspects, will reproach the naturalist (even while aware of the synthesis of meaning at the root of his philosophical activity) with having *absolutised* a domain of the natural[21] sciences. But he will nevertheless indignantly reject any accusation of having himself slipped into an initial absolutisation in his own synthesis. The logicist — who thinks that the synthesis of meaning is of a *purely logical* character, and that *cosmos* and *logos* are identical — reproaches the psychologistic absolutisation of any specific domain of thought that has not been conceived in its logical origin — the "psychologistic". Nevertheless he does not consider himself to have fallen into any "-ism" because he ascribes to each "domain of thought" its own autonomy.

The irrationalist philosophy of life, which assimilates every "reduction" of the law to a construction of thought that falsifies reality as it really is, and thinks it can correctly conceive authentic reality by situating itself in the psycho-subjective or historical "streams of life", is convinced that only its approach can discover *all* of reality. It will never accept that its own viewpoint also proceeds from an absolutisation of the speciality of meaning, synthetically abstracted.

The rich diversity of meaning that is presented within the cosmic coherence, as we shall see later, offers within its apriori structure numerous possibilities for elevating first one and then another of the aspects of reality to the rank of *common denominator* of all the others. For immanence-philosophy it will for-

---

[21] [Marcel always refers to what we call *natural science* as *cosmological science* (*science cosmologique*). We shall use the term *natural* throughout.]

ever remain incomprehensible why it has to seek the root of all these "-isms" in the depths of a personality that considers itself autonomous.

20. The tragedy of immanence-philosophy.

The Midas legend provides a useful illustration of all immanence-philosophy's "-isms". All that it touches with its philosophical thought based on the absolutisation of a single aspect of meaning is transformed, as if by magic, into an expression of this specific aspect of meaning. For the logicist, the created universe becomes *logos* (λόγος). For the psychologist, every aspect of meaning of reality becomes an expression of the *psychic*. For the historicist, everything appears under the fundamental aspect of *historical* development. For the naturalist, all reality becomes the sensible matter of our *moral duty*, etc., etc.

However, just as Midas was lost in the world that he moulded to his own choosing, so in immanence-philosophy the thinker is lost in the absolutisation of his own theoretical abstractions. Philosophical thought, now declared autonomous, is faced with the impossibility of arriving at a true conception of the totality of meaning. The Idea of Totality is filled with false content, and the thinker can no longer grasp in its authentic structure the speciality of meaning in its relation to the meaning of our world.

To conclude these preliminary remarks, to which we shall revert in detail later, we are in a position to say that the primary stumbling-block of all immanence-philosophy, taken in the broad sense we have given it, is this: *In the jealous care it takes to defend its point of view (the autonomy of philosophical thought) over against divine revelation, it fails to notice that it is engaging – in its apriori choice – in a religious transcendental approach. The internal flaw of all immanence-philosophy lies in its lack of any critical reflection on the starting point of its own thought. A genuine and radically transcendent philosophical thought is only possible if it rejects the notion of its own autonomy.*

21. Rickert's conception of the self-
limitation of thought.

Rickert, one of the leaders of the neo-Kantian school of
South-West Germany, nevertheless claims that we can never
become aware of the limits of thought by placing ourselves
beyond thought itself and, by directing our attention towards
it from that perspective, detecting its limits: "Insofar as we are
situated outside thought, we no longer know anything."[22] This
is undoubtedly true. We can even go further and say: It is
absolutely impossible for us, in the actuality of our self-
consciousness, to place ourselves outside our thought; for
without thought our human selfhood can no longer be known
in the temporal relations of our world. However, from the
immanence viewpoint Rickert lacks any idea of a transcendence of the selfhood. And our selfhood, as we have seen, can
never be removed from the act of thinking.[23]

---

[22] Heinrich Rickert, *System der Philosophie*, J.C.B. Mohr (Paul Siebeck), Tübingen,
1921, p.241, says: "It is certain that the heterological principle (for Herman Dooyeweerd, the requirement that the modal diversity be theoretically distinguished)
marks the limits of our thought in the problem of the ultimate unity of the world.
But even so it opens the possibility of liberating us from its chains. If through
thought we can determine the limits of thought, we ought to be able of going
beyond them as well." [Gewiß zeigt das heterologische Prinzip bei der Frage nach
der letzten Welteinheit die Grenze unseres Denkens, aber gerade dadurch eröffnet es
uns zugleich die Möglichkeit, uns von seinen Fesseln zu befreien. Sind wir imstande,
durch Denken die Grenze des Denkens fest zu stellen, so müssen wir auch imstande
sein, diese Grenze zu überschreiten.]
From the immanence viewpoint, these conclusions contain an evident contradiction.
Thought determines its own limits and is because of that able to go beyond them. In
these conditions what remains of a pure transcendental thought? It is no use
distinguishing, with Rickert, between a purely "heterological" thought and a
"monological-heterological" thought, the latter being able to go beyond the limits
of the former. When this type of monological thought seeks to conceive, in an
autonomous way, the unity of the cosmos in the subjective meaning connecting
"reality" and "value" it goes beyond the immanent limits of the activity of thought
as such. It gets lost in antinomy, which Rickert honestly recognises when he says
(ibid. p.260): "Thus we form a concept of that which, strictly speaking, cannot be
contained in a concept." [So bringen wir das in einem Begriff, was wir streng
genommen in einem Begriff nicht fassen können.]
[23] Heinrich Rickert, 'Wissenschaftliche Philosophie und Weltanschauung' in *Logos:
Internationale Zeitschrift für Philosophie der Kultur,* J.C.B. Mohr (Paul Siebeck),
Tübingen, Vol. XXII, I (1933), p.57 : "The universal knowledge which, as philosophy, necessarily makes the entire man its object, transcends man himself."
[...universalen Erkenntnis, die als Philosophie notwendig auch den ganzen Mensch-

For sure, if we want to know the limits of our thought, we ought, by thinking, to arrive at a transcendental theoretical Idea of its limits. But for all that, we do not in the least suppose, as does Rickert, that the limits can be set by thought. Neither can they be known by thought that is abstracted from its religious root and its inter-modal coherence of meaning.

A transcendent starting point is thus necessary for philosophical thought. Without it, it cannot carry out its task, namely, that of projecting onto our cosmic coherence, by means of a critical and theoretical reflection, a view of totality. To unearth this Archimedean point, the selection of which transcends it, philosophy has to go beyond its limits, which are the apriori immanent structure of its own thought. This first conclusion having been achieved, we shall now explain the transcendental critique of theoretical thought.

CSCSCS

---

en mit zum „Gegenstande" macht, indem sie sich über ihn stellt.] [Also in: Heinrich Rickert, *Philosophische Aufsätze*, Rainer A. Bast (ed.), p.345, Mohr Siebeck, Tübingen, 1999]

Chapter 1

The Problem of Time

1. The immanence in time of every
meaning aspect.

The aim of philosophy is to furnish us with a theoretical
view of the coherence of our temporal world, which binds
together all the aspects of meaning. This is a *temporal* coherence, to which philosophical thought is strictly bound, and
which alone confers on it its meaning.

Within this temporal coherence, as we know, reality displays itself through a diversity of modal aspects, each of which
is a modality of cosmic *meaning* in its own right. We have
already drawn attention to the aspects of number, space, movement, energy, organic life, feeling and sensory perception, as
well as the analytical and historical aspects and those of symbolic signification, social forms, together with the economic,
aesthetic, juridical, moral and faith aspects. Thus there are
fifteen aspects altogether, and the meaning of each is irreducible to any of the others.[1]

All these modal aspects are interlaced with each other in a
cosmic order of time which guarantees their coherence. As we
shall see, this order is necessarily bounded by concrete duration. We call cosmic time the indissoluble correlation between
order and *duration*. And on that account we establish a rigorous
and important distinction between cosmic time and each of its
particular modal aspects. Hence it is impossible for us actually
to transcend cosmic time, either in the concept – which only

---

[1] See the table located at the end of this volume in Appendix 1. It is only a very
simple and merely provisional layout of the fundamental terms. Later we will
discuss their structure, and demonstrate that they are mutually irreducible.

has an intentional meaning – or in the *transcendental Idea,* which is merely a limiting concept. We can only transcend cosmic time in the religious centre of our existence, even though, like all other creatures, we remain embedded in the temporal order, and so subject to time.

It is very remarkable that immanence-philosophy, in the sense we have defined it, has never been able, on account of its starting point, to take account of this universal *intermodal* character of time and the coherence of its modal aspects. The dialectical ground-motives which have ruled it, and which continue to do so, exercise a decisive influence on its various philosophical conceptions of time.[2]

> 2. The influence of the dialectical ground-motive on philosophical conceptions of time.

In the outline of our Introduction we briefly anticipated a few later conclusions in order to simply bring to light the influence of the dialectical ground-motives[3] of immanence-philosophy on its conceptions of time.

Classical Greek thought was already lost in a false dilemma: namely, whether time has a *subjective mental* or an *objective physical* character.

In a brief treatise[4] he devoted to time, Aristotle posed the problem in the framework of the Greek *form-matter* ground-motive. According to him, time is the measure or number or numerability of motion, conforming to the ὕστερον καὶ πρότερον, the before and after. He viewed motion as merely change of place or state, a striving of matter after form, and of poten-

---

[2] Cf. Herman Dooyeweerd, 'Het Tijdsprobleem in de Wijsbegeerte der Wetsidee' (*The Problem of Time in the Philosophy of the Law-Idea*), *Philosophia Reformata*, 1940, p.160ff, 193ff.

[3] Herman Dooyeweerd made extensive use of this term. By ground-*motive* he understood a basic principle, known or unknown, which guides and moves philosophical thought in a systematic and specific direction. A ground-motive is always fundamental and religious. It depends on the Archimedean point of thought, and conditions the way in which the fundamental questions of philosophy, the Ideas of Origin and Totality, are posed.

[4] Aristotle, *Physics* IV, 10, 219a, 29ff.

tiality after actuality. As long as it does not attain form, it is a plurality moving from before to after; it is without unity, and so without natural being, for being implies unity. The soul, however, in the subjective synthesis of the act of counting, can give unity to this plurality. Time thus cannot actually exist outside the soul. Aristotle's exposition does not give us any clear answer to the question whether time, in the local movement of things, has only a *potential* existence, in the plurality of the before-after stages.

Aristotle deified the *form-motive* by identifying the deity with pure form. The Ionian philosophies of nature, on the other hand, deified the *matter-motive*, that is, "eternal motion", the flowing stream of life, which cannot be fixed in any form. Time is then conceived, by Anaximander in particular, as a divine order of justice (δίκη) avenging the injustice of things which have taken birth in individual forms, by dissolving them into pure matter, and by making everything return to its formless *Origin*. "It is to the things from whence they come that beings are returned to destruction, according to necessity; they repay one another the punishment and penalty for their injustice, according to 'the order of time'".[5] The dilemma posed by Aristotle cannot arise here. Actually, the Ionian thinkers did not recognise any difference between the physical and mental realms. For them, "matter" was inanimate. Aristotle, on the other hand, regarded the soul as the form of the material body; "matter" was only a potentiality that could not have actual existence without a form which guaranteed the unity of being.

The internal dialectic of the form-matter ground-motive re-appeared in medieval Aristotelian scholasticism, which was also pulled in diametrically opposed directions as far as its conception of time is concerned.

On the one hand, Albert the Great defended an *objective-physical* concept of time, and assigned to the motion of things, independently of the soul, a form and a structure of its own, in

---

[5] [Marcel gives no reference for this quotation from Anaximander. It can be found in Diels and Kranz, *Fragmente der Vorsokratiker*, I (6th ed., 1951), p.89: ἐξ ὧν δὲ ἡ γένεσίς ἐστι τοῖς οὖσι, καὶ τὴν φθορὰν εἰς ταῦτα γίνεσθαι κατὰ τὸ χρεών. διδόναι γὰρ αὐτὰ δίκην καὶ τίσιν ἀλλήλοις τῆς ἀδικίας κατὰ τὴν τοῦ χρόνου τάξιν.]

its *numerus formalis*[6]. Thomas Aquinas, on the other hand, adopted a theory of *subjectivist psychologism* in line with Augustine.[7] Seen as the numerical measure of motion, time can only have real existence in the soul, though Thomas Aquinas conceded that as far as matter is concerned it has a *fundamentum in re*.[8]

Contemporary humanist philosophy poses the problem of time in line with the humanist ground-motive of *Nature-Freedom*. From the start the internal dialectic of this ground-motive drove philosophical thought towards a rationalist idea of time – viewed along the lines of classical physics as mechanical motion (the *Nature* motive) – on the one hand, or towards an irrationalist vitalist, a psychologistic or a historicistic, idea dominated by the *Freedom* motive. The opposition between objectivist and subjectivist views remains evident here.

In his *Critique of Pure Reason* Kant conceived of time as a transcendental form of intuition and sensory experience. By this form the impressions of consciousness – the objective-physical as well as the subjective-psychical – are moulded into an orderly series. Time and space are coordinated, space itself being also a form of intuition.

In the twentieth century, Einstein has given new impetus to the philosophical discussion about the meaning of time by his Theory of Relativity, where time acts as the fourth dimen-

---

[6] Albert the Great, *Physicorum*, Livre IV, tr. 3, c.16 : "Ad numerare tria exiguntur, scilicet *materia* numerata, et *numerus formalis*, et *anima* efficienter et formaliter numerans: ergo so non est anima adhuc numerus est secundum esse formale et secundum numerum numeratum; ergo, quo numerator est duplex, scilicet quo numeratur efficienter, et quo numeratur formaliter." – Time is this *numerus formalis*. In modern times, we find the same idea in the neo-Thomist P. Hoenen, S.J., in his *Philosophie der anorganische natuur*, Antwerp-Nijmegen, N.V. Dekker & Van De Vegt, 1940, p.284.

[7] Augustine, *Confessions*, XI, chap. 26, §33: "Inde mihi visum est nihil alium esse tempus quam distentionem: sed cuius rei nescio, et mirum, si non ipsius animae." [Whence it appeared to me that time is nothing else than protraction; but of what I know not. It is wonderful to me, if it be not of the mind itself.]

[8] Thomas Aquinas, *De instantibus*, ch. I, Opusc.xxxvi. Cf. H. Dooyeweerd, 'De Idee der individualiteits-structuur en het Thomistisch substantiebegrip', II (The idea of the structure of individuality and the Thomistic concept of substance), *Philosophia Reformata*, 1944-1945, pp.1ff.

sion of the world's physical space. Bergson maintained that the theory of relativity denatured time by reducing it to a spatial line. *True time*, according to Bergson, is a psychic durée of feeling, in which we experience it as created freedom of the *élan vital*, inaccessible to the thinking of natural science[9]. The actual durée has a psychic nature and is not composed of a mathematical uniformity of successive parts. Here, all the moments are interpenetrated qualitatively. Psychic "durée" is *real* or *absolute* time.

Modern phenomenology speaks of "real time" as an "*Erlebnisstrom*" and is opposed to the objectivist idea of time in modern mathematical natural science. For their part, Dilthey and Heidegger conceive time in a historical-irrationalist sense, though for Heidegger historical time has a dialectical-existentialist meaning.

In all these conceptions of time that we have enumerated, we note that time is always unintentionally identified with *one* of its modal aspects or *one* of its meaning-modalities. It cannot be otherwise when philosophical thought takes its starting point from a dialectical ground-motive that locks it in a religious dualism. Any *integral* conception of time is consequently excluded.

> 3. In each modal aspect time expresses
> itself in a unique way.

On the other hand, Reformed philosophy cannot, due to its starting point, reduce time to one of its modal aspects. As far as it is concerned, time expresses itself in a special manner in all aspects of reality, without exception. It follows that *cosmic* time has an *integral* character in our philosophy. This idea of time, which constitutes the foundation of the Reformed philosophical theory of reality, appears in the history of philosophy as completely new.

---

[9] These are the sciences which make the first four meaning-modalities (the numerical, spatial, physical and biotic) their field of enquiry. They are also known as the *cosmological (natural)* sciences. See Lalande, *Vocabulaire de la Philosophie*, Article "Cosmologiques (Sciences)".

Without going into detail of what will be the subject of future studies, we shall very briefly indicate the meaning of time in each aspect of reality; a meaning that – for each mode – is irreducible to any another.

In the numerical aspect of *quantity*, time asumes the modal meaning of *numerical relation*. In the series of numbers, there is an irreversible order of before-and-after, which does not depend in any way on our *subjective* manner of counting, but on a structural *constraint*[10] of the numerical modal aspect. In the series of numbers, the before-and-after does not represent a succession of movement, but a relation of time, of *quantitative* value. 2 is before 3, because 2 is smaller than 3.

In the *spatial* aspect, time has the modal meaning of *continuous extension*. The simultaneity of the parts of space must be distinguished modally from the order of time of *numbers*, on the one hand, and the *succession of movement*, on the other. This distinction does not exclude but presupposes a temporal coherence within the *cosmic* order of time between number-time and movement-time. Spatial simultaneity has nothing in common with a supra-temporality or *a-temporality*, with which Parmenides had already identified it in his conception of timeless *being*. Without a static spatial time, there can be no question of a movement-time.[11]

In the aspect of *movement*, time manifests itself in the modal sense of *succession of movement*. A static spatial simultaneity is only possible in a *relative* manner. *Absolute* rest is indeed only conceivable in the original sense of spatial extension. But motion presupposes this spatial extension, and is necessarily *founded* on it.

In the *biotic* aspect, time is manifested in the modal sense of *organic vital development*, with all the phases it goes through. The biotic time of development cannot be reduced to movement-

---

[10] The term *wetmatigheid* can be translated into English quite well by *constraint*, taken in Calvin's sense of that which denotes a limit, a measure, or an order imposed by a specific law.

[11] This is evident in the fact that Newton's idea of *absolute motion*, which inspired his mathematical concept of time, needed the static simultaneity of spatial coordinates to form a concept of identical durations of time for periods of motion.

time. Vital development, while founded on the modal functions of movement, is not as such "movement" itself. Math-
ematical-physical measures of time will always remain *outside*
the internal biotic order of time. They are unable to penetrate
the *internal* modal nature of the phases of growth, maturity, old
age and death, which have no homogeneous character and do
not submit to mathematical delimitation.

In the *psychical* aspect, time is manifested in the modal sense
of *sentient life*. The modal time of sentient life gives a special
and original character to the succession of sensory-moments.
Earlier feelings and sense impressions *do not disappear* to make
room for later ones, like the moments of motion. Either they
remain for a shorter or longer period in consciousness, or they
are suppressed in the subconscious or unconscious, where they
can continue to act in conscious sentient life. Associations of
feelings, because of their qualitative *sensory* nature, can never
be explained in a mechanistic way.

In the *logical* aspect, time assumes the analytical modal
meaning of *logical succession* (before-after) and *logical simultaneity*.
The order of time displays a normative modal meaning, as it
does in all the post-logical aspects. The logical order of earlier
and later (before-after, *prius et posterius*) and the order of logical
simultaneity constitute a genuine *modal* order of time which, in
the logical movement of thought, maintain their *normative*
character over against the psychical and pre-psychical aspects
of time.[12]

---

[12] The current view of the matter, which insists that we do not have a real order of
time here, is based on the assumption that logical relations are independent of time.
This view explicitly opposes the *logical* before-after to the *temporal* before-after. That
the abstract discursive form of a syllogism appears only in theoretical thinking does
not prove that the logical order of succession plays no role in pre-theoretical
thought. It would have to be shown that the principle of sufficient reason does not
apply to ordinary thinking, which is impossible. This principle cannot be applied
outside the modal order of time of logical succession. The premise logically precedes
the conclusion, not vice versa. This is well known, even in naive thought.

In the *historical* aspect, time has the modal meaning of *cult-ural development.*[13] Historical "periods" are periods of the real-isation of man's formative and controlling task. They cannot be delimited mathematically. The powerful cultural factors of an earlier period are incorporated in those of a later in the total form of a new image of time. In *tradition*, the time of historical development unites the past, the present and the future. Like all the other aspects of time, the historical order of time has a *normative* modal character. It imposes on humanity a normative formative task. To rest lazily in the historical present or to be mired in the past collides with the demands of the future. *Reaction* is an unhistorical return to a dead past, and is opposed to the norms of historical development.

In the *lingual* aspect, time is manifested in the modal mean-ing of *symbolic signification.* A pause, a slowing down or speed-ing up of delivery or gesture, the length of a light signal or sound, has symbolic meaning. Subjective and objective dura-tion are both subject to the normative order of time of the lingual aspect. The *transgression* of lingual norms draws atten-tion to the normative aspect of this modal order of time.

In the *social* aspect, time has the modal meaning of *social forms.* The right of precedence, for example, expresses civility or social politeness. Tact is the not doing something at an *inappropriate time.* Politeness demands that one does not turn up late to an invitation. Holidays possess a marked social character and entail numerous social obligations. The normative char-acter of social time is obvious.

In the *economic* aspect, time takes on the modal meaning of the *economy of value.* "Time is money", says the businessman. This manner of speaking is more than a metaphor, because it is a fact that the economic order of time is a *time concerned with saving*, that is, it seeks a normative apportioning of values. The phenomenon of economic rent is based on the fact that *present* goods are more highly valued than *future* identical goods. The

---

[13] *Culture* is understood here from the subject-side of its modal meaning: "directing or controlling formation" (*beheerschende vorming*), which is realised under the guid-ance of a normative freedom.

distinctions between *time-based wages* and *piece rates*, terms such as *futures market, discount*, etc., only have meaning within the modal framework of the economic order of time which, as such, cannot be reduced to any other modal aspect of time.

In the *aesthetic* aspect, time has the modal meaning of *the harmony of the beautiful*. The classical norm of the unity of time in Tragedy has only an *aesthetic* meaning. This order of time does tolerate any aesthetically-empty moment. If the author of a novel loses sight of this modal character of the aesthetic order of time and confuses it, for example, with historical order, he will no doubt compose a more or less accurate historical narrative, but not a work of art.

In the *juridical* aspect, time has the modal meaning of *right* or *justice*, of a balancing and harmonising of various interests. The non-observance of a time limit in the performance of an obligation, prescription[14], the deadline for claims or under-takings, the duration of contracts, the age of majority and minority, the validity of a law, retroactive effect, etc., are authentic juridical instances of time which have a normative juridical character.

In the *moral* aspect, time has the normative modal meaning of *moral love of one's neighbour*. It should not be confused with the religious fullness of love, which is the "fulfilment of the law". Delaying assistance that we could provide to someone who makes an urgent claim on us is ruthless and immoral. In its moral aspect, time is filled with the demands of love: love we owe to a country in danger, the duties of paternal and filial love, conjugal love, friendship, etc., *imperiously demand our time*. Christ's words: "You *always* have the poor with you, but you do not always have me", vividly illustrates the *opportunity for love* which, with death looming, demanded special sacrifices of His disciples.

In the aspect of *faith*, finally, time is reflected in its *transcendental limiting-function*. It points, in time, towards what is beyond time and is directed towards eternity. This modal meaning of faith is, as we shall see, related to Divine Revel-

---

[14] [*prescription*: a claim founded on use over a period of time.]

ation. In this eschatological aspect of time, faith groups the ἔσχατον (*eschaton*) and, in general, what is and what happens beyond the limits of cosmic time. In the first majestic words of the Book of Genesis: "In the beginning God created the heavens and the earth", faith-time points to the creative act of God, who calls time into existence. When we, as Reformed Protestants, believe that regeneration precedes conversion, we do not understand thereby a temporal order of succession in the sensory perceptive aspect of clock-time, but rather a time sequence whose meaning resides only in the limiting-function of faith. If our heart, the religious centre of our being, is not first regenerated by the Spirit of God, our conversion cannot subsequently come to light in our temporal behaviour. But regeneration can only be understood in faith-time, as the mystery of God's work in the sinner's heart, which is conceal-ed from his temporal existence.

Theology will always need this limiting-aspect of time within which temporal cosmic time is inextricably linked with the revealed supra-temporal Kingdom. It is therefore imposs-ible to identify the eschatological aspect of time, as some modern theologians do, with the historical aspect; which leads to a rejection of the central supra-temporal realm of human existence and Divine Revelation.

> 4. The correlation between temporal order and duration. The subject-object relation in duration.

Thus, from Herman Dooyeweerd's viewpoint, time in its cosmic meaning has a cosmonomic side and a special[15] or *concrete* side. Its cosmonomic side is the temporal *order* of succession or simultaneity. Its special side is the concrete *durée* (duration) which differs with each individual thing. However, duration remains constantly subject to order. So, in the aspect of organic life, the example of temporal order already given —

---

[15] [*special*: of a particular kind, peculiar, not general. The more usual sense of *exceptional* does not apply here.]

of birth, growth, maturity, old age and death – applies even to the most advanced organisms.

Because temporal order and duration are interrelated and can never be separated, the age-old opposition between the rationalist and irrationalist conceptions of time has no meaning for us. Indeed, the former absolutises the cosmonomic aspect of time and the latter its concrete subjective aspect.

We shall see how duration is expressed in a subject-object relationship. Suffice it to say for now that the *objective* duration can never exist *actually* without the subjective in the subject-object relationship. This is crucial for the problem of time measurement. What's more, the polar opposition between the subjectivist and objectivist conceptions of time disappears.

> 5. Every structure of temporal reality
> is a structure of cosmic time.

We will establish that all the fundamental structures of reality – the modal structures of the various aspects of meaning, as well as the typical structures of individuality – are grounded in the order of cosmic time, and are all specific structures of time. As such, they are necessarily subject to the concrete duration of things, events, processes, acts, social relationships, etc., that continually change with time.

The whole of empirical reality, with its great diversity of structures, is enclosed in universal cosmic time and determined by it. In each of these modal aspects, time is expressed in a specific manner that refers to both temporal *order* and *duration*. The *cosmic* character of time is expressed specifically in the intermodal indissoluble coherence of meaning, into which it fits the modal aspects, and which makes possible the important empirical *opening-process*.[16]

We shall see that the modal aspects are united by cosmic time in the order of succession which is expressed in the internal modal structure of each of them, and which reveals its

---

[16] [The editor's footnote on p.182 of *The New Critique of Theoretical Thought*, vol. II, explains this term: "The Dutch text has 'ontsluitingsproces'. The term 'opening-process' though occasionally replaced by the words 'unfolding-process, process of disclosure, or process of expansion,' seems to be preferable."]

temporal character especially in the *opening-process* to which we have just referred. But what do we mean by that?

In concrete reality, as we have noted, no modal aspect is independent of or isolated from any of the others. Just as the rainbow's refracted rays of light emanate together, so all the modal aspects are interrelated and *refer* to each other. They represent a dynamic unified whole, since the meaning of each modal aspect, under given conditions, is continually deepened and opened when it refers to the later aspects. Anticipatory structural moments[17] emerge, which reveal the internal coherence of meaning with the later modal aspects.

Both humans and animals, for example, have a psychic subject-function. In animals, it is the last subject-function. An animal does not think, speak, or believe, etc. If it feels pain, that feeling is strictly related to its pre-psychic and sensory organism. It is unable to deepen the meaning of its suffering, which it only feels in a *restrictive* function. Man, on the other hand, is also a *subject* in all the post-psychical modal aspects. His subjective feeling can appeal, by anticipation, to thought, justice, love, faith, etc. He is susceptible to the *opening-process*. Man can think about his pain and seek its cause; it may be the result of social conflict, injustice, lack of love, etc. He can believe that God is chastising him like a father, to lead him to eternal life. The feeling of pain does not remain *static*, but becomes charged with more and more meaning, which deepens in an expansive function as the anticipatory moments of the psychical aspect are brought to bear and refer it to the other post-psychical aspects.

The *closed* structure of the logical aspect, as we find it in the pre-theoretical mode of thought, does not involve these anticipatory structural moments, which are only expressed, in this aspect, in the theoretical attitude of thought. Only in theoretical thought can the internal connections with the historical, linguistic, economic and other post-psychical aspects open out and light up.

---

[17] The term *moment* is used here almost like sense C in Lalande, *Vocabulaire de la Philosophie*.

A final example: In a primitive closed juridical order, we find no anticipatory connection with morality. This explains why the principles of equity, of good faith, of good morals, of punishment commensurate with the fault, etc., are absent from it.

We shall see, at the appropriate stage, how this opening-process has a *temporal duration* and takes place according to the intermodal temporal order of the aspects of meaning.

6. The transcendental idea and the modal concepts of time. The logical aspect of the temporal order and duration.

Though it is possible to form a theoretical concept of the various modal aspects of time, we cannot grasp time itself in a concept in its universal cosmic sense. Since a concept is only possible in time, we can only *approach* cosmic time, by critical reflection, via a theoretical *limiting-concept*, as the necessary presupposition of the theoretical attitude of thought. We can thus only have a *transcendental Idea* of cosmic time in the theoretical discontinuity of its various modal aspects, which is the object of logical analysis.

In the logical or analytical aspect, cosmic time displays an analytical modal meaning. We have pointed out that the *logical* order of simultaneity and succession, just like the *physical* order, is a modal aspect of the integral order of time. The logical order only has meaning in the cosmic order of time, in its coherence with all the other modal aspects. So it makes no sense for us to oppose the *logical* anterior-posterior to the *temporal* before-after, as if the former had no real meaning as an aspect of time.

The theoretical concept brings together in a logical simultaneity the analysed features of what it defines. It is therefore subject to the logical principles of *identity* and *contradiction*, which express the normative analytical temporal order of simultaneity in the sense of logical implication and exclusion *(the excluded middle)*. Similarly, the theoretical logical movement of thought follows the analytical temporal order of anterior-posterior (the premises are logically prior to the conclusion), by being subject to the principle of *sufficient reason*.

It follows that nowhere, in the logical aspect or anywhere else, does cosmic time as such offer any concentration-point that could serve as a starting point for philosophical thought. In time, meaning is refracted into a rich diversity that can only come to a radical unity in the supra-temporal religious centre of human existence. This centre is the only area of our consciousness where we can transcend time, and from which we are able to acquire a real sense of time, which beings that are entirely immersed in time are utterly incapable of.

Some of Herman Dooyeweerd's followers do not appear to follow their master in this integral idea of cosmic time and its relation to the concentration-point of philosophical thought. They look for the concentration-point of human existence *in* time and assume that this religious centre must be *pre*-functional, and not supra-temporal. However, Dooyeweerd's answer is that in the horizon of *cosmic* time we do not have the least experience of anything pre-functional, that is, of anything that transcends the modal diversity of the aspects. Such an experience is only possible in the religious concentration of the root of our existence on the absolute Origin. Only then do we transcend cosmic time. Besides, how could man aspire to eternal things, if eternity had not been "put in his heart", as Scripture says? Even the idolatrous *absolutisation* of the temporal cannot be explained from the temporal horizon of human existence. For this horizon nowhere provides us with a point of contact for an Idea of the absolute, unless it is already bound to the supra-temporal. So this act of concentration presupposes a supra-temporal starting point in our consciousness.

That we transcend cosmic time at the root of our existence does not mean we have a static idea of the "supra-temporal", which we find in Greek metaphysics and humanism. We shall see that the central sphere of human existence is inherently *dynamic* in the fullest sense of the word. This is what is at the root of that tragic conflict between the City of God and the Earthly City that disrupts the history of the world. This it is that forms the central sphere of *events*. Indeed, it is important to note the distinction between *that which happens* and the *historical* aspect of cosmic time, which is only one of its temporal *modalities* of *meaning*.

7. Naive experience and the theoretical experience of time.

In the naive pre-theoretical attitude, we have an immediate, integral experience of cosmic time in the unbroken coherence of all its modal aspects – including the normative ones – and in its concentric relationship with our selfhood.

When my work is demanding and I look at my watch, time no longer has only an abstract objective aspect of movement for me, in this situation; on the contrary, I experience it in its continuous coherence with the aspects of number, space and movement, in the stream of organic life, in the duration of feeling as well as in its normative social aspect. If I make way for someone, I am intuitively aware of the temporal aspect of symbolic meaning and of the aspect of social relations in the temporal order. When I use the limited time available to me in an economic way, I acknowledge the economic aspect of time; it is the juridical (legal) aspect that drives me, when I try not to be late in fulfilling of my legal duties. When someone thinks of themselves as "late", they implicitly experience the normative aspects of the temporal order, and clearly demonstrate the integral nature of their naive consciousness of time.

However, in naive experience, we do not become explicitly aware of the various modal aspects of time; we only do so implicitly and simultaneously in their mutual union. The continuity of cosmic time here completely conceals the modal boundaries of its various aspects.

On the other hand, in the philosophical and theoretical attitude of thought, we can only approximate time and temporal reality by analytically separating their modal aspects, which nonetheless continue to express their coherence of meaning in their own internal structures.

C3 C3 C3

Chapter 2

The Second Way of a Transcendental Critique of Philosophy.

Part 1: The dogma of the autonomy of theoretical thought.

In our *Introduction*, we began by insisting that it is in the nature of philosophy to be directed to the fullness of meaning of temporal reality and to the selfhood. On this definition, we came straightaway to the question of the Archimedean point and the Origin. However, this view of the nature of philosophy is far from being universally accepted in philosophical circles. The first way of our transcendental critique could therefore be challenged by those who think of the task of philosophy differently.

In addition, we must justify in detail the "transition" by which we have relegated the theoretical problem of the foundation of philosophy to the central religious sphere, as well as the relationship between them. We would fail in our aim if, on account of diverging views, our approach were to be regarded as dogmatic.

If our transcendental critique is to actually embrace all possible views of the philosophical task, it is obvious that it must examine the theoretical attitude of thought as such. Indeed, no philosophy can escape this, as we shall see, even existential philosophy.

For these three reasons, we now enter upon the second way of a transcendental critique of philosophy.[1]

---

[1] The American translation of *De Wijsbegeerte der Wetsidee — A New Critique of Theoretical Thought —* has a number of important and substantial additions to the Dutch edition on this issue. Of course, we have taken account of these.

1. The dogmatic position of the autonomy of theoretical thought. Various
viewpoints. Their origin.

The *conditio sine qua non* of immanence-philosophy, of whatever school, is *the dogma of the autonomy of theoretical thought*. It is a certainly a dogma, since it is simply *assumed* that this autonomy stems from the very nature of such thought, so long as no attempt is made to justify it with a genuine critical study of the *internal structure* of the theoretical attitude of thought. Not only traditional metaphysics, but Kantian epistemology, modern phenomenology and phenomenological ontology as in Nicolai Hartmann, have been, and still are, locked in a theoretical dogmatism. The philosophers of the various schools regard essentially supra-theoretical *aprioris* as no more than elementary theoretical *axioms*, and they make no attempt to account for their fundamental significance for the entire theoretical vision of empirical reality.

Is such a claim justified, or do we not rather have good reasons to consider the so-called autonomy of theoretical thought as a fundamental critical problem?

What strikes us at once is that if everyone lays claim to the autonomy of theoretical thought, its meaning will be diverse and manifold. In Greek philosophy, for example, this autonomy has a different meaning to that of Thomist scholasticism. The meaning of autonomy in the modern humanist thought has nothing in common with that of Greek or Thomist thought. Whence arise these fundamental differences? Quite simply, they are differences in the *religious starting points* of these philosophies, which result in very diverse ways of understanding their so-called autonomy of thought.

Why does Greek philosophy claim autonomy with respect to the popular faith? Because, as far as it is concerned, theory (*theoria*, θεωρία) is the only genuine way to the knowledge of God. Faith (*pistis*, πίστις), which persists in clinging to mythological sensory representations, provides only an opinion (*doxa*, δόξα). Did not Plato insist that it is exclusively reserved for philosophers to approach the race of gods? Since the days of Parmenides' didactic poems, we see these two ways strongly opposed to each other. But all Greek philosophical *theory* nevertheless continued to be dominated by the same religious ground-motive that was *also* the basis of the popular faith and which, since Aristotle, we can call the *form-matter* ground-motive.[2]

How could we possibly understand the Thomist view of the autonomy of natural reason *(ratio naturalis)* – the scholastic ground-motive of nature-grace, which was entirely alien to Greek thought – apart from its religious background?

It is equally impossible to identify the fundamental differences between the modern humanist view of this autonomy and the Thomist view, without taking account of its religious background in the humanist ideal of science and *personality*. The latter finds expression in the ground-motive that has, since Kant, been called the *nature-freedom* ground-motive.

Thomism claims that, in the proper use of *natural reason*, philosophy can never contradict the supernatural truths of grace contained in the doctrine of the Church. However, although it makes use of natural reason, its claim implies an accommodation of Aristotelian metaphysics and its view of nature to ecclesiastical dogma. Nevertheless, this attempt at accommodation, which is typically scholastic, would not arouse any enthusiasm in a Kantian or Hegelian, any more than it would have in Aristotle if he had been familiar with Thomism.

In fact, the dogma of the autonomy of theoretical thought is absolutely incapable of explaining and justifying the fundamentally different conceptions it displays. How could it do so? And if it cannot, how can it any longer claim for itself the honour of being an unproblematic starting point for philosophy?

---

[2] For an extremely detailed study of this question, from the sources, cf. Herman Dooyeweerd, *Reformatie en Scholastiek in de Wijsbegeerte*, T. Wever, 1949, volume I, 496 pages. [Now available as *Reformation and Scholasticism in Philosophy*, Edwin Mellen Press, Lewiston, NY, 2004].

2. The dogma of the autonomy of
theoretical thought is an obstacle to
every philosophical discussion between the various schools.

If theoretical thought is autonomous, is it not surprising to
see the vehement objections which are always surfacing
between the various schools of philosophy? Because each
independent declares its own thinking to be *autonomous* (not
discerning its true starting point), a deep mutual understanding
between the various schools in philosophy is impossible. We
behold a fierce but unfruitful struggle, each side sticking to its
guns, without really understanding why, since the real starting
point of each one's thinking remains hidden.

If every philosophical trend that *claimed* to find its starting
point in theoretical thought alone actually had no apriori, no
deeper presupposition, it would be possible to convince an
opponent of his error in a purely theoretical way[3]. Now it is a
fact that a Thomist has never succeeded by purely theoretical
arguments in convincing a Kantian or a positivist of the ten-
ability of a theoretical metaphysics. Conversely, Kantian epistemology has never been able to convert a single Thomist to
critical idealism. In discussions between the various philosophical schools, one gets the impression of a dialogue between
the deaf, because they are unable to find a way – for themselves
or each other – of arriving at their true starting points, which
are inexorably *obscured* by the dogma of the autonomy of
theoretical thought.

Reformed philosophy believes that through its method of
critical self-reflection everyone has the opportunity of discovering their own supra-theoretical presuppositions. In this way
it can render a great service to the cause of philosophy in
general, and to the exchange of views between the various
schools that is indispensable for the progress of philosophical
thought.

---

[3] It is quite noticeable that in Lalande's *Vocabulaire de la Philosophie* the term *apriori* is
only explained as a function of reasoning (apriori–aposteriori), and the term *presupposition* is not even mentioned.

Certainly, by itself, this fact of experience is not yet evidence that an autonomous theoretical reflection is impossible for philosophy. However, it does demonstrate the need to make the alleged autonomy of theoretical thought into a *critical problem*, and no longer regard it as a so-called scientific *axiom* which needs no justification. This problem must be posed as an *absolute requirement*.[4] It is of paramount because it concerns empirical science as much as philosophy; both involve the theoretical attitude of thought.

> 3. The need for a transcendental (as well as a transcendent) critique of the theoretical attitude of thought.

The problem we have just raised is that of *a critical enquiry into the universally valid conditions that are necessary for theoretical thought and which are required by the very structure of this thought.* This critical enquiry will therefore take place *within* the *immanent* structure of thought, and it is just by this analysis that it will be possible to unmask all the so-called theoretical axioms, which actually originate from somewhere other than theoretical thought alone. It is therefore a question of a *transcendental*, as opposed to a *transcendent*, critique of science and philosophy.

A transcendent critique confronts, for example, the Christian faith with the results of modern science and the various philosophical systems. It notes, when appropriate, the real differences and conflicts between them. But that critique does not really touch the innermost character and immanent structure of the theoretical attitude of thought. Though transcendent, it yet remains dogmatic, as long as it does not address the fundamental question of whether the theoretical attitude of thought, with reference to its internal structure, can be independent of any supra-theoretical aprioris.

Actually, a transcendent critique is not really *critical*, and poses a double danger. The first regards certain statements as the result of an unbiased science and philosophical reflection

---

[4] [Marcel has: *question du droit*. He derived this from Dooyeweerd's use of the phrase *quaestio iuris* in the same context]

which, after a critical examination, appear to be the consequences of a hidden religious presupposition and anti-Christian attitude of faith. The second, with incalculable consequences, is that a complex of philosophical ideas, dominated by non-biblical ground-motives, will be welcomed into dogmatic theology and accommodated to the doctrine of the Church. Such a complex of ideas, if it has inspired the wording of some confessions of faith, may be passed off without examination as an article of Christian faith.

A *transcendent* critique is worthless to science and to philosophy, because it compares two different spheres *whose inner point of contact is left completely in the dark*, and is not subject to critical scrutiny. One could just as easily, and with no better outcome, critique science from the standpoint of art or politics.

Thus, to ensure from the outset a truly critical attitude in philosophy, a transcendental critique of thought must be carried out *at the very beginning* of philosophical reflection.

Part 2: The first transcendental problem of theoretical thought. The antithetic relation[5] of theoretical thought and the subject-object relation in naive experience.

In what ways do the theoretical attitude of thought and the pre-theoretical attitude of naive experience differ?

What we said in Chapter One about the problem of time will help us to sketch out an answer to this question.

4. The pre-theoretical attitude of naïve experience.

In the pre-theoretical attitude of naive experience, empirical reality presents itself entirely to us in the integral coherence of cosmic time. We do not dissociate the various aspects of reality from one another. We view them all together in their continuous, uninterrupted coherence. If at any time we be-

---

[5] [Remember: the word "object" in double quotes is always Marcel's equivalent of Dooyeweerd's *Gegenstand*. Similarly, Marcel refers to the *Gegenstand-relation* as the *antithetic relation*]

come aware of any of them, it is only implicitly. We grasp both time and reality together in a total typical structure of individuality.

In other words, in naive experience our logical function, as well as all our other functions of consciousness, is completely *immersed* in the coherence of cosmic time. Unlike scientific analysis, naive experience does not involve selective or discriminative thought. It apprehends reality directly in the concrete unity of individual things, social groups, events, and their relationships. It grasps immediately the typical total structures of mountains and rivers, trees and animals, houses and streets, tables and chairs, people who make up a family, a city, a craft guild, a church community, etc. All the modal aspects are grouped and typified in a characteristic manner and in an indissoluble coherence of time within a single whole.

The process of naive concept formation is not directed toward the modal aspects, but to *things* or *concrete events* that constitute *individual totalities*. It is not interested in abstract relations of number or space, nor in the effects of energy as such, but in things which are countable, spatial and subject to physical and chemical change. In the structure of naive exper-ience, the logical aspect is bound by an indissoluble coherence to the non-logical aspects. Consequently, the logical aspect is conceived as an inherent but implicit element of concrete reality. The same applies to the aspect of sensory perception, the cultural aspect of the history, the aesthetic aspect, etc.

How is this integral character of naive experience possible? It is solely on account of the *subject-object relation*, inherent in the structure of naive experience. In this relation, *objective* functions and qualities are unconsciously attributed to things and so-called natural events, in the modal aspects in which it is impossible for them to appear as subjects.

For example, while as adults we are free from animistic representations, and know very well that water itself is not alive, we still attribute to it — in the aspect of organic life — the *objective* function of being a necessary means of life. We know that a bird's nest is not alive, but we can properly represent it to ourselves as something related to the subjective life of a

bird; a nest is a typical object of life. A rose, as a subject, ha_ _ _
feeling, does not think or express an aesthetic judgement.
Nevertheless, we attribute to it the objective qualities of colour
and smell, objective logical characteristics, cultural qualities
and objective beauty.

Moreover, this subject-object relationship in the attitude
of naive experience and thought is grasped *as a structural
relationship of reality itself*. That is, things have objective
functions that are related to *possible subjective functions* these
things do not possess in the aspects of reality involved. The
sensory colour red is attributed to a rose, not in relation to *my*
or your individual sense perceptions, but for all possible
normal human perception of colour. Similarly, water is a
means of life for every conceivable living organism. But when
the subject-object relationship in the biotic aspect is individu-
alised, as in the example of the bird's nest, naive experience still
attributes objective functions to the things *themselves*, and in
accordance with the structural relation they have with *subjective*
life of the animal concerned. Similarly, the objective qualities
which are attributed to the bird's nest in the logical and post-
logical aspects are related to the *subjective* functions of human
nature, but in such a way that here also the individual typical
structure of this nest finds expression, characterised by a
specific relation with animal life. The nest is still a bird's nest as
regards its objective logical and objective aesthetic qualities,
even though it is a possible object of human culture with an
objective symbolic meaning expressed in its name.

The metaphysical concept of substance, that of the "thing
in itself", is absolutely foreign to naive experience, as is also the
abstract enclosing[6] of the reality of things in the modal aspects
that constitute the field of enquiry of physics, chemistry and
biology

---

[6] [That is, a *restricting* of meaning to *one* of its aspects. Dooyeweerd speaks of *acting
entirely in one aspect*. In Dutch: *handelen geheel in zijn physische zin-zijde* (to act entirely
in the meaning-aspect of physics) *Wijsbegeerte der Wetsidee*. II, p.43. In the *New
Critique*, it is translated as : *enclose entirely in its physical aspect*, II, p.46.]

Through the subject-object relationship, we experience reality in the full and integral coherence of all its aspects, as given in the temporal horizon of our experience. Naive experience leaves the typical total structures of this reality *intact*.

> 5. The antithetic structure of the theoretical attitude of thought; its intentional character; the origin of the theoretical problem.

By contrast, in the theoretical attitude of thought, we analyse empirical reality by breaking it up into its various aspects. In all its positive forms, theoretical thought has a typically *antithetic* [7] attitude, in which the logical or analytical function of our actual thought-act is opposed to the non-logical aspects of our experience. In turn, these aspects are "opposed" to our analytic function, and constitute its "object" *(Gegenstand)*. Remember that logical or analytical diversity presupposes a diversity of meaning at the base of any analysis. Logical analysis has nothing it can distinguish other than a previously given cosmic diversity of meaning, unless such analysis is to lose all meaning. Indeed, the logical aspect can only express its logical meaning in its coherence of meaning with all the other aspects. Thus, these non-logical aspects also belong to our *actual* act of thinking, which is concrete in time, and therefore should not be considered exclusively *outside* of the full temporal structure of the latter. In other words, *the antithetic structure of the theoretical attitude of thought can only exist within the temporal total structure of the act of thinking.*

---

[7] Herman Dooyeweerd uses the German word *Gegenstand* and its derivatives in the Dutch text (*Wijsbegeerte der Wetsidee*) as well as in the American translation (*A New Critique of Theoretical Thought*). This German word, usually translated as *object* in epistemological discussions, is used by Dooyeweerd for the way in which the non-logical aspects of reality are opposed to the logical function in the theoretical attitude of thought. Dooyeweerd very distinctly equates this term with *object* in the sense we have just described. In French, we felt unable to retain these German words. When we use "object" (in double quotes), it has the meaning of *Gegenstand*. But we will use most often French terminology.

This antithetic structure is purely *intentional*;[8] it does not have an *ontic* character[9]. The non-logical aspects are therefore in an intentional antithesis to the logical function of thought. Any attempt to grasp them in a logical concept meets resistance from them. It is precisely on account of this resistance that the theoretical problem arises.

In logical analysis, the aspect that is opposed to the logical aspect is theoretically distinguished from all the other aspects. If we use the symbol "X" for the aspect that thought is opposed to, and the symbol "Y" all other aspects, then "X" is placed immediately in an antithetic relation with "Y". This antithesis is the result of the necessary theoretical abstraction of the modal aspects from cosmic time. It does not correspond to the structure of empirical reality and remains *theoretical*. Indeed, time connects all aspects in a continuous coherence of meaning and cannot be eliminated *from reality*.

This resistance mounted by the non-logical aspects of the experience to the logical analysis of their structure is due to the fact that, even when theoretically abstracted, the modal structure of the non-logical aspect "X", which is set in opposition to thought, continues to express its coherence of meaning with the aspects "Y", which do not currently concern the philosopher or scientist.[10]

---

[8] The term *intentional* here carries the sense of a purely mental direction towards the *object* (*Gegenstand*). Its meaning is close to that given to it by phenomenology (Brentano, Husserl).

[9] The term *ontic* is not used here in Heidegger's sense, or in the usual sense of metaphysics. It relates only to empirical reality in its integral meaning, which embraces *all* modal aspects and individuality-structures.

[10] Herman Dooyeweerd notes that the modal structure of the analytical aspect is given as a whole and not in analysed moments. However, in the theoretical attitude of thought, we can analyse the structure of the analytical aspect, but only in its theoretical abstraction of the non-logical aspects, and in its opposition to them. For the analytical aspect, like all others, expresses in its own modal structure the temporal order in which the different aspects are arrayed. It follows that this structure is a unity in a multiplicity of analysable moments. The theoretical act by which we carry out this analysis is not identical with the *abstracted modal structure* of the logical aspect. The subjective analytical function of this concrete act is bound to its modal structure in its temporal coherence with all the other aspects. In its theoretical abstraction this modal structure has only an intentional existence in our act of thought, and can become the "object" (*Gegenstand*) of our actual logical

6. The first transcendental problem of
the theoretical attitude of thought.

From these remarks there follows a consequence of the
utmost importance: If a theoretical study of the modal diversity is only possible through the theoretical abstraction of its
aspects from cosmic time, that is, if a theoretical attitude of
thought is possible only through theoretical abstraction, it is
absolutely impossible any longer to regard theoretical reason as
an unproblematic given. From this arises the first transcendental
problem regarding the theoretical attitude of thought: the
problem of the antithetic relation or theoretical "objectification":

*What do we abstract in the antithetic attitude of theoretic thought
from the structures of empirical reality as these structures are given in
naive experience? And how is this abstraction possible?* [11]

Those who reject the integral conception of time we have
proposed will have to seek another solution to the critical
problem we pose. But this problem cannot be avoided or
shelved, once the theoretical attitude of thought is seriously
confronted with the pre-theoretical attitude of naive experience.

The theoretical attitude of thought, unlike naive experience, splits up reality into its various aspects. But a dogmatic
theory of knowledge, which regards the theoretical attitude of
thought as an unproblematic given, is obliged to destroy the
fundamental difference between the theoretical and the pre-
theoretical attitudes and, ultimately, *to identify the subject-object
relation with antithetic "objectification"*. [12]

---

function. Consequently, it is not the logical function itself that can become an
"object" *(Gegenstand),* but only the abstract (purely intentional) modal structure of
the logical function. We never get to a "transcendental logical subject" that can be
detached from the modal structures of time and be sovereign and "absolute".

[11] [Herman Dooyeweerd, *A New Critique of Theoretical Thought,* I, p.41]

[12] [Or, as Dooyeweerd puts it, "with the antithetic Gegenstand-relation", *A New
Critique of Theoretical Thought,* I, p.41]

Then naive experience becomes a *theory of reality*. However, the unavoidable necessity of *refuting* it becomes evident when it is identified disparagingly as an uncritical "naive realism". And this is then executed in accordance with the requirements of modern natural science and the physiological theory of the "specific energies of the senses". We will come back to this later.

Suffice it for now, and in line with our current purpose, that we have demonstrated the fundamental difference between the naive and the theoretical attitudes of thought, and now regard it as impossible for any philosopher to avoid the first transcendental problem that theoretical thought raises.

> 7. The relation between body and soul in man. The traditional concept may be imputed to the dogmatic ignoring of this first transcendental problem.

The dogmatic ignoring of the problem of analysis in the theoretical attitude of thought has had, and continues to have, important consequences for our entire vision of reality. Take a single example in the context of philosophical and theological anthropology: the traditional dichotomist view of human nature. This view, according to which man is composed of a material body and an immortal rational soul, is undoubtedly due to the error of supposing that the antithetic relation in the theoretical attitude of thought *answers to reality itself*.

Aristotle, in agreement here with Plato, tried to prove that the theoretical activity of thought – the *nous poietikos* (*the active intellect*, νοῦς ποιητικός) – should be entirely independent of and separated from the organs of the material body in its formation of logical concepts. For it to grasp everything but itself in logical universality and abstraction, the active intellect must be separate from the body. The theoretical activity of thought is here hypostatised in its *logical* aspect, conceived as *ousia* (οὐσία), an immortal substance.

Thomas Aquinas accepted Aristotle's theory but accommodated it to the doctrine of the Church. He argued that the rational soul – which, according to him, is characterised by the theoretical activity of thought – is a purely spiritual and immortal substance.

However, starting from the purely _intentional_ antithetic structure of the attitude of theoretical thought, Aristotle, Aquinas, and others proceed to a _real (actual)_ separation of the logical function from all the pre-logical aspects of the body. This is a dualistic conclusion inspired by the form-matter ground-motive, which we regard as incompatible with an integral view of empirical reality.

When the consequences of such an identification of the _intentional_ and the _real_ for the history of philosophy and for dogmatic and ethical theology (as well as all the pseudo-problems it creates) are assessed, the significance and consequences of our first transcendental problem for the theoretical antithesis become evident.

It is henceforth impossible to try and evade the questions it raises. For when we try to account for the thought-processes of the theoretical attitude of thought, we encounter further transcendental problems. The first problem concerns _how_ theoretical thought can overcome the antithesis in question. The first theoretical problem – which is about the resistance offered by the non-logical "object" to the logical function in its analytical activity – leads to the problem of the theoretical _synthesis_ of the logical and non-logical aspects (assuming that a logical concept of the non-logical "object" is possible). Antithesis (or analysis) and synthesis cannot be separated. This leads us to our second transcendental problem.

Part 3: The second transcendental problem of theoretical thought. The starting point of theoretical synthesis.

8. A critique of the starting points of theoretical thought is essential.

How is it possible for us to reunite synthetically the logical and non-logical aspects of experience, which we separated out in the theoretical antithesis? This is the second transcendental problem of theoretical thought.

By raising this problem, we subject all possible *starting points* of theoretical thought to a fundamental critique. This central problem leads us to ask whether the dogma of the autonomy of theoretical reason is *compatible with the intentional structure* of the theoretical attitude of thought.

To create a synthesis, we need a starting point. Now it is obvious that the *real* starting point for theoretical synthesis, whatever it may be, cannot be found in one of the two terms of the antithetic relation. It is clearly impossible that the antithetic relation, the *conditio sine qua non* of the theoretical attitude, could *in itself* be the synthesis-point between the logical aspect of thought and the non-logical "object" *(Gegenstand)* opposed to it. We have shown moreover that cosmic time, the guarantor of the indissoluble *coherence* of the modal aspects, does not offer any Archimedean point to theoretical thought.

So, to reduce the theoretically-separated aspects to a radical *unity* (or, from dualistic perspective, to a *pair* of supposedly radical unities) the starting point has to transcend the theoretical antithesis. Consequently, we strongly suspect that theoretical thought can hardly have *in itself* any genuine or valid starting point for theoretical synthesis. Hence, it could not be autonomous.

That is what we intend to demonstrate, by proving that the dogma of the autonomy of theoretical reason leads its adherents into an impasse.

9. The impasse of immanence philosophy: the source of theoretical antinomies and "-isms".

In order to maintain the supposed autonomy of theoretical thought, its advocates have only one solution to our problem: seek the starting point for theoretical synthesis *in theoretical reason itself.* So what possibilities exist for this so-called autonomous reason? Left to itself, as we know, it is unable to orient itself to the true Archimedean point from which it would be able to develop a genuine synthesis, and have a clear idea of the fullness and Origin of meaning. The postulate of autonomy, by definition, forces it to seek its starting point in *creaturely meaning* and *within time*. But because theoretical reason has an antithetic attitude, it is not faced with empirical reality, but with all the non-logical modal aspects of temporal experience. So from which of them will it select its crystallisation-point for theoretical synthesis – a choice it cannot escape? Indeed, there exist as many possible ways of synthesis as there are non-logical modal aspects; it is possible to have typically mathematical, physical, biological, psychological or even historical synthetic thought. Whichever theoretical reason settles on invariably leads to the *absolutising* of a particular modal aspect, around which it will crystallise the full meaning of empirical reality.

This is the source of all the "-isms" in the theoretical image of reality that makes reason autonomous. It cannot help but try to reduce all other aspects to *simple modalities* of the absolutised aspect.

All the "-isms" (whatever they are: materialism, biologism, psychologism, historicism, etc.) turn out to be essentially uncritical for two reasons.

In the first place, they cannot be justified *theoretically*. The antithetic structure of the theoretical attitude of thought tenaciously resists any attempt to reduce one aspect to another. In its attempt to break this resistance, every absolutisation inescapably leads theoretical thinking into *internal antinomies*. How could there be room for the absolute in the theoretical domain, when the theoretical attitude of thought is itself founded on an antithetic *relation*? No theoretical synthesis will ever erase this relation. It would be tantamount to erasing the theoretical attitude of thought itself. In any theoretical synthesis, logical analysis is dependent on the modal structure of the opposing non-logical aspect, and the synthesis, therefore, has a character that is partly logical and partly non-logical. The theoretical synthesis is certainly a *union*, but it is not the deeper unity of the logical and the non-logical. *It thus presupposes a supra-theoretical starting point that must transcend theoretical diversity.*

Secondly, given the range of possible modalities of theoretical synthesis, why does theoretical reason pick out one of them rather than another? Why is it directed towards one "-

ism" in preference to another? The act of *absolutising* a modal aspect, with a view to synthesis, cannot originate in the theoretical attitude of thought itself. *It thus presupposes a supratheoretical starting point that must transcend the theoretical diversity.*

By means of two lines of enquiry, therefore, we see that the second transcendental problem of theoretical thought remains unresolved, both for philosophy and the special sciences. The latter also has to carry out both a synthesis and an analysis. This lack of critical thinking leads to as much confusion in philosophy as in science.

> 10. A common denominator is indispensable for the theoretical comparison and distinction of the modal aspects.

It will perhaps be objected: You seek, we are told, a starting point for theoretical synthesis. But have not you imperceptibly passed from the problem of synthesis to that of a theoretical vision of reality? Are they not two different problems? Does science really require a theoretical vision of reality? Are not pure mathematics, logic, and ethics, for example, independent of such?

To answer this question, let us remember that the theoretical attitude of thought consists in separating the modal aspects of reality and opposing them to each other. In this process, the logical aspect of our act of thought is opposed to the non-logical aspects.

But how is a theoretical setting apart of the non-logical aspects possible without a penetration of their mutual relations and coherence? And how can these aspects be distinguished from each other, if they have absolutely nothing in common? An ordering or *comparison* of the non-logical aspects presupposes a common denominator.

In our view, the modal aspects can have no other common denominator than the *cosmic order of time*, which is expressed in the modal structure of each of them and guarantees its coherence with all the others. But from the immanence-standpoint, another denominator of comparison will have to be sought, for example, as we have seen, by reducing all the other aspects to simple modalities of a special absolutised aspect or, as was the case in Greek and scholastic metaphysics, by accepting a metaphysical concept of *being* as an *analogical unity* at the base of the diversity of the special aspects.

In any case, it cannot be denied that the theoretical vision of the mutual relations and coherence of these aspects implies, and consequently cannot presuppose, *a theoretical vision of reality*. This vision is, in fact, none other than that of the abstracted modal aspects in the totality of their coherence.

So our response to the former objection is to demonstrate that neither science nor philosophy can escape such a theoretical vision of reality.

Take, for example, pure mathematics. Immediately, the problem arises of how to conceive the relationship between the aspects of number, space, movement, sensory perception, logical thought and symbolic meaning. However, it is quite remarkable that, in accordance with their respective visions of this basic problem, pure mathematicians are split into different schools, such as: *logicism, symbolic formalism, empiricism, and intuitionism*. These differences[13] are not limited to the philosophy of mathematics alone. Logicism tries to reduce the aspects of number and space to the logical aspect, symbolic formalism tries to reduce them to the linguistic aspect, and empiricism tries to reduce them to the aspect of sensory perception.

In logic, theoretical schools abound. Here also different conceptions of the nature and limits of the field of logic are the result of the different theoretical visions of reality and its aspects. The place that the logical aspect occupies in the order and coherence of the different aspects implies a theoretical conception that depends on a choice of a starting point necessary for every theoretical synthesis. Depending on our initial choice, we end up with *psychologism, mathematicism, symbolic conventionalism, or dialectic historicism*, etc.

---

[13] For example, the famous Dutch mathematician Brouwer, leading light of the intuitionist school, completely eliminates an entire branch of scientific activity developed by the formalist and logicist theories (the theory of transfinite numbers).

The same applies to all the other special sciences: aesthetics, ethics, theology, etc. We shall return to this matter in a detailed study of each modal aspect. Simply to determine, for example, the disputed domain of ethics, without confusing it with the philosophy of law or theology, demands a theoretical vision of the relationships between ethical modal meaning and all the other modal aspects, not merely those of law and faith. One's view of every moral norm depends on a theoretical vision; which in turn depends on *the starting point* for theoretical ethical reflection.

From this it follows that each particular area of theoretical enquiry, whether or not it is "empirical" in the strictest sense, *presupposes a theoretical vision of temporal reality*. And this vision must necessarily exceed the limits of each special science and be of a *philosophical* character. At the same time it follows that *no special science can really be autonomous with respect to philosophy, considered as a theory of reality*. We will return to this in our final chapter.

11. The starting point of theoretical synthesis in the Kantian critique of knowledge.

Does this mean that we have proved, and that irrefutably, that theoretical thought itself, with respect to its inner nature, is dependent on a *supra-theoretical* starting point that radically excludes the autonomy of this thought?

This must not be accepted too hastily however, for we would be immediately rebutted with the fact that Kant supposed he could locate a starting point in theoretical reason itself, *which would be the basis for any possible theoretical synthesis*, and which would therefore be free of any absolutisation carried out from a special scientific viewpoint. We have to consider, then, whether the Kantian transcendental critique really demonstrates the autonomy of theoretical reason.

We have already addressed this issue with our introduction of the transcendental critical method of the Archimedean point. We have said that philosophical thought – theoretical thought directed towards the totality of meaning of our temporal cosmos – cannot come to a transcendental idea of this totality without analytical self-reflection.

The really critical issue, which we have only raised and which needs investigating, is *the relationship between the thinking selfhood and its theoretical logical thought-function.*

Is this functionalist manner of posing the problem satisfactory? Why direct our attention solely to the *logical function*, and not to the *integral act* of theoretical thought? For while it might be true that theoretical thought can be characterised by its theoretical logical aspect, it certainly cannot by any manner or means be identified with it.

In our examination of the internal structure of the theoretical attitude of thought in the preceding section (Part 2), we emphasised its antithetic character, and this enables us to resolve this new problem. Indeed, it is just the antithetic structure of the theoretical attitude of thought that forced Kant and his followers to oppose the logical function to the other modal aspects of the integral act of thought.

From the perspective of the *structure* of the theoretical attitude of thought, the problem is well formulated. But in their attempt to resolve it, Kant and his successors committed a fundamental error: they identified the *real act* with a *purely psychical temporal event,* which in turn becomes an "object" *[Gegenstand]* of the ultimate "transcendental-logical cogito". It was an error, because we know that the antithetic relation of "objectification" [i.e., the *Gegenstand*-relation] can only be an *intentional* relation between its logical aspect and its non-logical aspects located *within* the real act of theoretical thought. The real act itself can never become the "object" of its logical function, since the latter only exists within a real act of consciousness. Reduced to a mere theoretical abstraction, the real act cannot have any actuality, and sinks into nothingness. Therefore, the identification of this real act with its psychical aspect is untenable, and reveals a dualistic view of reality that cannot be explained in terms of pure epistemology.

Therefore, the transcendental problem of the origin of philosophical thought demands a further, much deeper, critical enquiry; one that does not depend on the first way relating to the Archimedean point.

Part 4: The third transcendental problem of theoretical thought. The concentric direction of theoretical thought toward the selfhood.

> 12. The problem of the starting point and method of a reflective critique in theoretical thought. The Kantian conception of the transcendental unity of apperception.

In order to discover the immanent starting point of all special synthetic acts of thought, in which the latter find their true unity, we must, according to Kant, divert our attention from the "objects" *(Gegenstände)* of our consciousness, and carry out an examination or critical self-reflection within theoretical thought.

This suggestion contains great promise. However, as long as theoretical thought in its logical function is directed merely to the opposed modal aspects of reality that constitute its "object", it remains unquestionably dispersed in a theoretical *diversity*. To acquire a concentric direction toward the ultimate unity of consciousness, which must lie at the root of all the modal diversity of meaning, theoretical thought must be directed *towards the thinking self*. Our selfhood, as we have pointed out, *functions* in all modal aspects of reality. But it is also nonetheless *a central and radical unity* which, as such, transcends every temporal aspect.

That is why no special science in the field of anthropology can ever answer the question: What is *man?* Each, in accordance with its viewpoint, will respond in a partial manner with a fragment of the truth, and offer us its conception of man – whether physical-chemical, biological, psychological, historical, linguistic, anthropological or sociological. But no special science, not even an encyclopaedic sociology, can ever tell us what man himself is in the unity of his selfhood.

Only the implementation of a critical self-reflection will lead us to the discovery of the true starting point of theoretical thought. With his maxim: "Know thyself", Socrates elevated this self-reflection to the status of a primary condition of philosophical reflection.

So the third transcendental problem of the critique of theoretical thought takes shape:

How is this critical self-reflection, the concentric direction of theoretical thought to the selfhood, possible; and what is its real character?

This is indeed a genuine transcendental problem, provided we do not lose sight of the fact that the theoretical attitude of thought, as regards its internal structure, is inseparable from the antithetic relation we have already examined.

Kant, who wanted to preserve the autonomy of theoretical reason, supposed, as we have seen, that in the logical function of the understanding it was possible to demonstrate the existence of *a subjective pole of thought*, opposed to all empirical reality, and which, as *transcendental-logical unity of apperception*, lies at the base, and is the *starting point*, of all synthetic acts of thought. The "I think", he insists, must accompany all my representations (i.e., surely, the "synthetic concepts of empirical objects[14]") if they are truly to be *my* representations. He meant this as a final transcendental-*logical* unity of consciousness, which can never become an "object", since every theoretical act of knowledge must proceed from this "I think". This is the "transcendental-logical subject of thought", which demands to be regarded as the universally-valid condition of every scientific synthesis.

Two things are now evident. The first is that the transcendental-logical subject is not identical with our real empirical act of thought which, according to Kant, can still become the "object" of this transcendental subject. The second, which follows from the first, is that the transcendental subject is reduced to nothing more than a *logical* point of consciousness,

---

[14] [Dooyeweerd identifies *objects* here with *Gegenstände*. See NC, I, p.53]

and is then stripped of all empirical individuality. And so Kant denies that we possess a real self-*knowledge* in the transcendental logical *concept* of the thinking self.

According to his epistemological conception, in fact, human *knowledge* depends only on impressions given in sense perception *(Empfindung)* received in the transcendental forms of intuition of space and time, and ordered by the logical categories into an "objective reality of experience". But while the real starting point for theoretical synthesis cannot be located *within* the antithetic relation of the theoretical attitude of thought, as we have shown, Kant's transcendental-logical ego remains trapped in the *logical* pole of this relation which, he believes, finds its counter-pole in the non-logical aspect of sensory perception. And since Kant is careful to fully explain to us that the logical aspect of thought and the aspect of sense perception are irreducible, it follows as a matter of course that we cannot find in the former any starting point to unite them theoretically.

Kant was therefore unable to demonstrate the existence of a starting point immanent in "theoretical reason", which meets the requirements of a genuine transcendental critique of theoretical thought. Because of his axiom that every synthesis must originate in the logical function of thought, Kant moreover abandoned every critical method of enquiry, and evaded the real problem of synthesis by simply replacing it with a dogmatic assertion. He could not do otherwise. The dogma of the autonomy of "theoretical reason" forced it on him, and compelled him to leave the *real* starting point of his theory of knowledge completely in the dark.

To our first transcendental problem, which he ignores, Kant has no answer. He is also unable to respond to the third problem we raised and ignores it also. It is not surprising that neither could he come up with a critical solution to our second problem.

If it is impossible to find in theoretical thought *as such* any starting point for the intermodal synthesis, this is because the concentric direction of this thought, necessary for a critical self-reflection, cannot have a *theoretical* origin. Like it or not, it must originate in my selfhood, the individual centre of my human existence.

Neither phenomenology, founded by Edmund Husserl, nor modern existentialism, has been able to dissociate the theoretical attitude of thought from the antithetic relation.

Phenomenology, in the steps of Franz Brentano, even affirms the intentional relation of *every* act of consciousness to an "object", but this fact has not the import that it might for us because the term *object* is understood by Brentano and Husserl in quite a different way to us; they attribute to feeling as well an intentional relation to an *object* (which could even be a melody).

However, as we have already hinted, the intentional antithetic structure, inherent in all theoretical thought, is undoubtedly present in the phenomenological attitude itself, as it opposes the absolute *"cogito"* (in the sense of an "absolute transcendental consciousness") to the "world" as its intentional "object" which depends on it. Scheler regards the antithetic relation – by which the human mind can oppose itself not only to the "world", but can even make the physiological and psychical aspects of human experience into an "object" – as the most formal category of the logical aspect of mind *(Geist)*.[15]

Modern humanist existentialism, too, can only grasp existence (as the free historical *ex-sistere*) in its theoretical *antithesis* to a "given reality of nature" (for Heidegger, the *Dasein*, the "ontological" manner of being, contrasted with the "given world" as the "ontic"; for Sartre, "nothingness" as opposed to "being"). Indeed, Heidegger himself is a phenomenologist, although his phenomenological method is irrationalist in the

---

[15] Cf. Edmund Husserl, *Ideen zu einer Phänomenologie und phänomenologischen Philosophie*, Halle, Max Niemeyer, 1913, p.92, [English trans.: *Ideas Pertaining to a Pure Phenomenology and to aPhenomenological Philosophy—First Book*, 1982 (1913), trans. Fred Kersten, The Hague, Martinus Nijhoff.], and Max Scheler, *Die Stellung des Menschen im Kosmos*, Darmstadt, Otto Reichl Verlag, 1930 (1928), p.58, [English trans.: *The Human Place in the Cosmos*, trans. Manfred Frings, Evanston, Northwestern University Press, 2009.]

hermeneutical sense of Dilthey's historicism; and phenomenology, as we have seen, implies the theoretical antithesis.

Given this antithetic attitude of existentialist thought, it is immaterial that the philosophy of existence tries to put a great distance between genuinely philosophical existentialist thought on the one hand and all scientific thought directed towards an "object" on the other. Although the natural sciences are also bound to the antithetic relation, existentialist thought gives the term "object" *[Gegenstand]* the meaning of "given object" *(das Vorhandene)*, which is quite different from our meaning.

For now, we cannot understand how the concentric direction of theoretical thought to the selfhood could obtain from the theoretical attitude of thought.

> 13. The concentric direction of theoretical thought toward the selfhood has a religious origin.

What, then, is our solution?

In our Introduction, we noted that the selfhood could not give this central direction to its theoretical thought without focussing itself on the true and absolute Origin (or one that is supposed such) of all meaning. This means that self-knowledge ultimately depends on the knowledge of God, though a knowledge that has nothing to do with a theoretical theology. Here we address the issue of the "transition" from the realm of theory to the central religious sphere, to which we alluded in our Introduction. We now set out to account for it.

First, we must recognise that self-knowledge and knowledge of the absolute Origin, or of a pseudo-Origin, both exceed the limits of theoretical thought and are rooted in the *heart*, the religious centre of our existence. However, this central supra-theoretical knowledge does not remain enclosed in the heart. By its very nature, it penetrates the temporal realm of our consciousness. Theoretical thought also is concerned in this central knowledge, in the transcendental process of critical self-reflection, and in the concentration of the theoretically-separated aspects of the antithetic relation upon the thinking selfhood. Indeed, we already know two things: first, that without a genuine self-*knowledge*, we cannot discover the true starting point for theoretical synthesis; second, because the concentric direction of theoretical thought can only originate with the selfhood, theoretical self-reflection presupposes this central knowledge. These two truths were totally neglected by Kant and modern phenomenology.[16]

However, only the biblical Revelation of man's creation in the image of God truly accounts for this fact. God reveals Himself as the absolute Origin who excludes all independent counter-powers that might be opposed to Him. He has expressed his image in man; in other words, he has concentrated all man's temporal existence in the radical religious unity of a selfhood in which the totality of meaning of the temporal cosmos was meant to be focused on its Origin. Consequently, the fundamental dependence of self-knowledge upon the knowledge of God originates in the essence of religion, the central sphere of our created nature.

14. The pretended vicious circle of our transcendental critique.

At this juncture, two objections could be made against us.

First: In its third step, is not your transcendental critique guilty of an unwarranted "leap" by taking the concentric direction of theoretical thought to be an effect of the religious sphere of our consciousness? Have you brought sufficient evidence for this? And what do you mean by religion?

Second: If your critique actually did prove anything, would you not hereby have mired yourself in a vicious circle? Does not a *proof* imply the autonomy of theoretical reason, which your critique regards as an illusion?

To the second question, Herman Dooyeweerd answers that what is undoubtedly *proved* is that the concentric direction of thought in its reflecting on itself cannot be derived from the theoretical attitude of this thought itself, but only from the selfhood, the individual supra-theoretical centre of our existence.

---

[16] The empirical fact that self-knowledge depends on the knowledge of God is established by Ernst Cassirer in the second volume of his *Philosophy of Symbolic Forms*, based on extensive anthropological and ethnological data.

So far, our critique has kept strictly within the theoretical sphere. It has highlighted a number of structural issues that have been completely ignored under the influence of the dogma of the autonomy of theoretical reason. These questions, once raised, can no longer be ignored by anyone able to appreciate the true worth of a resolutely critical standpoint in philosophy.

Of course, it is impossible that this transcendental critique should be free from any apriori, even in the question of whether self-*knowledge* is purely theoretical by nature. If it were thus free, it would refute its own conclusions.

But do our supra-theoretical presuppositions – which result in freeing theoretical thought from dogmatic "axioms" – conform to a truly critical attitude? If we have shown that the theoretical synthesis is only possible because of a supra-theoretical starting point (and we think we have demonstrated this irrefutably) then no one can dispute the need for these supra-theoretical presuppositions, a fact our critics will be forced to admit. The only thing that can be questioned is their *content*.

And how could the demonstrative force of our critique so far be anything other than *negative? What can be demonstrated* is that the starting point of theoretical thought cannot be located within this thought itself, but must be supra-theoretical or meta-philosophical. But it is impossible to prove *theoretically* that this starting point should be in the central religious sphere of our consciousness, for the simple reason that this enquiry is one of self-*knowledge* which, as such, transcends the theoretical attitude of thought. The only thing we can say is that this self-*knowledge* is necessary in a critical sense, because without it the true *character* of this starting point remains forever concealed from us. While it remains so, nothing will be more fatal to the critical examination of its true meaning for whatever internal direction philosophical thought might take under its impulse.

It would be a totally uncritical begging the question to claim that by abandoning the autonomy of theoretical thought our critique is locked in a vicious circle.

15. What is religion?

We come now to the first objection, and our reply to the first question: What do you mean by religion?

By religion we mean *the innate impulse of human personality to direct itself to the absolute Origin, real or assumed, of the temporal diversity of meaning, which is focused concentrically in itself.*

Since *in philosophical reflection* we clearly ought to account for the meaning we give to the word "religion", our definition has to be really theoretical and philosophical. It has of necessity a formal transcendental character that the concrete immediacy of religious experience cannot apprehend.

If, from the central religious sphere, we seek a theoretical approximation of religion, we can arrive only at a transcendental *Idea* or limiting-concept, whose content must remain abstract if it is to embrace all possible manifestations of religion, including apostate ones. Such an Idea invariably has the function of relating the theoretical diversity of the modal aspects to a central radical unity and to an Origin.

But here is a point we cannot emphasise enough. As the radically central sphere of human existence, religion transcends every modal aspect of reality, *including the aspect of faith.* It is not a temporal phenomenon which manifests itself *within* the temporal structure of practical life. It can only be approximated in the concentric direction of our consciousness, not in an ex-centric direction, nor as an antithetic "object". And this, be it noted, is regardless of its beliefs and their content. Indeed, we know that the faith-function, like every other function of our existence, is bound to cosmic time and to the temporal coherence of meaning, and it should never be identified with the religious centre of our existence. Nevertheless, the direction and content of faith cannot be understood apart from the religious ground-motive that directs it, nor apart from a divine revelation, whatever interpretation (genuine or apostate) is put on it. By its very nature, it is impossible to describe religion "phenomenologically". It is neither a "psychological phenomenon", nor an emotional sensory perception, nor the experience of the *tremendum*, as Rudolph Otto terms it. It is the ex-*sistent*[17] condition by which the ego is bound to its real or supposed-real firm foundation.

It follows that the manner of existence of the selfhood is religious in essence and is nothing *in itself*. True religion is a genuine *self-surrender*. Apostate man, who assumes that his selfhood is something in itself, loses himself in surrender to idols by absolutising what is only relative. When man aspired to be something *in himself* it was his downfall. As Calvin expresses it with his usual precision: "God formed man in his image and likeness, so that the light of His glory shone clearly in him...But the wretched, *aspiring to be something in himself*...God's image and likeness in him were erased".[18]

The absolutising of what is relative is a clear indication of the ex-*sistent* character of the religious centre of our existence, which is definitely expressed in every modal aspect of time, but which can never be *assimilated* or *exhausted* by them. Even in the religious absolutising of the historical aspect of our existence, which is tantamount to surrendering to a single aspect of time, we continue to transcend time.

Nevertheless, the autonomous ex-*sistere* of the selfhood that has lost itself in surrender to idols must be broken down by the *divine ex-trahere* from its apostasy, for man to regain his true ex-*sistent* position.

We can now answer the first part of the first question we were asked. Our conception of religion allows us to establish the fact that the concentric direction of theoretical thought must have a religious origin. Although it is always of a theoretical character, it has a religious origin, because it always depends on the "objectifying" antithetic relation. On the one hand, it springs from the tendency toward the Origin, which we find at the centre of human existence. On the other hand, as a consequence of the intrinsic structure of the theoretical attitude of thought, critical reflection – in the concentric direction

---

[17] Dooyeweerd here uses a well-known term from the modern philosophy of life. He stresses however that it is not meant here in the Humanist sense.

[18] John Calvin, *Epître à tous amateurs de Jésus-Christ*, [A Letter to all who love Jesus Christ] 1535, Ed. J. Pannier, Paris, Librairie Fischbacher, 1929, p.36.

of theoretical thought to the selfhood – necessarily appeals to a self-knowledge that is, as we have shown, beyond the limits of the theoretical antithetic relation.

We have thus demonstrated the internal point of contact between philosophical thought and religion, and we can consider it as an established fact that both the theoretical analysis and synthesis presuppose a religious starting point. Finally, we have just shown that it is unreasonable to demand theoretical proof of the religious character of this starting point: *any such evidence would be meaningless, because it presupposes the existence of this central starting point of theoretical thought.*

16. The supra-individual nature of the starting point. The communal spirit and the religious ground-motive.

We now come to the last stage of our transcendental critique.

We have established two facts: the necessarily religious starting point of thought, and the inherently ex-sistent character of the selfhood. These two facts lead to a momentous conclusion: that in reality it is not in the *individual* ego alone that we must seek the true starting point of philosophical thought.

In our Introduction, we remarked firstly that the selfhood must participate in the Archimedean point and secondly, that the full meaning of the temporal cosmos must be concentrated in this Archimedean point. But the selfhood is only the focal point of our individual existence, and not of the entire cosmos.

In addition, as a science, in the strictest sense of the word, philosophy is not a matter that concerns only the individual. It can only be developed in and through a *community*.

We have demonstrated in a number of ways the necessity for a *supra*-individual starting point. But that in no way diminishes the importance of critical reflection in theoretical thought, which is the only way of discovering the starting point for philosophy. For, ultimately, it is always the individual ego that stamps a concentric direction on its thought.

However, true self-knowledge reveals the ex-sistent character of the selfhood in a strict interdependence of the self with other selves in a religious community. In the individual ego, the central radical unity of our existence *points beyond* this selfhood to that which makes the whole of humanity spiritually *one in root*, in its creation, fall and at the same time redemption. The unity of our existence is, therefore, both individual and *supra*-individual.

According to our Christian faith, all humanity is spiritually included in Adam. In him the whole human race fell, and with it the entire temporal cosmos, which was concentrated in it. In Jesus Christ, the new humanity also is one in root, as members of a single body.

In other words, our self is rooted in the spiritual communion of humanity. It is not an autonomous "substance" or a "windowless monad". It lives in the spiritual community of the We which, in accord with the original meaning of creation, is directed to a divine Thou.

The Summary of the Law: "You shall love the Lord your God with all thy heart and with all your soul and with all your mind and with all your strength: you shall love your neighbour as yourself" undoubtedly shows the existence and the permanence of this spiritual community. This Summary of the Law, in its indivisible unity, is *religious* in nature and not merely moral[19]. But the existence of this religious command of love presupposes and posits that the neighbour is a member of the radically religious community of humanity in its central relationship with God, who created man in His image. This command is the root of all the modal aspects, which express God's Law in temporal reality.

However, a religious community is bound together by a common spirit. As a moral power ($\delta\acute{\upsilon}\nu\alpha\mu\iota\varsigma$), as a key idea, this spirit acts at the focal point of human existence. It takes shape in a religious ground-motive that provides a decisive primary

---

[19] Remember that the moral relations of love with our neighbour are only one of the modal aspects of society. They have meaning only in coherence with all the other aspects of our social life and, according to the diversity of social relationships, are differentiated in conjugal love, love of parents and children, social love of our neighbour, love of country, etc.

direction to the entire attitude of life and thought springing from it.

It goes without saying that in the historical development of society this ground-motive will take on specific historically-determined *forms*. But by virtue of its central religious significance, this ground-motive transcends the historical modal aspect and its relations, and consequently any actual historical formation. It would be trapped in a vicious circle if it attempted to explain this historical development in a purely historical manner, for by virtue of the internal structure of the theoretical attitude of thought an historical explanation presupposes a supra-theoretical central starting point, which is in turn determined by this religious ground-motive.

Since the fall and the promise of the coming of the Redeemer, two major currents have been at work at the heart of human existence. The first is due to the *work of the Holy Spirit* who, through the effective power of the Word of God incarnate in Jesus Christ, redirects to the Creator the creation which, by the fall, had fallen away from its true Origin. The Holy Spirit establishes a filial relation between man and his Heavenly Father. The religious ground-motive of this regenerating current is that of the Revelation of the Word of God, which provides the key to the interpretation of Holy Scripture, namely: *the ground-motive of Creation, the Fall and Redemption by Jesus Christ in the communion of the Holy Spirit.*

The second current is that of the *spirit of apostasy*, which seeks to estrange and divorce man from the one true God. It is an awesome religious power; it dominates the human heart and leads it in an immanent direction toward creaturely meaning. It is this that lies at the root of all deification of the creature. It is this that is responsible for the absolutising of the attitude of thought, which should always be relative even when it is theoretical.

By virtue of its idolatrous character, this religious ground-motive can have quite diverse contents.

17. The Greek *Form-Matter* ground-
motive and the modern Humanist
Nature-Freedom ground-motive.

In Western thought, the spirit of apostasy has manifested itself principally through two central ground-motives:

1. That which dominated classical Greek culture and thought. Since Aristotle it has been known as the *Form-Matter* ground-motive.

2. That of the modern Humanist conception of life and the world. Since Kant it has been known as the *Nature-Freedom* ground-motive.

Since the eighteenth century the latter has increasingly come to dominate Western culture and thought.

1. *The form-matter ground-motive*. This originated from the coming together of the ancient pre-Homeric Greek religion as the *religion of life* (one of many religions of nature), and the *cultural religion* of the Olympian gods. The ancient religion of life deified the eternally flowing stream of life, which could not be contained in any individual form. Periodically, generations of transitory beings arose from this stream but their existence, which was limited to an individual form, consigned them to the dreadful fate of death (ἀναγκή or ἡμαρμενή τύχη). This is the *matter-motive* of Greek thought, which found its most acute expression in the cult of Dionysus, which was imported from Thrace.

Secondly, the *form-motive* was the product of the later religion of Olympus, the religion of the form of measure and harmony. It was mainly based on the deification of the cultural aspect of Greek society. This motive found its deepest expression in the Delphic Apollo, the Lawgiver.

The Olympian gods were the Greek cultural powers personified. They left mother-earth with her eternally-flowing stream of life, and her menacing ἀναγκή. They acquired Olympus for their home, and had an individual immortal form, imperceptible to (human) senses. Nevertheless, they had no power over the fate of mortals.

The form-matter ground-motive was independent of the mythological forms it acquired in the old nature-religions and the newer cultural religion of Olympus. It dominated Greek thought from the outset.

We have already seen that the autonomy demanded by philosophical theory, in opposition to popular belief, implied only the emancipation from the mythological forms that were the product of sensory representation. In no way did it require philosophical thought to abandon the central religious ground-motive, which arose out of the coming together of the cultural religion and the older religion of life.

2. *The nature-freedom ground-motive*, which pertains to the modern humanist philosophy, was born of the religion of the free autonomous human personality, on the one hand, and the modern science-oriented religion of the domination of nature, on the other. To fully understand this ground-motive, it needs to be seen against the backdrop of the three fundamental motives that had previously given direction to Western thought:

a) the form-matter ground-motive

b) the ground-motive of creation, fall and redemption

c) the scholastic nature-grace ground-motive, introduced by Roman Catholicism for the purpose of synthesising the two former ground-motives.

The fact that the apostate current of thought manifests itself in various religious ground-motives is not at all surprising. By definition, in fact, it is incapable, in the absence of a concentric direction to the true Origin, of directing the attitude of thought and life towards the real totality of meaning and towards the real root of temporal reality. Every absolutisation is necessarily applied to a single aspect of meaning that has been torn from an actual temporal coherence. It is consequently empty and meaningless, *in*-significant (i.e., *signifying nothing*).

This is the awful truth that is revealed in the age-old conception of the Fall as both *privatio* (loss of meaning) and as negation *(non-*sense, *nothingness)*.

18. Sin. The dialectical character of the leading apostate ground-motives. Religious and theoretical dialectic.

However, we do not have to accept that the central *power* of the spirit of apostasy is a "nothing" or nothingness. This power lies firmly *within* the boundaries of creation, and cannot operate beyond the boundaries imposed on it by the divine order of meaning. Only by virtue of the religious concentration-impulse in the human heart is it possible for the human heart to direct itself to idols. The power of sin is *linked to the religious concentration-law* of human existence, and can only exist or operate in accordance with that law. That is why the apostle Paul says that without law there is no sin, and that there is a *law* of sin.

Consequently, there can be no inner contradiction, no dialectical relationship, between creation and fall, if they are understood in their Biblical sense. A contradiction would arise if, and only if, sin had a *real* power *in itself, independent of creation and its laws* – which will never happen.

On the contrary, the very nature of the idolatrous ground-motives binds them to an inescapable internal religious antithesis. We know that every aspect of meaning is by definition *relative*. So what happens when a particular modal aspect is absolutised, and an attempt is made to reduce all the other aspects to simple modalities of the absolutised aspect? Actually, these aspects do not allow it to happen, as it impinges on their true meaning. They in turn begin to claim, in the religious consciousness, an absoluteness identical but *opposed* to the deified aspect. The deification of any (relative) aspect evokes the others as its *correlates*.

At this point a *religious* dialectic appears within these ground-motives. They are actually composed of two conflicting and irreconcilable religious motives. Human thought gravitates endlessly to one then to the other, moving from one pole to the other in opposite directions. Herman Dooyeweerd submitted this religious dialectic to a detailed examination in the first volume of his *Reformation and Scholasticism in Philosophy*, and demonstrated that it is quite different from the theoretical dialectic inherent in the intentional antithetic relation of theoretical thought.

While theoretical antithesis is inherently *relative*, antithesis in the religious sphere always is by nature *absolute*. Theoretical antithesis leads to theoretical synthesis. But does the religious antithesis allow any genuine synthesis? Where could it find a starting point from which this synthesis might begin, since such a starting point must be of a religious nature? And how could any philosophical attempt to overcome this religious antithesis in the starting point by means of a dialectical theoretical logic end in a positive result? Such an enquiry is absolutely and radically *uncritical*. Even so, this applies to every so-called "dialectic" philosophy, from Heraclitus to Hegel, in so far as it sought an ultimate synthesis of its conflicting religious motives. It is indeed a squaring of the circle, and for the following reason.

A theoretical synthesis of a religious antithesis is always subject to the intrinsic law of a religious dialectic. In other words, as soon as philosophy returns to the way of critical self-reflection these supposed syntheses are automatically dissolved into the polar antithesis within their starting point. In Greek antiquity, the efforts to eliminate the religious antithesis between the form-motive and the matter-motive by means of a dialectical logic only resulted, in the later stages of Greek thought, in a polar antithesis. Hegel also sought to "think together" the antithetic motives of nature and freedom. But against this synthetic dialectic Proudhon declared the verdict already delivered by Kant and repeated by Kierkegaard: "The antinomy cannot be resolved".

19. The religious dialectic of the scholastic nature-grace ground-motive.

A more complex religious dialectic appears in the fundamental scholastic ground-motive of *nature-grace*, introduced into philosophy and theology by Roman Catholicism, and unfortunately taken over by Protestant scholasticism.

This ground-motive was originally a synthesis between the central ground-motive of the revealed Word and that of the Greek (especially the Aristotelian) conception of nature (the form-matter ground-motive). But it also lends itself readily to a combining of the revealed Word with the humanistic nature-freedom ground-motive. In this attempt at synthesis the Christian ground-motive automatically loses its radical integral character.

In the scholastic vision of human nature, there is no room for the biblical revelation of the heart considered as the centre and root of our temporal existence. When it proclaimed the autonomy of natural reason in the "natural sphere" of knowledge, Thomistic scholasticism was oblivious to the fact that, *ipso facto*, it subjected philosophy to the domination of a religious ground-motive that no accommodation to the doctrine of the Church could ever neutralise. Such a ground-motive will always exercise its corrosive action in the whole sphere of thought.

The Greek ground-motive that here dominates the view of nature has itself undergone some scholastic accommodation to the Christian doctrine of creation, and the Humanistic ground-motive has, likewise, undergone an accommodation to the doctrines of creation and fall. Thus, the internal dialectic of the Greek ground-motive on the one hand and the Humanist ground-motive on the other are concealed, as a component, in the dialectical tension between "nature" and "grace".

In scholastic anthropology this component is very clearly expressed, as we have already noted, in the dichotomistic relation of body and soul, whether this conception is dominated by the "form-matter" ground-motive or the "nature-freedom" ground-motive.

The internal dialectic of the nature-grace ground-motive drove scholastic thought in the fourteenth century from the Thomist pseudo-synthesis *(natura preambula gratiae)* to the Occamist antithesis, according to which there is no point of contact between nature and grace.

Recently, this ground-motive has disclosed its polar tendencies in "dialectical theology". Karl Barth and Emil Brunner are in disagreement as to whether it is possible to find a "point of contact" for grace in "nature". In response to Brunner's affirmative, taking a synthetic approach, Barth opposed an inexorable NO. However, in his *Dogmatics*, Barth has abandoned this radically antithetical conception of nature and grace.[20]

> 20. The necessary primacy of one of the antithetic components of a dialectical ground-motive.

A real synthesis of the conflicting religious principles that operate simultaneously in a dialectical ground-motive is impossible. In its quest for unity, there remains only one way open to philosophical thought, that of assigning religious *primacy* or *precedence* to *one* of these two principles. When a philosophical current becomes aware of the religious antithesis posed by its starting point, it has to devalue and exclude the divine attributes of the opposing principle if it assigns primacy to one of them.

The ancient Ionian philosophy of nature proclaimed the primacy of the *matter-motive*. It originated in the archaic period during which the old religion of nature and life, which had been abandoned by the public Olympian religion of the *polis* (πόλις), but reappeared brilliantly in the religious revivals of the Dionysian and Orphic movements. Consequently, the Ionian thinkers must have been very aware of the religious conflict in the form-matter ground-motive. That is why, in their philosophy, the principle of form is entirely divested of its divine character. For them, the true God is the formless and eternally-flowing stream of life, usually represented by a "moving element" *(water, fire, air)*. In Anaximander, it is conceived as an invisible *apeiron* (ἄπειρον) flowing through the stream of time and taking vengeance for the injustice of transitory beings (which had escaped from it by taking on an individual form) by

---

[20] The development of the religious dialectic in the form-matter motive of Greek philosophy and of the nature-grace motive of Christian Scholastic philosophy are studied in detail in the first two volumes of H. Dooyeweerd, *Reformation and Scholasticism in Philosophy*. The transcendental critique of modern Humanistic philosophy and its nature-freedom motive are developed in the second part of the first volume of *De Wijsbegeerte der Wetsidee* (*A New Critique of Theoretical Thought*), to which we refer the specialist as we cannot do them justice in this all-too-short Prolegomenon.

returning them to their original formlessness. The deepest conviction of these philosophers may doubtless be expressed by the famous words (in a typical Greek variant) of Mephistopheles in Goethe's *Faust*:

Denn alles was (in Form) besteht,
Ist wert das es zu Grunde geht.

For all that comes, by form, to be,
Deserves to perish wretchedly.

Aristotle, however, agrees with Socrates and Plato in assigning primacy to the form-motive. The deity becomes a "pure Form", and "matter" is completely stripped of any divine quality, because it is now merely the metaphysical principle of imperfection and potentiality.

William of Ockham was fully aware of the inner conflict between nature and grace and expressed both disdain for and condemnation of "natural reason". There is no room here for metaphysics or natural theology. Whilst jealously maintaining the autonomy of natural reason, Ockham assigned the primacy to the *grace-motive*, but not in the synthetic hierarchical sense of Thomism.

Modern humanistic philosophy lacks, at the outset, a clear notion of the religious antithesis between the motive of the domination of nature by autonomous science, and that of an equally autonomous freedom of personality. Rousseau was the first to devalue the ideal of science, attributing the primacy to the freedom motive, as the true origin of the religion of feeling. Following Rousseau, Kant deprived "nature", as understood by natural science, of all divine character, and even denied its divine origin. For him, God is a postulate of practical reason, and so of autonomous morality completely dominated by the Humanist freedom-motive. Nowadays, the modern philosophy of life and the Humanistic philosophy of existence seriously devalue the motive of the autonomous control of nature, and assign an absolute religious primacy to the freedom-motive, though in a sense quite different from Rousseau and Kant.

> 21. The meaning of each component
> of a dialectical ground-motive depends
> on that of its counterpart.

We shall conclude these remarks by observing that the meaning of each of the antithetic components in a dialectical ground-motive depends on that of its counterpart.

Consequently, it is impossible to grasp the meaning of the Greek matter-motive in isolation from its form-motive, and vice versa. Likewise, the meaning of the Scholastic nature-motive and that of its grace-motive mutually determine one another, and the same is true of the Humanistic nature- and freedom- motives.

This fact is of great importance in a critical study of the history of philosophical thought. The term "nature" in Greek thought bears a completely different meaning from what it does in modern humanist philosophy. In a Thomist discussion of the problem of freedom and causality, the term "freedom" does not have the Humanistic meaning, and its concept of "causality" has nothing in common with that implied by the classical Humanistic motive of the domination of nature.

CΒCΒCΒ

Chapter 3

The Central Significance of the Transcendental Basic-Idea of Philosophy.

Part 1: The transcendental basic-idea of philosophy.

> 1. The religious ground-motive controls philosophical thought by means of three transcendental Ideas that are indissolubly linked.

By demonstrating that the religious ground-motives are the real starting point for philosophy, our general transcendental critique of the theoretical attitude of thought has completed its main task. It remains to consider how these religious ground-motives control the immanent development of philosophical thought.

This they do through a triad of transcendental Ideas which correspond respectively to the three transcendental problems we have just studied. So, is theoretical thought able to focus successively on the necessary presuppositions for its development, without the thinker having to actually detect them through critical self-reflection?

While the theoretical concept of a modal aspect is directed to the modal diversity of meaning and separates the chosen aspect from all the others, the transcendental theoretical Idea is directed to the coherence (first problem), the totality (second problem) and the Origin (third problem) of all meaning, respectively. The theoretical Idea does not in any way cancel the theoretical setting apart or the antithesis of the modal aspects. It retains a theoretical character (first problem). But within the theoretical attitude of thought, it relates the aspects, which have been set apart and opposed to each other by analysis, concentrically to their mutual relation and coherence of meaning, to their radical (or at times broken dialectically) integral unity (second problem), and to their Origin (third problem). In other words, it relates them to the necessary presuppositions for the formation of a theoretical concept of modal speciality and diversity of meaning.

The transcendental ideas, which occur at the stages of critical reflection we have just described, form an *indissoluble unity*. Indeed, the question of how we think of the mutual relation and coherence of the modal aspects of meaning as theoretically separated and opposed to each other (first problem), is dependent on whether or not we accept the integral religious unity in the root of these aspects, which gives to their totality of meaning a concentric expression (second problem). But the second question depends on a third: How do we view the Idea of the Origin of all meaning. Is it to have an integral character or one that is dialectically split; in other words, do we go for a single Origin or one of two opposed principles (third problem).

It follows that we can think of the three transcendental Ideas, which contain the answers to these three fundamental problems, as three branches of one and the same *transcendental basic-Idea*.

This basic-Idea is certainly fundamental for philosophy. But it is so also, albeit in an indirect way, for the foundation of all sciences. In their theoretical conception of reality and in their methods of concept formation and question-raising, they are always dependent on philosophy.

The content of this Idea, in so far as it is directed to the Origin and unity (or duality) in the root of the temporal diversity of meaning, is directly determined by the religious ground-motive of theoretical thought.

Our transcendental critique can be immensely useful for the exchange of views between the various schools of philosophy. It allows for the establishing of a *real point of contact* which, as we have shown, is excluded by the dogmatic insistence on the autonomy of theoretical reason. By ruthlessly unmasking every theoretically-camouflaged supra-theoretical apriori, which each school imposes on every student on pain of

being considered a simple amateur, our critique strikes a n.._
blow at dogmatic exclusiveness, and precludes any school from
laying claim to a monopoly of philosophical truth.

*The primary requisite of critical thought is to make a sharp distin-
ction between theoretical judgements and supra-theoretical judgements
which alone make them possible.*

Before initiating a serious discussion with any philosophical current of thought it is therefore essential to examine with
the greatest care the transcendental basic-Idea at the root of its
thought-process, because an apriori that dominates its every
thought is definitely hidden there.

Immanence-philosophy will gain nothing by refusing to
think critically about this transcendental basic-Idea. For, all
things considered, the latter reveals its apriori influence in the
way in which each philosophical problem is posed. Should not
every philosopher seek to account, in a critical manner, for the
meaning of his statements and questions? He who genuinely
does so will, for sure, encounter the transcendental basic-Idea
of meaning and of its Origin, which is at the root of his
philosophy.

> 2. The analogical metaphysical con-
> cept and the transcendental Idea of the
> totality of meaning. Critique of the
> metaphysical concept of the analogy
> of being.

Thomist metaphysics will deny the religious character of
the transcendental Idea of the totality and Origin of modal
diversity in its intermodal coherence. It will object that our
thought must have a transcendental concept of totality that is
immanent and autonomous, as a whole that is greater than the
sum of its parts. We gladly concur, but in what sense must we
understand this concept? Is not the whole transcendental
problem of the relation of modal diversity to the totality and
radical unity of meaning concealed in just this concept? The
geometric concept of totality is very different from the
physical-chemical one (in particular the concept of atom), as
well as those of biology, psychology, linguistics, etc. These
necessarily-special scientific concepts, which are only con-

cerned with the modal aspects, cannot adequately approximate the totality in its relation to the modal diversity and to the intermodal coherence unless, from the outset, I opt to go down the paths of those "-isms" our transcendental critique has unmasked.

We presume that Thomist metaphysics would approve this argument. But it will make haste to add that the transcendental concept of totality is implied in the metaphysical concept of being, whose nature is not generic or specific but analogical. In saying that being is a whole in which everything participates, the concept of the whole is taken in this transcendental analogical sense. As such, it is the metaphysical presupposition of every generic and specific concept of totality.

We object that this concept does not meet the requirements of a transcendental Idea in a truly critical way. As such, a purely analogical concept of totality really lacks the concentric direction inherent in the transcendental basic-Idea of meaning. In theoretical thought, it does not direct the modal diversity modal toward the unity of its root, because it is eccentrically[1] dispersed by this diversity. For this simple reason, therefore, it cannot replace the transcendental basic-Idea.

In addition, the metaphysical concept of being in the Aristotelian sense is not an autonomous concept of theoretical thought, as is claimed here. When subjected to a transcendental critique it proves to be dependent on the dialectical form-matter ground-motive and to have a religious character. Pure matter and pure form are the two poles of the primary (so-called transcendental) division of being. Pure matter is the principle of potentiality and imperfection; pure form is identified with God, pure actuality, and the unmoved Mover of material nature.

Without doubt, Thomism accommodated this Aristotelian concept of divinity to the Christian doctrine of creation. The metaphysical Idea of being and totality then gives rise to a transcendental Idea of the Origin undergirding a "natural

---

[1] [That is, *away* from the centre as opposed to *concentrically*, *towards* the centre. It does not have the modern meaning here of *bizarrely*.]

theology". It claims to prove the existence of God as Prime Mover; but these proofs clearly take their starting point from empirical data in nature and – leaving aside the unjustifiable logical leap from the relative to the absolute – presuppose the idea of God that is to be proved. The Ionian philosophers of nature and Heraclitus, who deified the principle of "matter" of the eternally-flowing stream of life, never entertained the idea of a prime mover as first cause of empirical motion. This was not a logical fault on their part, since they attributed the religious precedence to the "matter" motive.

Consequently, we discover that in Thomism, autonomous metaphysics has to replace the transcendental critique of theoretical thought. Its metaphysical axioms and "proofs" are only the religious presuppositions of a dogmatic theoretical elaboration, masked by the dogma of the autonomy of natural reason.

Presumably Aristotle himself was fully aware of the religious character of his form-matter ground-motive, from the decidedly religious manner in which he speaks in his *Metaphysics* of the mystical moments of union between human thought and the pure divine Form in theological theory. Thomas Aquinas however could not have seen this because his conception of the autonomy of natural reason (dominated by the nature-grace ground-motive) was based on an understanding of autonomy wholly different from Aristotle's.

We conclude that the metaphysical concept of the whole and its parts, implied in the analogical concept of being, is only a pseudo-concept. It does not explain how the theoretical diversity of meaning can be concentrated into one unity. A purely analogical unity, as implied in the analogical concept of being, is not a unity at all, because it remains dispersed in the diversity of the modal aspects. It cannot even explain the coherence that exists within this diversity, because such coherence is the primary presupposition of a genuine analogy.

Finally, an analogical concept can only be used in philosophy if it is qualified by a non-analogical moment of meaning that determines its special modal meaning. We shall return to this when we discuss the theory of the modal aspects.[2]

In our philosophy, there is no room for an analogical concept of being in a metaphysical theological sense. Being can only be attributed to God, for creation is only meaning. Reality or existence has only a dependent "way of being". A genuine concept of being is impossible. The *word* "being" has no unity of meaning. When, in our *Introduction* we called meaning the being of created reality, the word "being" only designated the *essence*, which in no way transcends the limits of meaning. Only the transcendental basic-Idea ruled by the central ground-motive of Divine Revelation can relate the various modal aspects of meaning to the Divine Being of the Origin. But this Idea is not an autonomous concept and is incompatible with every theology.[3]

Part 2: The philosophical basic-idea as transcendental foundation of philosophy.

3. The theoretical character of the transcendental basic-Idea and its relation to naive experience.

For us, the contents of the transcendental basic-Idea of philosophy are the fundamental determination of the relation between the Origin, totality and diversity of modal meaning in the coherence of the various modal aspects. We could ask the question whether we have not made too abstract a conception

---

[2] We do not wish to complicate this exposition. Herman Dooyeweerd studied in detail the concept of totality in the philosophies of Edmund Husserl, Hermann Cohen, Heinrich Rickert and Theodor Litt, and demonstrated that all attempts at the logical formulation of this concept lead to an impasse because a transcendental basic-Idea is always at the root of such a concept, *A New Critique of Theoretical Thought*, Vol. I, p.73-82.

[3] For a discussion of the theological use of the analogy of being, cf. H. Dooyeweerd, 'De transcendantale critiek van het theoretisch denken en de thomistische theologia naturalis' (*The transcendental critique of theoretical thought and Thomistic natural theology*), *Philosophia Reformata*, 1952.

of the basic-Idea and why, first of all, it does not refer to the naive experience of reality.

The characteristics of naive experience are well-known. It does not theoretically isolate the different modal aspects. It grasps reality in its individual structures, in the concrete unity of these structures and their different aspects. It is the only mode of experience in which reality is actually delivered to us as it exists in the coherence of all its structures. And it is precisely this *concrete* reality that forms the primary *datum* that philosophy has the task of studying. It is therefore impossible to ignore naive experience as a factor in philosophy, which is why it could appear inadequate to simply identify the transcendental basic-Idea with the theoretical antithesis of the modal aspects of reality. If every philosophical view of empirical reality has to confront the datum of naive experience and to account for it, does it not follow that the content of the transcendental basic-Idea must be related to *naive experience itself* and consequently to the diversity and coherence of meaning of the individual structures of reality?

In the first place, we reply that philosophy must *account for* naive experience, and consider its datum as a fundamental philosophical problem. If philosophy restricted itself to the attitude of naive experience, it could never account for this datum. Philosophical knowledge is *scientific* knowledge that is attained only as a result of a *synthesis* of meaning. Because philosophy cannot renounce its theoretical attitude of thought, its transcendental basic-Idea is necessarily linked to the theoretical antithetic relation *[Gegenstand-relation]* in which reality is split up into its various aspects. To study the typical individual structures, philosophy must conduct a theoretical analysis of their unity, and these structures in turn become a *philosophical problem*: that of their temporal unity in the diversity of the aspects of reality.

Secondly, the transcendental basic-Idea involves a twofold relation: one with the law-side[4] of reality, the other with

---

[4] [Marcel here could be more literally translated as *cosmonomic aspect of reality* and *concrete subject aspect*. The translations I have used are more intelligible and in keeping

its factual subject-side. And since, by definition, the latter is individual, the transcendental Idea is also at the same time a basic-Idea of *type* and *individuality*, although it remains subject to the theoretical antithetic relation.

> 4. A special science cannot explain naive experience, nor offer an autonomous conception of the modal structures of the different aspects or of the structures of individuality. Science and philosophy.

This leads us to clarify one of the essential tasks of philosophy and the extent of the possibilities inherent in any special science.

In modern scientific thought, the naive concept of a thing is broken up into functional concepts, each of which is studied in keeping with its specific law. This method promotes an understanding of the functional coherence of phenomena within a special modal aspect. Its results have been significant because, through a penetrating analysis and synthesis, the meaning-aspects of reality – especially those of number, space, movement, organic life, and mental life – have gradually unfolded the secret of their functional immanent law.

However, under the influence of the classical humanist science-ideal there appeared an urge to eliminate the typical structures of individuality and to dissolve all empirical reality into a continuous functional system of causal relationships. From then on, not only was this absolutising of the scientific concept of function able to inflict serious damage on philosophical thought, but the more this scientific thinking deeply penetrated one or another aspect of reality (that it had set apart and isolated from the others), the more it found itself unable to provide an explanation of *naive experience*, or a view of *the unity of truth*.

The unity of temporal reality is not given "antithetically" in a mosaic of meaning-aspects that have been isolated from

---

with both the Dutch and English versions of Dooyeweerd's magnum opus. I will use the above style throughout this work.]

one another. From its position outside the purview of naive experience, special science loses sight of all true reality. Set within the speciality of the meaning-aspects, it is incapable of accounting for naive experience, and even its own possibility. Without a true view of reality, no science is possible. This means that an autonomous scientific thought does not exist.

The theoretical isolation of an aspect of reality that constitutes the field of enquiry of a special science is only possible (because of the intermodal coherence of cosmic time which is expressed within it) in the light of a transcendental Idea of its coherence with the other aspects and of the radical unity of the modal diversity. So also, no science as such can ever have an autonomous conception of the modal structures of the various aspects, nor of the typical structures of an individual totality. A theoretical analysis of its structures also requires a theoretical view of totality, which must be philosophical. The structure of a special aspect is a temporal unity in a diversity of structural modal moments, which can only display their modal meaning in their structural coherence and totality. The modal structures of reality cannot be grasped theoretically in special scientific concepts, because each of these concepts *is itself a philosophical problem*. The concepts of time and space that Einstein uses in his theory of relativity have a special synthetic meaning very different to those of other sciences such as biology, psychology, history, etc. This difference in meaning, and hence the real meaning of these concepts in the structure of the physical aspect, can only be elucidated in a philosophical enquiry into this structure, an enquiry that implies a theoretical view of totality. Nevertheless, a philosophical conception of this modal structure is found implicitly at the root of physics and it is this that enables it to focus in on its own field of enquiry.

So, philosophy alone is able to grasp, by means of its view of totality, the different aspects that have been set apart by theoretical thought, though still bound together in their mutual coherence. It alone, too, can account for the possibility of every special science, not excluding naive experience.

5. Naive experience and philosophy.

On the other hand, naive experience grasps temporal reality in a real and universal way that is intuitive rather than theoretical. It is itself situated within this temporal reality and the actual coherence of all its aspects, and totally lacks any systematised knowledge of the latter. If in its basic religious standpoint it views reality in the light of the Word of God and from the outset takes account of the relationship between God and creation, then naive experience will indeed possess a radical and integral view of temporal reality, conceived concentrically in its true religious root and in its relation to its true Origin. Without being able to demonstrate scientifically why, this naive experience will fiercely oppose any attempt by special theoretical thought that, flouting its own limits, tries to excise from it any of the aspects of meaning it experiences in the reality of things. However, because it lacks any theoretical notion of modal diversity, naive experience does not satisfy any of the requirements of the transcendental basic-Idea underpinning philosophical thought. But the concrete unity of things, which it experiences directly and immediately, will never be a problem for it.

That is why, even when naive experience is made into a theoretical problem, the transcendental basic-Idea of philosophy can have no other content but what we have discovered in our transcendental critique. Indeed, from a methodological point of view, philosophical enquiry into the modal structures of the meaning-aspects, as they are abstracted from temporal reality, must necessarily *precede* the philosophical analysis of the individuality-structures, and the latter imply the theoretical problem of the temporal structural unity in the diversity of its modal aspects.

The reformed philosopher, remember, does not oppose naive experience to philosophy. The world of experience and the world of the philosopher are neither different nor contradictory, even though the prevailing philosophy as a matter of course opposes appearance to reality and essence, and truth to fiction. Philosophy is related to, and refers to, naive experience and concrete reality, that is, to reality as it is lived. Its task is to subject the distinctions and relations, of which naive experience has an immediate awareness to scientific analysis, and to *set apart or abstract* the various aspects that naive experience knows together. A scientific understanding of the universe is not, in itself, superior to naive knowledge of it. Between naive experience and philosophy we do not have opposition but simple *distinction*: the former is found *within* reality, the latter operates *directly with the individual aspects* of that reality. Scientific thought deepens naive thought and brings out its full potential, and thus enriches and expands it.

> 6. Reflexive thought and the apriori limits of philosophical thought. The transcendental basic-Idea is a *conditio sine qua non* of philosophy.

In any case, philosophy cannot abandon the antithetic relation inherent in the theoretical attitude of thought. Such is a misconception that one current of modern immanence-philosophy would have us accept. It contrasts philosophy, regarded as reflexive thought focused on the "transcendental-logical subject of pure thought", with every kind of "objective" thinking *(gegenständliche Denken)*. Then it conceives the latter as the "naive" way of thinking. It is specific to special science, which is entirely lost in the study of its "objects" without ever reflecting on the activity of the pure thinking self, which itself can never be an "object". This difference between philosophical and objective scientific thought rests in the first place on an unfortunate confusion of terms: the object *[Gegenstand]* is here taken to be the "field of enquiry" or the object of enquiry. And secondly, it rests on a fatal identification of the real naive attitude of thought with theoretical thought. Moreover, even this "pure thinking self" cannot be divorced from the antithetic relation.

What distinguishes philosophy from science is that the former is focused on the totality and unity at the root of temporal meaning. And we know that this concentric direction of theoretical thought is possible only through a genuine critical self-reflection that acquires a religious knowledge of the selfhood, beyond the theoretical horizon.

Once again we find that the transcendental basic-Idea is the *conditio sine qua* non of philosophical thought. Philosophy cannot do without a transcendental foundation. As we have maintained all along, its refusal to account for the very conditions of its own possibility is, in our eyes, fundamentally uncritical.

To make special science into an epistemological problem, and so into a philosophical one, and to refuse to examine the necessary presuppositions of philosophical thought, is to be trapped in a vicious circle. Is not the transcendental problem implied by every science, namely the possibility of an inter-modal synthesis, a fortiori one of philosophical thought? And does it not, at every stage of its enquiries, confront fundamental issues concerning the relationship of the Origin, the totality, the modal diversity and the intermodal coherence of meaning?

What's more: since philosophical thought cannot become its own "object" philosophy, by raising the fundamental critical problem of its own possibility, necessarily encounters its own immanent limits within cosmic time. Therefore it can only account for its limits by directing its theoretical thought to its supra-theoretical presuppositions. A really *reflexive* thought is thus characterised by a critical self-reflection of the transcendental basic-Idea of philosophy, in which philosophical thought points beyond and above itself to its own apriori conditions within and beyond cosmic time.

As soon as reflexive theoretical thought is conceived as a "free" act that transcends every structural limit, on the assumption that these limits only apply to the realm of the antithetic relation, we are back to the illusory conception of the sovereignty and autonomy of philosophical reflection.

The "object" *[Gegenstand]* cannot be identified with "temporal reality". We must not forget that cosmic time is the condition of the antithetic relation. The structural limits of philosophical thought transcend the antithetic relation, because they are founded in cosmic time, which cannot be determined by thought. For thought presupposes cosmic time.

Philosophy must *reflect* on its transcendental basic-Idea in order to discover its undeniable apriori limits that stamp on thought its ultimate well-defined character in the cosmic coherence of meaning. Philosophical thought is incapable of autonomously determining its own apriori conditions. On the contrary, it is itself determined and limited by its transcendental focusing on its presuppositions. Its limit is set by its intentional and its ontic structures in cosmic time.

In the basic-Idea of philosophy, we are engaged in reflexive thought *while thinking* to the limits of philosophical thought. This Idea is, in the full sense of the word, a *limiting* concept par excellence, the ultimate transcendental foundation, the *conditio sine qua non* of philosophy, by which we retreat *into ourselves* in thinking. We can reflect critically on the limits of philosophical thought only because, *in our selfhood*, we transcend them as limits of *philosophical* knowledge.

However, the presuppositions of philosophy, towards which the basic-Idea of philosophy points, are themselves infinitely more than an Idea. Idealism, which elevates the Idea itself to the rank of totality of meaning, is possible only from the immanence perspective. Nevertheless, its transcendental *foundation*, its philosophical basic-Idea, continues to point *beyond the Idea* towards that which exceeds the transcendental limits of philosophy, since it is only this *that makes philosophical idealism possible*. But the immanence standpoint has renounced this last stage of critical reflection.

> 7. The relation between the transcendent and the transcendental points of view. The original meaning of the transcendental ground-motive.

We can now provisionally summarise our conception of the limits of philosophy.

A religious presupposition is at the root of all philosophy. It is what gives content to the transcendental basic-Idea of philosophy. And this Idea, as Idea, *points* beyond its own limits to this presupposition. It is, therefore, *transcendent*, while philosophical thought is *transcendental*. The choice of Archimedean point necessarily crosses the boundary of the temporal coher-

ence of our cosmos. As long as philosophy, as such, is being
directed by its basic-Idea, it remains within this boundary,
because it is only possible by reason of the temporal order of the world.

Taken in this sense, *transcendent* and *transcendental* are not
mutually exclusive. Indeed, since the starting point of philosophy cannot be located within theoretical thought, the actual
transcendental direction of this thought presupposes the central transcendent sphere of our consciousness, from whence it
springs. Genuine and radically transcendental philosophical
thought is only possible with the rejection of its autonomy,
and it is only by conceiving in this way the relation between
the transcendent and transcendental conditions of philosophy
that justice is really done to the *original critical meaning* of
transcendental thought.

8. Kant and the transcendental idea.

In his *Transcendental Dialectic*[5] Kant examines the function
of the transcendental Ideas of theoretical reason, and gives his
epistemology its true transcendental direction. He then
explains how these Ideas point to an absolute totality that transcends the immanent limits of "objective experience", while at
the same time in their theoretical knowledge they keep within
its immanent limits. Here too we see a dawning of the three
transcendental Ideas in their radical unity: The Idea of the
universe, which in Kant is limited to the realm of "nature" and
corresponds to our Idea of the integral coherence of meaning
in cosmic time; the Idea of the unity of the human selfhood,
and that of the absolute Origin *(Urwesen)*.

However, Kant does not accept that these transcendental
Ideas, in their unity, are the true basic condition of his
"critical" philosophy. He does not see that in their theoretical
use their actual content must rest on supra-theoretical presuppositions that vary with the religious ground-motives of the
theoretical thought involved. Their meaning is only logical

---

[55] [*Transcendental Dialectic* is the third part of the *Critique of Pure Reason*. It has for its
object that reality which lies beyond our experience; namely, the essence of God,
man and the world.]

and formal. They have only a regulative, systematic function for logical concepts (their categories), which rest apriori on sensory experience.

Having reached this critical point, why did Kant now abandon the genuine transcendental ground-motive? First, for sure, because he held to the autonomy of theoretical thought. But even more because he was aware that there was an irreducible antithesis in his *Nature-Freedom ground-motive*, and he refused to develop a dialectical synthesis from it.

Moreover, he did not see that his theoretical epistemology was based on a transcendental basic-Idea whose content depended on this religious ground-motive. Undoubtedly, his conception of the autonomy and spontaneity of the transcendental logical function of thought is dominated by the Humanist freedom-motive, while his conception of the purely receptive character of the sensory function of experience, and of its subjection to the causal determinations of science, depends on the nature-motive. In his conception of the apriori relations of the transcendental categories and of sensory experience, Kant accepts the synthesis of natural necessity and freedom, while he rejects it in his ethics. A detailed study of his theory of knowledge shows that he could not account for the possibility of a synthesis of the logical and sensory functions of consciousness, not on account of any pure theoretical critique of knowledge, but because of the fundamental dualism in his religious ground-motive.[6]

Like it or not, the transcendental ground-motive implies the focusing of theoretical thought, by means of a critical self-reflection, on its transcendental basic-Idea which points above and beyond its own theoretical limits to its transcendent presuppositions. Kant is no exception. In his "dialectic of pure reason" the transcendental Ideas, within their theoretical limits, actually point to the transcendent realm of the "noumenon" in which the Ideas of autonomous free will and God

---

[6] In the first edition of his *Wissenschaftslehre*, Fichte tried to solve the difficulties inherent in Kant's dualistic conception. Cf. H. Dooyeweerd, *A New Critique of Theoretical Thought*, Vol. I, p.90.

obtain a "practical reality". While Kant accepted only such limits to theoretical thought as it imposes on itself (with the exception of its dependence on sensory perception) the transcendental Idea of freedom, in its dialectical relation with the category of causality, is in fact the basic condition of his transcendental logic, although he never admitted it. And it is this same Idea which, in his *Critique of Practical Reason*, has "practical reality" on the grounds of "reasonable belief".

A genuine transcendental ground-motive is therefore to be found at the root of Kant's critique, and is its basic condition.[7]

> 9. The transcendental limits of philosophy and the criterion of speculative metaphysics.

Since the limit of philosophical thought is set by its intentional structure on the one hand and its ontic structure in cosmic time on the other, any philosophy that does not account for this limit necessarily degenerates into *metaphysical speculation*. That is to say, it seeks the absolute and the supratemporal *within* the cosmic order of time, through an absolutising of special modalities of meaning.

In the absolutising of the logical function of theoretical thought, and in the assertion that the laws of special modal aspects (e.g., the laws of number, space, logic, morality, aesthetics), have an absolute validity even for God, we observe the outworking of a speculative metaphysics. The ancient Platonic doctrine of Ideas, the modern theory of absolute values, the doctrine of "truths in themselves" and "*Sätze an sich*", Husserl's "absolute consciousness", the traditional doctrine of the immortality of the soul conceived as a complex of temporal functions, the modern deification (rational or irrational) of the "spirit" *(Geist)* in the psychical, logical and post-logical (non-sensory) functions of mental acts; all these theories are speculative and metaphysical in character, *un-*

---

[7] In *A New Critique of Theoretical Thought*, Vol. I, p.91, Dooyeweerd devotes a section to the decline of the transcendental motive in the Marburg School's methodological logicism, in Litt's conception of reflexive thought, and in Husserl's *egology*.

critical, and lack any conception of the immanent limits of philosophical thought. They all begin with an absolutisation of modal aspects that have already been abstracted by theoretical thought from the temporal coherence of meaning. In an illegitimate and unacceptable manner, they all attribute to this absolutised meaning the mode of subsistence of the Origin, whether conceived as "being", as non-substantial actuality or as "validity", and without regard to whether the absolutising is carried out on the actual-individual *subject-side* of a particular domain of meaning or its *law-side*. We will have occasion later to highlight all that is fundamentally fallacious about these metaphysical speculations.

Every speculative philosophy is bound to clash with Calvin's judgement: *Deus legibus solutus est, sed non exlex.* "God is not subject to the laws, but not arbitrary."[8] This axiom imperiously reminds human reason of the limits God has set within the temporal universe. It is the alpha and omega of every philosophy that wants to be critical not only in name but in fact.

It is of the utmost importance to emphasise the transcendental character of a genuinely critical philosophy, and to exclude all interference from speculative metaphysics in the domain of the Christian religion and theology. Philosophy is bound to the cosmic order of time. It can only be a *subject* that never elevates itself to the Throne of the Legislator or lays claim to fathoming God's Counsel. It is subject to the law of time. It is not the activity of a sovereign reason unaccountable to anyone. Philosophy's honour is to be a servant of Almighty God, never of theology. Its condemnation is always its failure to submit to the constraints of its calling.

---

[8] Cf. P. Marcel, *Le fondement de la loi et de l'obligation morale chez Thomas d'Aquin, Duns Scot et Calvin* [The foundation of law and moral obligation in Thomas Aquinas, Duns Scotus and Calvin], 1936, ch. III, p.100-106.

Part 3: The law-idea as transcendental basic-idea of philosophy.

10. The origin of this terminology.

Herman Dooyeweerd coined the Dutch term *wetsidee* for the Idea of transcendental philosophy; that is, *Law-Idea, idea legis,* or *cosmonomic-Idea.* His choice derived from the discovery that the major systems of ancient and medieval philosophy as well as many of the major systems of modern philosophy, that of Leibniz among others, expressly oriented philosophical thought towards the Idea of a divine world-order, variously called natural law *(lex naturalis),* eternal law *(lex aeterna),* and pre-established harmony *(harmonia praestabilita),* etc. Indeed, it is from this law-Idea, which implies also the Idea of subjectivity, that it took an apriori position with respect to all the central core problems of philosophical thought. Usually this law-Idea has been largely conceived in a rationalist and metaphysical manner.

It became an exciting task to demonstrate that every genuine philosophical synthesis is actually *based* on this law-Idea, even when its author is unaware of it. Indeed, philo-sophical thought, which is intrinsically subjected to the temporal world, absolutely has to have an apriori view of the Origin and the totality of meaning of the *law*, as well as of its *subjectivity* (its inseparable correlate). Philosophy must have an apriori view of the mutual relations and coherence of the various aspects of meaning, in which the divine order and its subjects are disclosed.

11. Objections to the expression "law-Idea". Reasons for employing it.

It is true that the choice of the expression "law-Idea" may lead to some misunderstanding. H. G. Stoker[9] said that the idea

---

[9] H. G. Stoker is professor of philosophy at the University of Potchefstroom (South Africa). Cf. *The New Philosophy at the Free University* (1933) and *The Philosophy of the Idea of Creation* (1933). The famous Dutch philosopher and scientist Philippe Kohnstamm supported the same idea after his adherence to the Philosophy of the Cosmonomic-Idea.

of law was too narrow and that it would have been better to use the more comprehensive Idea of *creation*.

But Herman Dooyeweerd had good reason to stick with his terminology:

1. When dealing with the *preliminary questions* of philosophical thought, the basic-Idea of philosophy must be able to demonstrate, for every thinker without exception, the necessary conditions of *every philosophical system*. Therefore the term used for this basic-Idea must be universal and not have any special content derived from the ground-motive of the Christian religion.

2. A cosmonomic-Idea is actually at the root of every philosophical system. This would not be the case with an Idea of creation, which could not be accepted by a thinker who denies creation or who, all things considered, feels it should be removed from philosophical thought.

3. The term "Idea of Creation" is not adequate for determining the *content* of the Christian basic-Idea. The Fall and redemption through Jesus Christ in the communion of the Holy Spirit both play a vital role in the central ground-motive of the Christian religion.

4. The term "law-Idea" has in its favour the fact that by pointing to the Origin and meaning of the law (*nomos, νομός*) or of the cosmic order, and by highlighting its relationship with subjectivity, it expresses in a first rate manner the restrictive nature of the transcendental basic-Idea. As Socrates has already put it[10], the law is, *ex origine*, a *limitation* of the subject.

By its aptitude for a critical focusing on the preliminary questions concerning meaning (its Origin, totality and modal diversity) in the relationship of the cosmic order to its subject, the term "law-Idea" is really the core criterion from which the

---

[10] Socrates, in Plato's famous dialogue *Philebus*. [Marcel is probably referring to *Philebus* 26b7-10: ὕβριν γὰρ που καὶ σύμπασαν πάντων πονηρίαν αὕτη κατιδοῦσα ἡ θεός, ὦ καλὲ Φίληβε, πέρας οὔτε ἡδονῶν οὐδὲν οὔτε πλησμονῶν ἐνὸν ἐν αὐτοῖς, νόμον καὶ τάξιν πέρας ἔχοντ᾽ ἔθετο. "O my beautiful Philebus, the goddess, methinks, seeing the universal wantonness and wickedness of all things, and that there was in them no limit to pleasures and self-indulgence, devised the limit of law and order (Jowett translation)."]

different starting points and currents of philosophy can be rigorously defined. It alone allows a line of demarcation to be drawn in a satisfying manner between, first of all, immanence-philosophy in all its nuances and the Christian standpoint of transcendence and secondly, between a truly *transcendental* philosophy that is aware of its immanent cosmonomic limits, and a speculative metaphysics that believes it can transgress them. Finally, it makes possible a recognition, first of all, of the criterion of rationalism *within immanence-philosophy itself*, a criterion which absolutises the natural and moral laws at the expense of individual subjectivity, and secondly, of the irrationalism that tries to reduce law to a dependent function of the individual creative subjectivity.

5. Though linguistically this term appears to refer only to the law-side of the cosmos, it is nevertheless obvious that it equally refers to the subject-side of reality in all its individuality. The cosmic "law" only has meaning in its relation with the subject-side of the cosmos; and the special laws, in relation to the subjects that are subject to them. Subjects whose being, actions, or functions are not determined by laws do not exist. In other words, the cosmonomic-Idea implies the Idea of the *subject*, which points toward the concrete (factual) side of reality, in accordance with the fundamental relationship that unites the totality, diversity and coherence of meaning.

In the final analysis, it is not what term to use, but its content, that matters. So if someone does not consider these explanations convincing and has qualms about using them, Herman Dooyeweerd sees no objection to just using the term "transcendental basic-Idea".

12. The law-Idea, the modal concepts of law, subject and object.

The law-Idea, in its broadest sense, together with the transcendental idea of subjectivity, also determines the content of the special modal concepts of laws and of subject and object used in various branches of science.

These (special modal) concepts only relate to a single special aspect, and unlike the law-Idea, do not in themselves point beyond the diversity of meaning towards the transcendent

Origin and totality. But whatever their special meaning, according to the modal aspects considered by theoretical thought, they always depend on a law-Idea.

In pure mathematics, for example, the logicist school conceives of the numerical and spatial laws as purely analytical. The series of real numbers is regarded as continuous in accordance with the logical continuity of the principle of progression. But this mathematical concept of law depends on a law-Idea that is logicist and rationalist.

In biology, the mechanistic school conceives of the special laws of organic life as pure physical-chemical laws. But this concept depends on a law-Idea based on the Humanist ideal of deterministic science, in its classical form.

In the "pure theory of law" *(reine Rechtslehre)* of the neo-Kantian scholar Hans Kelsen, the legal rule is identified with a logical judgement of the form: "If A... then there ought to be B". The legal subject and its subjective right are broken up into a logical complex of legal rules. But this legal concept of law is governed by a dualistic Humanistic cosmonomic-Idea, according to which there is an unbridgeable gulf between two ultimate types of law. These are the natural laws and norms which, proceeding from fundamentally different logical categories of transcendental thought, "create" the various fields of scientific enquiry. This dualistic cosmonomic-Idea is governed by the dialectical nature-freedom ground-motive, though in an antithetic conception that differs from Kant's.

Also note that the three scientific concepts we have just mentioned are of a rationalist type: the subject-side of reality within the special modal aspects is reduced to the law-side. In addition, the laws of the special aspects considered in legal and biological research are conceived in a purely functionalistic sense. There is no room here for typical laws corresponding to the structures of individuality, on account of the law-Idea that governs these special scientific concepts. We shall return to this problem later.

Part 4: The positive content of our law-idea. The cosmic order of time and the principle of the internal sovereignty of the law-spheres.

What positive content does the transcendental basic-Idea of philosophy receive from the central ground-motive of the Christian religion?

The Archimedean point of our philosophy is located in Christ, the new root of mankind, in which through regeneration we participate in our restored selfhood.

13. The law as a boundary between the "Being" of God and the "meaning" of creation.

The *totality of meaning* of our temporal cosmos is in Christ, considered in his human nature, which is the *root* of regenerated mankind. In Him our *heart*, from whence spring the issues of life, confesses the sovereignty of God the Creator of all his creation. In Christ, our heart bows before *the law*, in its central religious unity and in its temporal diversity, which originates in the holy will of the Creator. This law is the forever-uncrossable boundary between the *Being* of God and the *meaning* of his creation. In other words, with respect to the law, there exists an *essential* distinction between God and the creature. Sovereign Origin of all things, God is at no point and in no way subject to the law. This *subjection* is rather the authentic trademark of all that is created, whose existence is limited and defined by the law. As to his human nature, Christ was himself born *under the law*, but he is not under it with respect to his divine nature. No creature can ever transgress the boundary *imposed* by the law upon its creaturely existence. Even when it seeks – in a revolt it considers "noble" – to dispense with the law and depart from God, the creature remains nonetheless strictly and inviolably subject to His laws.

In its faithfulness to Scripture, Calvinism emphasises strongly from the outset that *the law* is an insurmountable barrier between the Creator and creation. But far from falling into the trap of absolutising the law, it is precisely in this conception of law that Calvinism expresses, with remarkable

penetration, its fundamental religious idea of God's sovereignty over all creation. The transcendent totality of meaning
of our cosmos exists only in religious dependence on the
absolute *Being* of God. It is not an *eidos* in the sense of Plato's
speculative metaphysics, nor *being* isolated in itself. Its mode of
existence remains *ex-sistential*, that of heteronomous meaning
which does not find its *raison d'être* in itself, but *points beyond
itself* to its divine Origin, without which it sinks into *nothingness*.

There is therefore not the slightest danger that by focusing
on the problem of *meaning*, the Philosophy of the Law-Idea can
be regarded as a "meaning-idealism". It has been objected that
meaning cannot *live*, *act*, or *move*. But is not this life, this action,
this movement, as the mode of being of created reality,
precisely *meaning* that points beyond itself, and that never finds
rest in itself? The *totality* of meaning, which transcends philosophical thought, also has its necessary correlate in the Being of
the Origin. In fact, one cannot understand the modal aspects of
reality or even concrete things otherwise than in their *meaning*,
that is to say, their way of being, which is always relative and
points to their temporal coherence and to the totality and
Origin of all relative things. If the pre-logical aspects of reality
were not aspects *of meaning* related to the logical aspect, then
thought could never form a *concept* of them.

14. Sin and the logical function of
thought.

Sin is a rebellion against the Lord of our cosmos. It is
apostasy which breaks with the fullness of meaning; it is the
deification, the absolutising, of meaning that seeks to acquire
the attributes of the very Being of God. And because our
world in its diversity and temporal coherence of meaning is
bound by the divine order of creation in the religious root of
mankind, without which it no longer has either meaning or
reality, the apostasy of the heart, the religious root of this
world, implies the apostasy of all creation which was concentrated in our human race.

The disruption of the fall gradually penetrated all temporal
aspects of reality. None of them can escape it; neither the pre-

~~ogical aspects, nor the logical aspect, nor the post-logical aspects. That is obvious as soon as we find they are placed, by virtue of the cosmic order of time, in an indissoluble bond, which refers to a radical religious unity. Only by losing sight of this bond could we come to the opposite conclusion.

Any attempt to free the logical function from the consequences of sin must be unmasked as contrary to the biblical concept of the fall. If it fails to do this, Christian thought will be overwhelmed by the dialectical ground-motives of immanence philosophy. These will strip it of its Christian character. We will return to this.

St Paul says that by the fall, human thought (νοῦς) has become a νοῦς τῆς σαρκὸς, a "carnal mind" (Col. 2: 18), because it cannot be separated from its apostate religious roots. And thought includes its logic function. Without doubt, the *logical laws* of thought, and the structural modal law of the logical aspect are not at all affected by sin. The effects of apostasy appear only in the *subjective* activity of thought, which remains *subject* to these laws. But in sin, we are continually inclined to make the aspect of logical meaning independent, and to violently sever its connection with the other aspects, and to transgress its modal boundaries.

> 15. The contents of the Law-Idea. Reformation of the cosmonomic Idea by means of the central ground-motive of the Christian religion. The illustration of light-refraction.

From a Christian perspective, our law-Idea responds as follows to the three transcendental questions of philosophy:

1. *What is the Origin* of the totality and modal diversity of meaning of our cosmos, on the law-side and on the subject-side?

– The holy and sovereign will of the Creator God, who has revealed Himself in Jesus Christ.

2. *What is the totality of meaning* of all the modal aspects of the cosmic order, their supra-temporal unity beyond the diversity of meaning?

– On the *law-side*, it is the obligation, based on the sovereignty of God, to love and serve God with all our heart and our neighbour as ourselves.

– On the *subject-side*, it is the new religious roots of our humanity in Christ (which excludes nothing at all of our created universe) in submission to the fullness of meaning of the divine law.

3. *What is the mutual relation* that unites the modal aspects of reality?

– That of *internal sovereignty*, wherein each sphere of law is absolutely irreducible to any other, in the cosmic coherence of the various aspects of meaning. And the latter has itself been constituted, in the temporal divine order of the world, into a cosmic order of time.

To make this law-Idea more concrete, we shall use the illustration of light-refraction, already referred to in our Introduction, but which of course must never be interpreted in a physical sense.

White unrefracted light represents the time-transcending *totality of meaning* of our cosmos on its law- and subject-sides. Just as white light originates from a light source, so the totality of meaning of our cosmos has its starting point in an Origin by which and for which it was created. The prism, which refracts the light into a spectrum of coloured rays, is *cosmic time*, through which the fullness of meaning is refracted into its various temporal aspects. Just as the seven coloured rays do not owe their origin to each other and do not originate from one another, so the temporal aspects of meaning are, with respect to each other and to their own meaning, *sovereign in their own domain*.

In the religious fullness of meaning, there is *only one* law of God. There is also *only one* sin against God and *only one* creation that has sinned in Adam. But under the boundary-line of time the fullness of meaning, on its law- and subject-sides, breaks up like white light through a prism into a rich variety of meaning-aspects, each sovereign in its own domain, each in its own modal structure expressing the fullness of meaning in its own modality.

16. The law spheres and their internal
sovereignty.

From now on we shall call the modal aspects of temporal
reality *law spheres*. This expression, which should not be taken
in a geometrical sense, means the set of laws that govern each
modal aspect in its own domain. It highlights the fact that no
aspect is reducible to any other aspect and that in this sense
each aspect is sovereign in its own domain. We call this
sovereignty: *internal sovereignty*.[11]

The acceptance of the fundamental philosophical principle
of internal sovereignty in each modality is dependent on the
Christian viewpoint of transcendence, itself dominated by the
religious ground-motive of creation, fall and redemption. The
immanence viewpoint is incompatible with this cosmonomic
principle.

This incompatibility does not stem from an inability on
the part of immanence-philosophy to recognise that the totality and profound unity of meaning must transcend its modal
diversity and that the modal aspects, *which it accepts as such*, can
never originate from each other. Every thinker, whoever he
might be, has to distinguish various modal aspects in temporal
reality and be careful not to confuse them.

But in our transcendental critique of theoretical thought,
we saw that the immanence viewpoint necessarily leads to an
absolutising of the logical function of thought, or to one of a
particular theoretical synthesis. Therefore, the isolated modal
aspect chosen as the common denominator of all the others, or
of a part of them, is torn from the intermodal coherence of
reality. Whether conscious of it or not, the thinker makes this
aspect independent and elevates it to the rank of an Origin that
transcends meaning. Over against this unlimited sovereign
authority, the other aspects are unable to assert their own
internal sovereignty. *Mathematical logicism* will only confer relative autonomy to the logical domains of thought. *Psychologism*
will only regard the psychological domains as irreducible,

---

[11] [This will be confusing unless it is realised that Marcel's *internal sovereignty* is
synonymous with Dooyeweerd's *sphere sovereignty*]

understood transcendentally or otherwise; *historicism*, those that relate to historical development, etc.

If the thinker is aware of the implacable antithesis in his hidden religious starting point, his philosophical system will veer towards a patent dualism. Instead of a single common denominator, he will choose two, related antithetically. In its usual three directions, the transcendental basic-Idea will highlight the dualist character of this religious ground-motive, but will not try to overcome it. We see once again the impossibility of accepting in this situation the principle of internal sovereignty in the various law-spheres.

Because of its Archimedean point, immanence-philosophy is obliged to construct various *absolutisations* of the modal aspects. We will have occasion to explain how and why these absolutisations are apparently possible.

However, immanence-philosophy does not let itself be attacked without trying to defend itself. So, conversely, it reproaches our Christian starting point with not being itself able to escape an absolutising of *religious meaning*. We shall examine this reproach and demonstrate that, on our own standpoint and that of immanence-philosophy, this charge is untenable.

> 17. The Christian religion cannot be absolutised in any way, by virtue of its fullness of meaning.

In the first place, the Christian religion, by virtue of its fullness of *meaning*, is incapable of any absolutisation. It is *religio*, that is, a link between the *meaning* of creation and the *Being* of the Origin. These two cannot exist on the same plane. He who tries to make the religious totality of meaning independent of its Origin is guilty of a contradiction in terms. He who declares that God at least is absolutised hardly knows what he says.

Secondly, this criticism usually arises from a confusion between *the temporal meaning of the aspect of faith*, enclosed within a law-sphere, and the *fullness of meaning of religion*, which transcends the limits of cosmic time, and cannot be enclosed in a modality of meaning.

Finally, outspoken critics of transcendence in philosophy, like Heinrich Rickert, recognise that religion, in its fullness of meaning, does not lend itself to any coordination with fields such as law, morality, science, etc. And it would be difficult to deny that viewing religion as an autonomous realm of thought would totally destroy its meaning.

As to the contention that the recognition of the religiously-dependent nature of philosophical thought leads to the destruction of its meaning, immanence-philosophy would have to demonstrate it in a far more convincing way than by mere religious assertion of the autonomy of philosophy.

> 18. Internal sovereignty in the inter-
> modal coherence constitutes an im-
> portant philosophical problem.

It is a fundamental transcendental principle that the internal sovereignty of the modal aspects is strictly related to our transcendental Ideas of the Origin, totality and unity of meaning. This principle also derives from our transcendental Idea of cosmic time, which implies, as we know, a cosmic coherence of the aspects of temporal reality. This coherence is ruled by the divine temporal order imparted to our world, not by philosophical thought.

The principle of internal sovereignty discloses a quite remarkable issue. Indeed, it might seem that the internal sovereignty is incompatible with the intermodal coherence that guarantees the cosmic order of time. The key to this important problem is, we shall see, in the modal structure of the various aspects, which have a cosmonomic character. The same cosmic time that guarantees internal sovereignty also guarantees the intermodal coherence of meaning between the modal aspects and their law-spheres. Thus the corollary of the principle of internal sovereignty is the principle of *internal universality*.[12]

---

[12] [To be identified with Dooyeweerd's principle of *sphere universality*.]

19. Potentiality and actuality in cosmic time. Why does the totality of meaning only split up through the prism of time?

All the structures of temporal reality are, as we have said, structures of cosmic time. As structural laws, they are founded in the cosmic order of time, and are principles of temporal *potentiality* or *possibility*. In their realisation in individual things or events as concrete transitory structures they possess *duration* and *actuality*.

Everything that has a real existence has many more potentialities than just those that have already been actualised. Potentiality as such is found on the concrete subject-side; its principle, however, is on the cosmonomic-side of time. The concrete subject-side is always related to individuality, actual and potential, which can never be reduced to a general rule. But it remains dependent on its structural laws, which determine the margin or latitude of its possibilities.

H. G. Stoker, and later Dr. Kohnstamm[13], raised the question why it is precisely in cosmic time that the totality of meaning is refracted into interdependent modal aspects. The reason seems to be, for Herman Dooyeweerd, that the fullness of meaning, as radical totality and unity, is not and can never be truly given in time since all temporal meaning refers beyond itself to its supra-temporal fulfilment.

In the correlation of order and duration, we must insist once more, it is the true meaning of cosmic time to be a successive refraction of meaning in its interdependent modal aspects. The internal sovereignty of the law-spheres makes no sense in the religious fullness and radical unity of meaning. So,

---

[13] Ph. A. Kohnstamm, in his essay: *Pedagogy, Personalism, and Philosophy of the Cosmonomic Idea* (anniversary anthology published in honour of Prof. Dr J. Waterink, Amsterdam, 1951), p.96ff, in which the author, a renowned Dutch thinker, who died shortly after, made known for the first time his adherence to the Philosophy of the Law-Idea. He had, however, a reservation on the question of the idea of time. This reservation was based on his supposing, quite correctly, that the Bible does not ascribe even to God any supra-temporality in the sense of Greek metaphysics. But the conception of the supra-temporal defended by Dooyeweerd is radically different from the Greek conception, as we have seen in a previous chapter.

love, wisdom, justice, power, beauty, etc., are interpenetrated and identified in a radical unity. We begin to understand somewhat this state of affairs in the focusing of our heart on the Cross of Jesus Christ. But this radical unity of the various modalities is impossible within time regarded as the successive refraction of meaning.

That is why every philosophy that tries to dissolve this totality of meaning in Ideas of reason or absolute values always becomes entangled in antinomies by means of which the cosmic order of time wreaks vengeance on any theoretical thought that attempts to transgress its immanent limits.

20. The logical function is relative in a cosmic, not a logical, sense.

Similarly, the attempt to approximate cosmic time other than in a *limiting*-concept must necessarily lead to antinomies, because the concept presupposes time. With regard to its fundamental logical aspect, the concept is *discontinuous*, and is unable to grasp the cosmic *continuity* of time, which exceeds the modal limits of its aspects. In its modal speciality, the logical function is actually *relative*. This is not a logical relativity, but a cosmonomic temporal relativity. In order to interpret the *cosmonomic coherence* in a *logical-dialectic* sense, philosophy must in any case begin with a *logical* relativising of the fundamental principles of logic, and thereby it sanctions the antinomy.

21. In his *Critique of Pure Reason*, Kant eliminates the cosmic order of time.

By deifying "theoretical reason", the autonomous Archimedean point of his philosophy, Kant eliminates the cosmic order of time from philosophical thought, especially epistemology. He thus relegates to the background the fundamental critical question of all philosophy: that of its own possibility. This elimination was to become much later the source of subjectivism.

In his *Prolegomena to Any Future Metaphysics*, Kant said of his *Critique of Pure Reason*: "This work is difficult and requires a resolute reader to plunge gradually into a system that sets nothing at its foundation as given except reason itself, and thus, without relying on any fact, seeks to develop knowledge from its original seeds".[14] What Kant demanded of the reader is quite simply to renounce the preliminary issues of critical thought. "Theoretical reason", the evident product of theoretical abstraction, must be accepted as a given. The possibility of this theoretical thought is not even considered. The cosmic order of time, the only guarantee of the meaning relations of this thought, is lost sight of. And we can demonstrate that a really *critical* critique of theoretical reason[15] is *impossible* apart from a transcendental idea of the cosmic order of time.

Part 5: The importance of this law-idea for the modal concepts of laws and their subjects.

> 22. The modal concepts of law and its subject. The subject, in so far as it is *subject to laws.*

Herman Dooyeweerd's Law-Idea (Cosmonomic-Idea) is of paramount importance for determining the actual content of the *concepts of laws and their subjects*, which we will soon have at our service *in their modal speciality of meaning.* Law, we have seen, takes its origin from the holy God's creative sovereignty and constitutes the absolute boundary between the Being of the Origin and the *meaning* of all that is created, which can only be "subject", that is, *subjected* to a law. It follows that the transcendental meaning of the relation between the divine law and its subject will be expressed in every concept of modality, both on its law-side and on its subject-side.

We now have both time and occasion to evaluate the significance of this conception in the positive development of Reformed philosophy. To understand the following critical remarks it will be sufficient if the reader bears in mind the

---

[14] [Immanuel Kant, *Prolegomena zu einer jeden künftigen Metaphysik* (Prolegomena to every future Metaphysics), in Works, Ernst Cassirer edition (*Immanuel Kants Werke*, Berlin, Bruno Cassirer, 1922), IV, p.23.]

[15] [A direct allusion to Kant's magnum opus, the *Critique of Pure (i.e., theoretical) Reason.*]

provisional explanations we have given of the subject-object relation as perceived intuitively by naive experience, and if he recalls that in every modal aspect where we find this relation, the subject-side embraces both the subjective and objective functions that temporal reality discloses in that aspect.[16]

> 23. Humanist immanence philosophy has completely disrupted the meaning of the concepts of modal laws and their subjects.

Humanist immanence-philosophy, of the rationalist or irrationalist type, could not but completely lose sight of the concept of modal subject in its relations with the modal laws, and thereby cause untold damage to the philosophical analysis of reality. In it, the subject becomes *sovereign*, either in the metaphysical sense of "substance" *(noumenon)*, or in the transcendental-logical or phenomenological sense.

In Kant's "theoretical" philosophy, for example, the subject is a subject only in an epistemological sense. It is the origin of the form of the theoretical laws of nature; the "transcendental subject" is the *legislator* of nature in a transcendental-logical sense. After the destruction of the traditional metaphysics of nature, the pre-psychical aspects of reality are separated in a synthesis of logical and sensory functions of consciousness. Their structural modal laws are replaced by the transcendental apriori *forms* of the *theoretical intellect* and *subjective sensibility*, in an apriori synthesis. That numbers, spatial figures, energy effects, and biotic functions might actually be modal subjects subject to the laws of their own sphere is a notion foreign to all modern immanence-philosophy.

In Kant's "practical" philosophy, the subject, in the metaphysical sense of *homo noumenon* or pure will, becomes the autonomous legislator of moral life. Because of the dualistic conception of his transcendental basic-Idea, Kant could not

---

[16] We will have the opportunity later to observe that there are no objects in the numerical sphere, because there are no pre-numerical spheres that could find themselves in it as objects. We shall also examine the special nature of this relation in the limiting sphere of faith.

agree to the idea of a radical unity of the order of creation overarching the polar opposition between natural laws and norms.

Since immanence-philosophy abandoned the ancient metaphysics of nature, two features have come to characterise its theoretical concept of the subject:

1. The subject is conceived only in the special sense of the epistemological and ethical functions of consciousness. Empirical things and events are regarded only as objects of sensory perception and theoretical or practical thought. This is the inevitable consequence of the reduction of "empirical" reality to the logical and psychical aspects of consciousness, abstracted by theoretical thought from the coherence of cosmic time. The reduction results from the elimination of the cosmic order of time and the advancing of the (so-called *critical*) "principle of consciousness" *(Satz des Bewusstseins)*[17], wherein the possibility of our knowledge is limited to subjective and objective *contents* of *consciousness* which are received only through sensory perception and formed by logical apperception.

2. The subject loses its original meaning of "being *subjected* to a law that does not originate from itself". As "transcendental subject" or "ideal subject", it is crowned autonomous self-sufficient legislator, in perfect agreement with the humanist Ideals of science and personality.

In the classical rationalist conception, the empirical subject is reduced to a complex of causal relations by which it is completely determined. The "laws" are identified with the "objective". The empirical subject becomes an "object", which in turn

---

[17] [Neither Dooyeweerd nor Marcel give any clue as to the origin of this phrase. The reference is to Karl Leonhard Reinhold (1757-1823), Austrian philosopher and professor of Critical Philosophy at the University of Jena, 1787-94. This "first principle" of his Elementary Philosophy is expounded in three major works: *Versuch einer neuen Theorie des menschlichen Vorstellungsvermögens* (1789), *Beiträge zur Berichtigung bisheriger Missverständnisse der Philosophen, Erster Band* (1790), and *Über das Fundament des philosophischen Wissens* (1791). I am grateful to Prof. Ernst-Otto Onnasch of Utrecht University, for pointing out to me that, though Reinhold based the whole of his *Versuch* on the *SdB*, he first used the term itself only in the *Beiträge* in 1790. Reinhold has long been neglected, but a new (first) *Complete Works (Gesammelte Schriften)* is being undertaken through Schwabe Verlag, Basle.]

is identified with the antithetical object of the ultimate "transcendental subject of thought".

Modern "realist" positivism interprets the concept of law, norms as well as natural laws, in the sense of a scientific judgement of probability. Here again, this concept is completely divorced from the structures of the law-spheres, and from the structures of individuality, which are founded in the cosmic order of time. This positivism sees law as "autonomous" products of scientific thought which, by way of a logical "economy", tries to order the facts which are merely a sensory datum.

24. Rationalism and irrationalism.

In the irrationalist currents of humanist thought, concepts of laws and of their subjects are quite different from those of rationalism.

The *rationalist* types of immanence-philosophy try to dissolve the *individual subjectivity into an order of universally valid laws* whose origin is sought in sovereign reason. Rationalism is the absolutising of a general rule.

The *irrationalist* Humanist types, on the other hand, are not in the least interested in "laws" as a product of thought or reason. However they fall into the opposite extreme, looking on this "theoretical order" as a pragmatic falsification of genuine reality. In its creative *subjective individuality*, this "reality" is not bound to universally valid laws, and derides all "concepts of thought". It is an attitude dominated by an irrationalist attachment to the freedom-motive.

Thus, rationalist types absolutise laws while irrationalist types absolutise subjective individuality.

25. The concept of the subject in irrationalist phenomenology and in the philosophy of existence.

The conceptions of subject and selfhood in the irrational current of modern phenomenology (Scheler) and in the philosophy of existence (Heidegger, etc.) are a typical phenomenon.

Here Kant is accused of having conceived of selfhood in *substantial* terms as legislating subject, and so of not having penetrated to its *pure* actuality.[18]

In a very lucid manner, Scheler[19] describes the selfhood as "pure actuality"; as such, it transcends the cosmos considered as a "world of things", which he also reduces to the physical-psychical aspects, abstracted from temporal reality.

Scheler and Heidegger have a static conception of reality as regards the "given world of things". They only reject it firstly as to "free personality", and secondly as to "free human existence".

This view of the concepts of subject and the "world of things" *(Dingwelt)* in general, shows once more that modern phenomenology and humanistic existentialism are themselves in accord with immanence-philosophy. An Archimedean point set in the "transcendentally purified actual consciousness" or in "existential thought" ultimately assigns sovereignty to the "transcendental ego".

But when we consider the place of man in the cosmos, we will have the opportunity to see that the actuality advocated by modern phenomenological thought cannot and should not be set in opposition to subjectivity, because it constitutes the latter's real nucleus. In other words, in every modal aspect of our cosmos, even the pre-logical, actuality attaches to the meaning of the subject-functions found in them. The notion that temporal reality should be a static and fixed given *(Vorhandenes)* comes from a failure to appreciate the dynamic character of reality in the coherence of its various aspects.

---

[18] Martin Heidegger, *Sein und Zeit*, p.320, §64: "The ontological concept of subject does not characterize the *personality of the ego as such, but the identity (Selbigkeit) and permanence (Beständigkeit) of something that already exists.* To determine the self ontologically as *subject* is to treat it as something that already exists. The being of the ego is seen as the reality of the *res cogitans*" (that is, thinking substance). [English trans.: Martin Heidegger, *Being and Time*, trans. Joan Stambaugh (2nd ed. 2010), New York, State University of New York Press.]

[19] Max Scheler, *Der Formalismus in der Ethik und die material Wertethik*, 3rd Ed. 1927, p.397ff. [English trans.: Max Scheler, *Formalism in ethics and non-formal ethics of values*, trans. Manfred Frings, Evanston, Northwestern University Press, 1985 (1973)]

In Herman Dooyeweerd's estimation, on the other hand, this dynamic is guaranteed by the mode of ex-sistence of all created things, as meaning which finds no resting place in itself, and by the opening-process of temporal reality, which we shall examine later.

> 26. In ancient Greek thought the concept of law and subject is based on the form-matter ground-motive.

The various ideas of laws and their subjects in humanistic immanence-philosophy which we have discussed are attributable to the dialectical character of the nature-freedom ground-motive. The ideas of Greek thought, which were dominated by the form-matter ground-motive in its original religious meaning, have nothing comparable. Greek thought knew nothing of the modern concept of natural causal law, or of the autonomous subject, in the Kantian sense of law-giver.

Under the primacy of the matter-motive, the law of nature had from the start the juridical sense of justice (δίκη): every individual form had to be dissolved into "matter" by the standard of proportionality. This δίκη was conceived as an *anangke* (ἀναγκή), the inexorable fate to which all forms are subjected.

Under the primacy of the form-motive in the later cultural religion, the concept of law, in the general sense of order, acquires a teleological turn with respect to "natural subjects". Introduced by Socrates, this notion was developed in a metaphysical way by Plato and Aristotle. It is opposed to the extreme view of the Sophists who saw law in a purely conventional way in human society, and who denied any laws to "nature", the flowing stream of becoming.

In his *Metaphysics*, Aristotle identifies the subject with "substance," composed of form and matter. Natural law rules the striving of all matter for its own substantial form.

In his *Philebus*, Plato sees natural law as the *peras* (πέρας), imposed on the *apeiron* (ἄπειρον), the formless stream of becoming, which receives from it the character of an ability to be (γένεσις εἰς οὐσίαν). This is the Pythagorean conception, even as regards its ethical law.

Like the humanist nature-freedom ground-motive, the Greek form-matter ground-motive, in view of its dialectical character, could never lead philosophical thought either to a transcendental cosmonomic Idea (conceiving the divine law in its radical religious unity), nor to the radical unity of the human subject (overarching the modal diversity of its temporal functions). The transcendental Idea of the Origin was itself trapped in the polar dualism of matter and form. Lacking the biblical ground-motive of creation, the Greek idea could never conceive of the subject as "subject", that is to say *subject to divine law*, taken in its full biblical sense. In Plato and Aristotle, the teleological law of the form-principle has its original opposite in the ἀναγκή of the matter-principle. At most, "natural law" in the Greek sense is conceived as a subjective participation of rational material substances in divine thought, as the Origin of all cosmic forms. But this is, rather, a Thomistic interpretation of Aristotle's conception.

Finally, the scholastic concepts of law and subject in the modal diversity, are dominated by the dialectic nature-grace ground-motive, and dependent on an accommodation of either the Greek or humanistic conceptions to the Christian conception.[20]

CBCBCB

---

[20] Herman Dooyeweerd engages in detail with this scholastic idea in the critical section of the first volume of his *Philosophy of the Law-Idea (De Wijsbegeerte der Wetsidee)*, which is devoted to the origins of humanist thought.

Chapter 4

Philosophy and WorldViews

Part 1: The place of the *Philosophy of the Law-Idea* in the historical development of philosophy.

> 1. Radical antithesis and cooperation between Christian thought and the various currents of immanence-philosophy.

The *Philosophy of the Law-Idea*, as we have seen, requires a rigorous reflective critique from those who engage in philosophical enquiry. This transcendental critique of theoretical thought leads to the discovery of a radical antithesis between the transcendental basic-idea of a philosophy ruled by the central ground-motive of the Christian religion, and immanence philosophy in all its forms. This antithesis draws a wholly different boundary line from that previously assumed, and it can brook no compromise.

Now that we know the controlling role of the basic-Idea in the internal direction and development of all philosophical thought, we understand the absolute necessity, for a truly Christian philosophy, of the rejection of supra-theoretical presuppositions and "axioms" of immanence-philosophy in all its forms. The *Philosophy of the Law-Idea* cannot consider as its own the problems of immanence-philosophy that are attributable to its own fundamental dialectical ground-motives; it must discover the path determined by its own basic-Idea.

However, the antithesis of the starting points and basic-Ideas does not mean that a philosophy which wants to be intrinsically reformed is bound to break all contact with Greek, scholastic or modern humanist philosophy. On the contrary, the *Philosophy of the Law-Idea* can maintain the deepest relationships with other currents of philosophy, relationships far more fruitful than can ever be achieved between the various trends in immanence-philosophy. Because of its radically critical position, which allows it to make a clear distinction between philosophical judgements and apriori supra-theoretical judgements, Christian philosophy will never break the community of thought that closely connects all philosophical schools. As we have seen, philosophical dogmatism, which transforms religious presuppositions into theoretical "axioms", and requires their prior acceptance as a prerequisite for any discussion, is alone the cause of such ruptures.

Consequently, how, and on what basis, can philosophies so radically different in their religious ground-motives and basic-Ideas cooperate within the framework of their common philosophical task? To answer this question, we have to consider some objections.

> 2. A partial truth cannot exist autonomously, but is always based on the totality of meaning of truth.

Two times two is always four, it is often said, whether a Christian or a pagan draws the conclusion.

This argument is at once raised against any idea of a Christian science or philosophy, but it is obvious that it could just as easily be made against the general result of our transcendental critique of theoretical thought, which is that theoretical thought is always dependent on a religious apriori.

We readily grant that this argument would be a sorry affair if it was intended to really refute the results of our transcendental critique of theoretical thought. As such, it is nevertheless very interesting because it draws our attention to a fact that helps us clarify the necessary basis of cooperation between the various schools of philosophy in accomplishing the common task.

Note first that the proposition 2 x 2 = 4 is not true "in itself" but only in the context of the laws of number and the logical laws of thought. This context, as we know, is possible only in the universal coherence of meaning of all the law spheres, and supposes a totality of meaning of which the numerical and logic aspects are, each in its way, a modal refraction in cosmic time. *No partial truth is self-sufficient.* A partial *theoretical* truth is true only in its coherence with other theoretical truths and, in its own relativity, this coherence presupposes the totality of truth.

It follows that even a philosophical conception of the mutual relationship and coherence of the numerical and logical aspects, consequently of the modal meaning of number- and logical-concepts, is influenced from the outset by a transcendental basic-idea and by the religious ground-motive that determines its content.

Secondly, it is certain that the judgement 2 x 2 = 4 refers to a state of affairs which, in the numerical relations, is independent of any subjective theoretical view and its supra-theoretical presuppositions. It is certainly not true that this "state of affairs" is a "truth in itself", or has some "absolute validity". Just like the proposition that establishes it, this fact depends on the cosmic order of time and the intermodal coherence of meaning that it guarantees, apart from which it is meaningless. It is founded in this *order* and not in a theoretical view of the numerical aspect and its modal laws.

With its temporal laws and all the structural facts that are founded in it, this cosmic order is the same for every thinker, whether Christian, pagan or humanist. As soon as they are discovered, the structural facts impose themselves on everyone, and it would make no sense to deny them. All schools and trends of philosophy have in common the task of accounting for them in a philosophical manner, that is to say, in the light of a transcendental basic-Idea. They are interdependent and should learn from each other, even in respect of errors they have committed in the theoretical interpretation of structural facts and laws founded in the temporal order of our cosmos. Immanence-philosophy can discover many facts which have hitherto escaped the notice of a philosophy led by a truly Christian basic-Idea, and vice versa. Therefore there may, and should, be a noble and healthy competition between all the trends of philosophy.

The Philosophy of the Law-Idea does not claim any privileged position. Our Christian ground-motive and the content of our basic-Idea which the latter determines do not provide us with any guarantee that we shall not commit a fundamental error in accomplishing our task. On the contrary! Better than anyone we can recognise our fallibility, for the simple reason that the fall and sin are key factors in our Christian ground-motive, and we consider it impossible that a Christian philosophy could ever lay claim to infallibility. Rather, this danger threatens immanence-philosophy, and humanism in particular, to the extent that it places the ultimate standard of truth in theoretical thought. We will come back to the problem of truth.

> 3. The idea of a *philosophia perennis.*
> Philosophical thought and historical
> development.

However, we are presented with a second objection. "You assume", we are told, "a radical antithesis in philosophy between the Christian point of view and that of immanence. What remains then of the old idea of the *continuity* of philosophy, that even modern Thomism, however isolated, has zealously maintained? Is not a truly Christian philosophy obliged, whatever you say, not only to break contact with the historical development of philosophy from Greek thought to the present day, but also to set itself outside this development? If this is so, then your claim for a *reformation* of philosophical thought, from a Christian perspective, is doomed to failure from the outset, because reformation is not an *ex nihilo* creation".

We treat this objection with the seriousness it deserves, and in the first place we ask the question: "What do you mean by the *continuity* of philosophy?" We just say, in fact, that philosophical thought as such is closely and necessarily related to the historical development which our genuinely philosophical basic-idea proposes. No thinker, whoever he may be, can put himself outside this development. Therefore our transcendental basic-Idea, as defined above, recognises this *continuity* and firmly rejects the proud illusion that a thinker could begin with a clean sheet by making a clean sweep of the age-old development of philosophical reflection.

But in any case the postulate of the *continuity* of philosophy cannot be turned against the fundamental religious ground-motive of philosophy, with the intention of enclosing it in a kind of historical relativism: we cannot confuse the religious *ground-motive* with the various and variable *forms* it has received. This would inevitably be to fall into historical relativism with respect to truth itself.[1]

Whoever takes the trouble to familiarise themselves with the philosophy of Herman Dooyeweerd, quickly discovers how it is related to the historical development of philosophical and scientific thought, at least with regard to its immanent philosophical content, even though this Master never *follows* immanence-philosophy. The development of his philosophy, starting with the fundamental principles of internal sove-reignty, for example, would have been impossible without the earlier development of modern philosophy and the different branches of science. And consequently it is precisely this philosophical idea of internal sovereignty that Dooyeweerd opposes from the outset to the humanist conception of science. Again, we will be easily convinced that his transcendental critique of theoretical thought has a close historical connection with Kant's *Critique of Pure Reason*, even though it is often opposed to the theoretical dogmatism of Kantian epistemo-logy.

The development of the Philosophy of the Law-Idea is consequently necessarily related to historical development. To penetrate ever deeper into the richness of meaning of the cosmic order is the common task of all philosophies, even those which are irreconcilably opposed to ours, and we ourselves are ambitious to make our contribution to the construction of this majestic building.

However, we must never forget that the *religious starting point,* and hence the whole direction that philosophical thought

---

[1] We encounter this relativism in the philosophy of Dilthey in connection with worldviews, and in a manner more striking than in Oswald Spengler.

receives from it by means of the three-fold transcendental basic-Idea, are inseparable. *It is therefore essential that Christian philosophy, in its smallest details, never gives up this religious starting point if it wants to avoid sinking into accommodation like scholasticism, which we have demonstrated to be fatal to every idea of a Reformed Christian philosophy.*

Every serious philosophical school, we are convinced, contributes to some extent to the development of human thought, and none can lay claim to a monopoly. In the history of the world, no serious current of thought has appeared, however apostate in its starting point, which has not received a special calling by which, if necessary against its will, it was bound to contribute to the fulfilment of God's plan for the development of human faculties to which He assigns, even within the fallen creation, the accomplishment of their appointed task. In the development of our philosophy of history, we will be eager to emphasise this.[2]

> 4. Antithesis between viewpoints and the theory of worldviews in immanence-philosophy.

Finally, the idea of an antithesis of viewpoints is not in itself foreign to immanence-philosophy, especially in its modern form of a theory of worldviews *(Weltanschauungslehre)*.

Many antitheses are actually developed by it, including the oldest: between idealism and naturalism. Curiously, idealism, in its Kantian and post-Kantian forms of transcendental "critical" idealism, believes that this antithesis can be resolved to its advantage by a pure theory of knowledge, without resort to any belief in a freedom that transcends the limits of theoretical reason. But we only have to reflect on the activity of thought

---

[2] It is not possible for us to discuss the immanent historical meaning of God's providence in history before undertaking an analysis of the modal structure of the historical aspect. The view we have expressed about the historical task of immanence philosophy presupposes the acceptance of God's providence, which raises some complex problems for philosophical thought that will engage our attention later. Let us just say that this notion implies the biblical Augustinian idea of a continual struggle in the religious root of history, between the *Civitas Dei* and the *civitas terrena*.

to see immediately that every attempt to reduce theoretical thought to a natural object presupposes a "transcendental subject of thought" or a "transcendental consciousness" without which the objective experience of natural phenomena would be impossible. In the light of our transcendental critique of theoretical thought it is obvious that this alleged purely epistemological refutation of naturalism is based on supra-theoretical presuppositions. We know that the "transcendental subject" is only an absolutisation of the logical function of thought, and that this absolutisation arises from the humanist freedom-motive which the autonomy of thought implies.

Many modern thinkers, however, have tried to neutralise this conflict between the various schools of philosophical thought. They expected to achieve their goal by turning philosophy itself into a "theory of worldviews" that would be neutral and not takes sides with respect to the various antitheses.

For this purpose Dilthey[3] devised three types of "philosophical worldview" which, according to him, continually re-appeared in the course of history:

1. Materialistic positivism (Democritus, Epicurus, Hobbes, the Encyclopaedists, Comte, Avenarius).

2. Objective idealism (Heraclitus, the Stoics, Spinoza, Leibniz, Shaftesbury, Goethe, Schelling, Schleiermacher, Hegel).

3. Freedom-idealism (Plato, Christian philosophy, Kant, Fichte, Maine de Biran).

Rickert[4], for his part, has a more differentiated classification of "worldviews", along the lines of the neo-Kantian philosophy of values, and considers the following types:

---

[3] Wilhelm Dilthey, *Die Typen der Weltanschauung*, Berlin, 1911 [In : Wilhelm Dilthey, *Gesammelte Schriften*, Göttingen, Vandenhoeck and Ruprecht, 1931, VIII, pp.75-118 (6th ed. 1991)]. [English translation in: William Kluback and Martin Weinbaum, *Dilthey's Philosophy of Existence: Introduction to Weltanschauungslehre*, Bookman Associates, New York, 1957.]

[4] Heinrich Rickert, *System der Philosophie*, J.C.B. Mohr (Paul Siebeck), Tübingen, 1st ed., 1921. Windelband (South-West German school of neo-Kantianism) also argues that philosophy is the science of worldviews. (*Wissenschaft der Weltanschauung*). Cf. Wilhelm Windelband, *Einleitung in die Philosophie*, J.C.B. Mohr (Paul Siebeck),

1. Intellectualism
2. Aestheticism
3. Mysticism
4. Moralism
5. Eudemonism
6. Eroticism
7. Theism and polytheism

The characteristic feature of these and all such classific-
ations is that, being constructed on the immanence standpoint,
they destroy the only genuine radical antithesis, namely that
between the immanence-standpoint itself and the Christian
transcendence-standpoint, and that they reduce our Christian
starting point to one of the many "-isms" of immanence-
philosophy. At the same time, unless the creator of these syst-
ematisations is a decided relativist with respect to worldviews,
any opposition that appears *relative* to us will be declared
absolute on the immanence-standpoint.

Indeed, as far as we are concerned, worldviews in immanence philosophy clash in a merely relative manner, and they
only become irreconcilable as the result of a religious absolutisation derived from a dialectical ground-motive.

In modern humanist philosophy, idealism and naturalism
are in a *polar* opposition that from the outset lies concealed in
the fundamental structure of its transcendental basic-Idea
common to them both, and which is itself due to an antithesis
within its religious ground-motive. It expresses itself in an
internal antinomy between the science-ideal and the personality ideal, between nature and freedom.[5]

However, aestheticism and moralism are not aually in
polar opposition but are simply the result of a hypostatisation
of the modal aspects concerned and display within the human-

Tübingen, 2nd ed. 1920, p.19ff. [English trans.: Wilhelm Windelband, *An Introduction to Philosophy*, trans. Joseph McCabe, London, T. Fisher Unwin, 1921.]

[5] Dooyeweerd presents a proof of this assertion in the second part of Volume I of
Philosophy of the Law-Idea, Dutch edition (*De Wijsbegeerte der Wetsidee*), p.139-461,
American edition (*A New Critique of Theoretical Thought*), p.169-495.

ist ground-motive two different manifestations of free autonomous personality.

It is only in appearance that the "theistic" types appear to
abandon the immanence-position. Every theistic philosophy is
in fact directly based on *a metaphysical idea of God* which proceeds from hypostatised theoretical thought ($voῦς$).[6]

In Aristotle's theistic philosophy the divine $voῦς$, pure act
and "pure Form", transcendent first cause, prime mover and
ultimate end of the world, is nothing but hypostatised theoretical thought under the direction of the Greek form-motive,
and presented in a theistic disguise. Such is the *idol-Idea* of this
immanence-philosopher.

The same can be said of Descartes' and Leibniz's "theistic"
philosophies. However, when either of them deifies theoretical
thought, they do so on the basis of the Humanist nature-
freedom motive, which gives their "theism" an entirely different character to Aristotle's.

But whether it is governed by the ground-motive of
Greek or modern humanist thought, we wonder what such a
philosophical "theism" has in common with the radical Christian attitude in philosophical questions concerning life and the
world.

> 5. The consequences of our transcend-
> ental critique for the history of philo-
> sophy. The only possible antithesis in
> philosophy.

On pain of rapidly sinking into inextricable confusion we
cannot, in our study of the history of philosophy, classify the
Greek, medieval scholastic, and modern humanistic systems in
accordance with the abstract schemas of Dilthey or Rickert,
without taking account of their differing religious ground-
motives.

The philosophical meaning of the terms idealism, materialism, intellectualism, mysticism, etc., depends entirely on the

---

[6] In Dooyeweerd's thought *hypostatise* is taken as *meaning B* in Lalande's *Vocabulaire de la philosophie,* article. *Hypostase.* This rather inelegant word was used by Bergson. It is basically synonymous with *to deify.*

transcendental basic-Ideas and religious ground-motives that
govern their content. Greek idealism, for example, which is
governed by the primacy of the religious form-motive, is very
different from the mathematical idealism of Leibniz, which is
governed by the humanist ideal of modern science, implied in
the dialectical nature-freedom ground-motive. The terms
"matter" and "nature" in Greek thought have a different
meaning from that of modern humanist philosophy. Anaximander and Anaximenes were materialists in the sense of the
Greek matter-motive; they were not so in the sense of Hobbes,
whose materialistic metaphysics was governed by the mechanistic science-ideal of pre-Kantian humanism. Democritus
was in no way a materialist in the modern humanist sense. His
"atoms" were "ideal forms" in accordance with the Greek
form-motive, conceived in a uniquely mathematical sense. The
Greek ideal of goodness-and-beauty (καλοκάγαϑον) is no more
comparable with Schiller's humanist aestheticism, which is
dominated by the religious nature-freedom ground-motive,
than Kantian moralism is with Socrates' ethical thought.

It is very dangerous to engage in a supposedly purely-
theoretical analysis of Greek or medieval philosophical currents based on general frameworks that take no account of the
religious ground-motives of Western thought. Though unaware of the fact, the modern humanist ground-motive of
nature-freedom is used as the criterion in the interpretation of
ancient and medieval thinkers. Neither Dilthey nor Rickert
has escaped this pitfall. That is why our transcendental critique
of philosophical thought is also of great importance for the
history of philosophy.[7]

In the light of the transcendental basic-Idea, there is only
one ultimate and radical antithesis in philosophy, that between
the absolutisation or deification of meaning in apostasy from
God, on the one hand, and the return of philosophical thought

---

[7] Cf. on this subject the works of D. H. Th. Vollenhoven, Dooyeweerd's brother-
in-law, Professor of the history of philosophy at the Reformed Free University of
Amsterdam, in particular: *Het Calvinisme en de Reformatie van de Wijsbegeerte*, H. J.
Paris, Amsterdam, 1933, and *Geschiedenis der Wijsbegeerte* (several volumes) T. Wever,
Franeker, 1940ff.

to God in Christ, which requires the notion of complete relativity and the heteronomy of all that participates in the creaturely mode of meaning, on the other. Since this is an ultimate antithesis, there is no room whatsoever alongside it for equivalent antitheses.

Obviously there is a radical difference between the religious ground-motives of ancient Greek thought and modern humanist thought. But these ground-motives do not negate the possibility of an antithesis in the ultimate radical sense of that which separates the Christian religious ground-motive from all apostate religious ground-motives. We are able to establish that the religious antitheses we discovered in each of the dialectical ground-motives display in fact a *polar tension* between their components, which has nothing in common with the antithesis between the Christian and secular starting points.

These kinds of polar tensions are radically excluded from the transcendental basic-Idea of every genuinely Christian philosophy for which there can never be, in principle, the problems of idealism versus naturalism, aestheticism versus moralism, rationalism versus irrationalism, or mysticism versus theism. All these "-isms" can only exist in terms of the immanence-standpoint.

Insofar as such "-isms" have so far found a place in Christian philosophical thought, because of the absence of an integral Christian cosmonomic-Idea, they can only be atavisms in the true sense of the word, the rudiments of secular thinking that is incompatible with a truly Christian attitude.

Part 2: The distinction between philosophy and worldview. The criterion.

6. The boundary line between philosophy and worldview from the immanence-standpoint. Disagreement regarding the criterion.

Can a worldview be confused with philosophical thought? Should it? Can we say that philosophy is nothing but an elaborate worldview, a "guide to a happy life" (*Anweisung zum seligen Leben*) in the form of a philosophical theory? While we agree that the absolute antithesis we formulated is inevitable in the domain of worldviews, must not philosophy – on account of its theoretical character and in order to maintain it – avoid every choice of position lest the boundary that separates it from every worldview is obliterated?

Once again, we are here confronted with the dogma of the autonomy of theoretical thought. These questions demand of us a clear idea of the relationship between philosophy and worldview.

It is very difficult to open a discussion on this point with immanence-philosophy. There are profound differences in its conception of what a worldview and its relations with philosophy could or should be.

Heinrich Rickert, for example, sets out to investigate the nature of a worldview axiologically from his theoretical philosophy of values. Its essential characteristic in his view depends on the choice of a personal a-theoretical position regarding the question: "What is for you the highest value?"

Theodor Litt, another defender of the autonomy of theoretical philosophy, complains that Rickert has transgressed the limits of genuine philosophy in his theoretical philosophy of values. In his opinion, value is *ex-origine* a-theoretical; any founding of absolutely-valid theoretical truth on a value must be rejected. For Litt, values have no place in philosophical thought either as one of its determining factors or even as its decisive factor. To talk of *values* is, in his opinion, "evidence of the fact that the subject has not abandoned his concrete personal relation with the totality of reality in order to achieve pure knowledge".[8] By this criterion, immanence-philosophy in its secular development has been plagued with worldviews, and its purification has hardly begun.

In Nietzsche's philosophy of life, we find exactly the opposite. Here, philosophy's task is to provide a "classification

---

[8] Theodor Litt, *Einleitung in die Philosophie*, Teubner, Leipzig and Berlin, 1933, p.261.

of values". Philosophers are "leaders and legislators".[9] Philosophy becomes thereby an "art of living" and as such has in common with theoretical science only the fact that both are expressed in concepts.

Modern existentialist philosophy, which was powerfully influenced by Søren Kierkegaard, follows the same trend in its conception of the relationship between philosophy and world-view. For Karl Jaspers, philosophy was, from its inception, much more than just a "universal theory". "Philosophy gives impulses, draws up tables of values, adds meaning and purpose to human life, and gives man a world in which he feels safe; in a word, it provides a worldview." Only a "prophetic" philosophy, capable of providing this worldview by drawing up tables of values as norms, is entitled to the name of *philosophy*. In his opinion, this term is commonly used today for what could be better and more clearly described as universal logic, sociology and psychology, all of which, as theory, have no appreciation of values. Consequently Jaspers' famous book, which sets out to provide a *theory* of possible worldviews and to *understand* their meaning psychologically, is called: *The Psychology of Worldviews*.[10]

We find, therefore, two opposing trends: one that distinguishes philosophy from worldviews axiologically and one that identifies them. In the former it is argued that philosophy should at all times be directed towards a theoretical value, in the latter that all valuation whatsoever should be excluded.

Nevertheless, we maintain a respectful distance from a genuinely axiological criterion, for the one that has been proposed is heavily loaded with the *transcendental basic-Idea* of the philosophers under consideration. A "concept of value", in an objective idealist sense, or even in a subjective psychological sense, reveals an *immanentist* origin. For those of us who, from the outset, have raised the question of the possibility of

---

[9] Friedrich Nietzsche, *Genealogie der Moral*, Leipzig, Verlag von C. G. Naumann, 1887, p.38. [English trans.: Friedrich Nietzsche, *The Genealogy of Morals*, trans. Horace Barnett Samuel, New York, Courier Dover Publications, 2003.]

[10] Karl Jaspers, *Psychologie der Weltanschauungen*, Berlin, Springer Verlag, 3rd ed. 1925, pp.1-7.

philosophy and have established the need for a critical reflection on the transcendental basic-Idea, a criterion springing from
a philosophy that pays no attention to the importance of its
own basic-Idea is unacceptable.

> 7. For Theodor Litt every worldview
> is an "individual impression of life".

Every man, says Litt, has his own "worldview", which is
nothing but an impression of life, entirely dependent on the
view of experienced reality formed by the community in
which he lives. Community life creates an atmosphere of
common beliefs that influence everything that is said, thought
or done, without their ever being subjected to any criticism.
These views of community life and the world take on the most
varied forms, from the mythical image of the world to the
dogmas of religion or the worldly wisdom of a popular view of
life. In its origins, philosophy is very intimately involved in
such general views of the world. Nevertheless, to safeguard the
purity of its scientific consciousness, it has to sharply distinguish itself from them. It restricts itself, in fact, to universally
valid theoretical truth, and this truth is found only in the
domain of theoretical thought.[11]

Litt's view of worldviews hardly carries us very far, for
the very prejudices come into play here that we saw in the case
of the criterion of value. In other words, determination of the
relationship between philosophy and worldviews is ruled by a
transcendental basic-Idea, whose importance this thinker
ignores for want of critical reflection.

Moreover, when Litt refers to the requiring of "universal
validity" for a worldview as a "lack of logical integrity" (which
in his opinion appertains only to "theoretical truth") this *ad
hominem* argument hardly impresses us. It is obvious that his

---

[11] Litt's definition of worldviews agrees fairly well with the one Georg Simmel
gives to philosophy as a "temperament, seen through a world picture", or a revelation of "what is profound and final in a personal approach towards the world in
the language of a world picture" (Georg Simmel, *Hauptprobleme der Philosophie*, G. J.
Göschen, Leipzig, 1910, pp.23, 28). This remark is interesting, for Simmel is a prop-
onent of the historicist and relativist philosophy of life to which Litt, despite appearances, is very close.

conception of the *meaning* of theoretical truth bears the stamp of a transcendental basic-Idea issuing from a supra-theoretical choice of position and, on his own admission, *from a worldview*.

What of ourselves? What relationship do we see between philosophy and worldviews?

The concept of a worldview goes beyond the domain of vague representations that are now depreciated, now over-valued, only if it is understood in the sense of necessarily involving a view of totality. In our opinion, an individual "impression of life", fuelled by whatever convictions, is not a worldview.

An authentic worldview has, undoubtedly, a close affinity with philosophy, because it also is directed towards the totality of meaning of our cosmos. It also implies an Archimedean point, a religious ground-motive, and the religious commitment for our selfhood. But unlike philosophy, its specific attitude of thought, its view of totality, is not theoretical, but *pre-theoretical*. It does not conceive reality in abstract terms, but engages the typical structures of individuality directly, without theoretical analysis. It is therefore not the prerogative of a privileged class of "philosophical thinkers": it concerns every man, including the simplest.

It would be a very big mistake to see in Christian philo-sophy no more than a philosophically elaborated worldview. At the same time, we would misconstrue their mutual rela-tions. The Revelation of the Word of God no more gives us a detailed Christian worldview than it does a Christian philo-sophy. To the one as to the other, it gives simply the starting point in their central ground-motive and hence their *direction*, but a truly *radical* and *integral* direction in which nothing escapes and which determines everything. And exactly the same applies for the direction and particular manner of consid-ering every issue which *apostate religious* ground-motives impress on philosophy and every worldview.

While they cannot be identified, philosophy and world-view are thus inextricably united in their root. Their respective tasks are totally different; philosophy cannot take the place of a worldview, nor vice-versa. They must mutually understand each other, and that from their common religious root.

But philosophy has the special task of giving a *theoretical* account of every worldview. We will come back to this shortly.

Part 3: The postulate of neutrality and the "theory of worldviews".

It is very interesting to discover the influence of *the personality-ideal* in the postulate of neutrality, a key factor in the humanist transcendental basic-Idea.

On a number of occasions already we have established that it is by means of this postulate that the various trends of modern immanence-philosophy attempt to evade any critical reflection of the transcendental basic-Idea of their philosophy.

The postulate of neutrality arises from the strict distinction made by Kant between theoretical reason and practical reason, and his attempt to emancipate the free autonomous personality from the tyranny of the humanist science-ideal, which was itself founded on the humanist religious freedom-motive.

But the postulate of neutrality does not have a *theoretical* origin, but rather a most decidedly *religious* one.

Before proceeding to a critique of it, we shall first examine the theoretical arguments invoked in its defence.

9. Rickert's argument for the postulate of neutrality.

Herman Dooyeweerd believes that Rickert, in his *System der Philosophie,* has produced its best and most detailed defence. We shall now summarise this philosopher's arguments.

Philosophy, as to its inner nature, is the theoretical science that has the task of understanding the cosmos theoretically as a totality, although it is divided by theoretical thought into two completely distinct spheres: the spatio-temporal or *natural reality* perceptible to the senses, the other *timeless values* that have *absolute validity*.

Philosophy must be limited strictly to a theoretical attitude of knowledge. It therefore did not proclaim any world-view as "conviction", "faith" or "imperative". Imperatives and norms have nothing to do with theory: the concept of a normative science is self-contradictory.

In Rickert, "reality", which he reduces to its psycho-physical aspects, is not considered in the objectivising manner of the special sciences. The latter must determine what reality is as "pure reality", that is, as a conscious, *immanent given*, the "psycho-physical". Since there is no other reality, philosophy has nothing to say about it.[12]

Nevertheless, reality for Rickert is more than "pure reality". As theoretical *form*, in which the understanding conceives an empirical sensory material of consciousness, reality is a *category of thought*, which is not *real* but which possesses *validity* (*Geltung*).

Rickert said that Kant adopted this "critical" viewpoint in relation to reality, when he proclaimed[13] the transcendental subject to be "universally valid", stripped of all individuality in the synthesis of its forms of thought and intuition of being, the formal origin of the true "*Gegenstand*" of knowledge. Only this type of "validity" or "value" can be used to build its "universe" epistemologically and it is crucial for the *objectivity* of reality acquired on the basis of a critical philosophy.[14]

Even more clearly, the theoretical Idea of the *totality of reality*, conceived by Kant as an *infinite task* for thought, reveals its *value*-character. If this totality is "absolute totality", it is so only by virtue of the value that holds.[15]

---

[12] Heinrich Rickert, *System der Philosophie*, J.C.B. Mohr (Paul Siebeck), Tübingen, 1921, p.170.

[13] [Marcel has misunderstood Dooyeweerd here. What Dooyeweerd said was that Kant proclaimed the "universally valid" transcendental subject to be the formal origin of the true *Gegenstand* of knowledge. See *De Wijsbegeerte der Wetsidee*, I, p.94 and *A New Critique of Theoretical Thought*, I, p.130.]

[14] Heinrich Rickert, *op. cit.*, p.175.

[15] Heinrich Rickert, *ibid.*

For the problem of the "totality of reality" to be susceptible of philosophical solution, it must be posed as an *epistemo-*
logical problem. Philosophy does not deal with reality "as
such", but with the problem of *the knowledge of reality*. It seeks
to understand the theoretical values which in fact *are* not, but
which *hold good* and guide our understanding of reality, so that
the latter acquires stability and consistency. In other words, the
philosophical problems of reality must be conceived only as
concerns regarding the theory of knowledge, as *theoretical prob-*
lems of meaning and value. Theoretical philosophy of reality is an
epistemology; it seeks to interpret the meaning of knowledge
and this is only possible in terms of *values*.

However, it would be wrong to restrict the task of philosophy just to the study of these purely theoretical values. As a
theory of values, philosophy must be directed to the totality
(Vollendung), and must necessarily include the universe of
values within its horizon, and move towards a system of
values. Hence it must also consider the *a-theoretical* values:
morality, beauty, holiness, etc., so that it can interpret the
meaning of all life in a theoretical manner.

According to Rickert, the material content of this value
system can be deduced from general axiological forms. The
development of such a system involves a *material* through
which we first acquire a notion of the *multiplicity* of values. It is
by orienting itself to *the historical life of culture* that philosophy
discovers this multiplicity.

To understand this line of thought, we must observe that,
according to Rickert, *philosophy*, as a theory of totality, has the
task of reunifying, by means of thought, the "world of natural
reality" and the "world of valid values", which were first
separated by theoretical thought. When we are not thinking,
when we are "concept-free", we experience this unity immediately; but if there were an irreducible dualism in theoretical
thought, philosophy could not become a real philosophy of
"totality".

There must be, then, a theoretical meeting point between
values and reality, a *third sphere* capable of uniting the other
two. This is what Rickert supposes he has discovered in the

concept of meaning which, in his opinion, is "logically prior" to the theoretical separation of reality and value. Meaning itself is neither reality nor value; it exists as a synthesis, which occurs in the act of valuation. Meaning, signification *(Bedeutung)*, belongs to all "acts" so far as the subject chooses a position in them with respect to values. In the "immanent meaning of the act", value and reality go hand in hand synthetically. In itself, immanent meaning is never *value*, but through it reality is *related to values* and values are "connected" to reality.

In the concept of *meaning*, the distinction between value and reality is never effaced; they are simply combined into a higher synthesis. "Value" is *meaning*, but has a *transcendent, timeless, absolute* character. On the other hand *meaning*, as meeting-point between value and reality, is "immanent meaning", and in it alone does the subject find its place. "Reality" is merely the *object* of the transcendental epistemological subject; and in the sphere of values there is no subjectivity at all.

To find the multiplicity of values, philosophy must be oriented towards the realm of the immanent meaning which is only manifest in the *historical life of culture* through cultural goods that constitute what is "truly objective"; and this life must be studied in a theoretical and objective manner by the science of history.

The science of history studies culture as "reality endowed with values" *(wertbehefte Wirklichkeit)*, although in fact it turns away from absolute values. As such it presents philosophy with the material it needs to construct its systematic theory of values. From the cultural "goods" of history philosophy abstracts general *values* which will serve to define the problems philosophy has to solve as a doctrine of the *meaning of life*. It has to operate with an "open system" that can make room for new values.

Therefore, only the absolute universal validity of the theoretical value of truth can be demonstrated convincingly for any thinking being. It alone has an internal guarantee of this validity. A relativistic conception of this value theoretically refutes itself since it has to appeal to an absolute truth, if it is to be taken seriously.

On the contrary, the universal validity of a-theoretical values of this open system – beauty, personal holiness, holiness impersonal morality and happiness – cannot be proven, because any evidence falls within the theoretical domain. As the theoretical science of totality, philosophy can give us a theoretical view of these values, in a theoretical system, but without being able to say anything about the practical priority of any of them: it will only give us a *formal order* of "degrees of value" *(Wertstufen)*.

If philosophy established the supremacy of a particular value, it would fall into "prophetism" inconsistent with its theoretical starting point which must be free from any prejudice. It would become a worldview, even if it declared the theoretical values that dominate its field of enquiry to be the highest, dominating all of life. Instead of thinking philosophically in a theoretical style, it would begin to preach a form of intellectualism, as happened with Enlightenment philosophy.

However, philosophy cannot help but include worldviews in its theoretical enquiry. Its object is the *totality* of the cosmos, to which the subject belongs, that is to say the whole man in his relations with the cosmos, the subject who chooses a position in life with respect to values. Hence, philosophy must also be a theory of worldviews, a *theory of the total meaning of life (Theorie des vollendeten Lebens)*, and hence also a philosophy of values.

As a "theory of worldviews" philosophy will merely develop the various possible types of worldview theoretically. It will therefore only identify the consequences of the precedence of a particular value, that is, to furnish us with theoretical clarity regarding the meaning of each worldview. But it will be careful not to take sides, because "it is for each individual to choose for himself the worldview that best suits his personal extra- or supra-scientific nature".[16]

---

[16] Heinrich Rickert, *System der Philosophie*, J.C.B. Mohr (Paul Siebeck), Tübingen, 1921, p.407. Neither in his essay *Wissenschaftliche Philosophie und Weltanschauung* (in *Logos: Internationale Zeitschrift für Philosophie der Kultur*, J.C.B. Mohr, Tübingen, Vol. XXII, 1933), p.37ff, nor in his *Grundprobleme der Philosophie* (J.C.B. Mohr, Tübingen,

10. Critique of the foundations of
Rickert's theory.

The foundations of Rickert's theory of worldview seem
well established. He seems to defend zealously the limits of
theoretical philosophy against any attempt to make of theory
something more than pure theory. His rejection of every
intellectualist foundation for philosophy and his distinction
between philosophy and worldview seem well documented. In
addition, Rickert shows such little regard for intellectualist
prejudices that he recognises theoretically the need for religion
to permeate the whole of life and maintain its ruling value on a
level above all others. He also recognises that the axiological
point of view does not exhaust the essence of religion.

And yet, a formidable obstacle lurks in this plea for the
theoretical neutrality of philosophy, and it is fatal to his whole
conception of the essence, task and place of philosophy.

Rickert's postulate of neutrality can have *complete* meaning
if and only if the "theoretical value of truth" – the value that
alone can dominate philosophy in his opinion – has an absolute
validity in itself, independent of the temporal cosmic order,
independent of every other value, and above all independent of
the religious fullness of truth.

The obstacle in question is the presupposed identification
of "truth" with *theoretical accuracy* and (in the apriori presupposition that flows from it) the notion that truth so understood has
an absolute "value" in itself: "In philosophy", he says, "we see
a theoretical attitude of mind, and we seek in it nothing other
than what we call truth. We assume therefore that truth has an
intrinsic value, or that it makes sense to seek the truth for the
sake of truth. Hence, we assume also that there is a truth of
timeless validity: this is a presupposition that arouses some
opposition in our day. It implies the belief that there is a truth
in itself, an absolute truth, which can serve as a yardstick for
every philosophical conception of the world[17]."

1934) does Rickert modify his viewpoint. Cf. Dooyeweerd, *A New Critique of
Theoretical Thought*, Vol. I, p.129, footnote 1.

[17] Heinrich Rickert, *System der Philosophie*, J.C.B. Mohr (Paul Siebeck), Tübingen,
1921, p.39. [Wir sehen in der Philosophie ein theoretisches Verhalten und suchen in

It would be quite petty of us to taunt the author with the word "belief", which appears in this quote, and to argue that, on his terms, "belief" belongs in the realm of worldviews not philosophy. For Rickert is firmly convinced that truth is the unique value whose absolute universal validity can be proved theoretically.

But how can it be argued that the absolute validity of this value, i.e., "theoretical truth", could be theoretically demonstrated? Indeed, does not every theoretical proof imply a norm that guarantees its accuracy? (Herman Dooyeweerd hesitates to say an absolute truth-value, having in itself its own validity). How does one prove what is presupposed in the proof? We will return to this.

11. The inherent antinomy in Rickert's theory of values.

For now, we will be satisfied with showing that this absolutisation of theoretical truth in an absolute value resting in itself inevitably leads, on our author's standpoint, to an irreducible antinomy.

It is Rickert's wish to relate philosophical thought to the "totality of values". Over against this totality, the "truth-value", in Rickert's *theoretical* conception, is only a type of (transcendent) meaning in the (transcendent) diversity of values. If this is so, the theoretical truth-value cannot, under any circumstances, be posited as "in itself" because it always presupposes the *totality* of values. The idea of an absolute theoretically "truth-value" resting entirely in itself is self-contradictory and destroys itself.

In addition, the diversity of values presupposes that there is a coherence of meaning between them. How else could they belong to the same totality of values? And if this is so, what

---

ihr nichts anderes als das, was wir Wahrheit nennen. Dabei setzen wir voraus, daß die Wahrheit einen Eigenwert besitzt, oder daß es einen Sinn hat, nach Wahrheit um der Wahrheit willen zu streben. Darin steckt die weitere Voraussetzung, daß es Wahrheit gibt, die zeitlos gilt, und schon diese Voraussetzung wird in unserer Zeit Anstoß erregen. Sie schließt die Überzeugung ein, daß es in sich ruhende, oder absolute Wahrheit gibt, an der alle philosophischen Ansichten vom Weltall zu messen sind.]

significance can be given to the postulate of the "theoretical purity" of my philosophical thought, if the theoretical "truth-value" – which alone can give meaning to this thought – cannot satisfy this postulate without destroying itself? How can a particular value, severed from the coherence that binds all the others and set by itself, retain any meaning? If it cannot, the postulate of the autonomy of theoretical thought is then reduced to an absurdity, and it shows once again the impossibility of finding the real Archimedean point of immanence-philosophy in "pure" theoretical thought.

12. The test of a transcendental basic-Idea.

Let us now apply the test of the transcendental basic-Idea to Rickert. We note that the metaphysical concept of value in his system is seen to be ruled by a specifically supra-theoretical choice in respect of the Origin and totality of meaning of the various modal laws, in particular the spheres of normative laws. Here's how.

A norm *as law* (mandatory) is necessarily related to a subject: it is thus *relative* and so cannot be the absolute Origin of meaning. Since referring norms to the sovereignty of God induces a conflict with the secret religious proclamation of the sovereignty of the human personality, it is inevitable that an Idea of reason is hypostatised as a value sufficient unto itself. This value appears elevated to the Origin of the laws. But in fact, it is the apostate selfhood which, in the Idea of value, promotes so-called "practical reason" to the dignity of sovereign Origin.

As we have seen, absolute value is nothing but the hypostatisation of the norm (in its modal speciality of meaning) which to this end is separated from the subject, on the one hand, and from God as the Origin, on the other and, like a Platonic Idea, rests in itself. However, this "value" is never conceived with Plato as a "being", an exemplary form with respect to the perceptible cosmos, but as a "holding good".

The real root of this axiological metaphysical theory is the *humanist personality-ideal*, which plays a fundamental role in the religious ground-motive of humanism. After a long battle, this ideal gained through Kant's "primacy of practical reason" the ascendancy over the humanist science-ideal of the intellectualist Enlightenment. Theoretical philosophy, Rickert explicitly declared, should in no way lord it over the autonomous freedom of personality in its choice of a worldview.

In Rickert, a religious ground-motive lies at the root of his postulate of theoretical neutrality. This ground-motive is expressed in a transcendental basic-Idea. It would be possible to show the apriori influence of this Idea on the whole of Rickert's thought, in his concept of law and subject, his view of reality, his metaphysical idea of value, his notion of time, etc.

> 13. Without prying into matters that concern no man, the philosophy of the Law-Idea alone leads each thinker to a fundamental self-criticism.

We can see that the enquiry into the transcendental basic-Idea to which a philosophical system is related, leads simultaneously to a radical exposure of the antitheses in philosophical thought and to the discovery of some unpalatable truths. Immanence-philosophy should not complain about this. For it, too, demands that philosophical thought should search for the truth and nothing but the truth. However, it fiercely resists any attack against the autonomy of theoretical thought.

The reader should not, however, lose sight of the fact that the radical criticism of the philosophy of the Law-Idea has nothing in common with a judgement directed against the personal religious attitude of any thinker. Such a judgement does not belong to man and in no way corresponds to the intention of our philosophy. After all, are not we Christians well-acquainted with an apostate selfhood as well as one refocused on God that engage in a mighty struggle every day in our own hearts?

However, the radical criticism that the philosophy of the Law-Idea demands of every thinker reveals the *real* truth at just this point: The proclamation of the autonomy of philosophical thought means that that thought has turned away from Christ, the new religious root of our cosmos. And this attitude, which cannot come from Christ or be inspired by Him, springs from the root of existence that has turned away from God: the *sinful heart*.

Part 4: The pretended self-guarantee of theoretical truth.

We should not be content, however, with having refuted Rickert's plea for the postulate of neutrality. Indeed, it has not escaped the attention of its other defenders that its real foundation in Rickert's philosophy of values exceeds the limits of a "purely theoretical" thought. Theodor Litt, in particular, believes that the Idea of value, as such, is merely a "worldview" concern.

So we have to penetrate to the root of an argument for this postulate that is not based on a philosophy of values. It is actually found in the pretended self-guarantee of the absoluteness of "theoretical truth".

Rickert, too, as we have seen, focuses all of his argument on this "self-guarantee"; but in the axiological turn in his demonstration he revealed his weak point and laid himself open to criticism. Leaving this aside, let us simply ask whether in some other way one could lay claim to establishing the "self-guarantee of theoretical truth" on a "purely theoretical" conception of philosophy.

We have had occasion to observe that this alleged self-guarantee *can never be proved* theoretically. Theodor Litt, too, has discovered the pitfall that remains hidden from the defenders of the absoluteness and self-guarantee of "theoretical truth" when they suppose *it should be possible to demonstrate them in a theoretical way*. Litt goes so far as to accuse those who believe this self-guarantee to be demonstrable of *relativism*, insofar as they seek to relate "truth" to something that is not itself truth, something other than the truth and, if possible, *more than* the truth.

In his opinion, all that can be theoretically demonstrated is the internal contradiction in which every relativistic conception of truth involves itself.

In fact, this would not mean very much, or even anything at all, for the defence of the autonomy of theoretical thought, if Litt had also [not[18]] extricated himself from an apriori ident-ification of absolute self-guaranteeing truth with *theoretical accuracy*. For if the truth is not exhausted by its relation to theoretical thought, on the contrary, if "theoretical truth" is only a refraction of meaning (*heteronomous*) of the fullness of the whole truth, that is to say its *religious fullness*, then his argument that "relativism" destroys itself returns immediately against anyone who denies the fullness of truth.

Litt nevertheless sought, and with infinite care, to protect himself against any misunderstanding of his true thinking. For him, autonomous truth is only valid in exclusive correlation with the "cogito", the "I think (theoretically)". In that way, he also sought specifically to cut off any "hypostatisation" of truth as an idea or "value" that would have *being* or *validity* apart from subjectivity.

In other words, "absolute autonomous truth" holds only in and for theoretical thought. Yet this judgement is clearly the epitome of contradiction. How can a truth whose validity is made relative to *theoretical* thought be absolute and autonom-ous? The philosophy of values at least escaped this contra-diction by hypostatising truth as an absolute value, elevated in itself above any connection with subjectivity. By restricting the validity of truth from the outset to its relation with theor-etical thought, Litt falls into this fundamental *relativism*, which he believed he had definitively avoided by absolutising *theoretical* truth.

It is very interesting to see how he tries to justify himself in the light of this accusation. For him, relativism is, in all its forms, an internally contradictory scepticism which, in its arguments, must simultaneously presuppose and destroy the authentic concept of truth: "To destroy it", he said, "because what they call in their own terms 'truth' is not truth; and to presuppose it, because this act of destruction is an intellectual

---

[18] [The *not* (Fr. *ne*) here is surely a typing error. Litt identified absolute truth with theoretical accuracy.]

action, which can only be meaningful if the 'truth', in its original sense, is accepted as possible and accessible[19]." And if scepticism sees no contradiction here, it is just because it has not arrived at the final stage of critical reflection with respect to theoretical thought. Through reflective thought, it merely puts forward the claim to validity which is inherent in the judgements of thought directed to "objects" *(Gegenstände)*, and forgets that the judgements of reflective thought also claim for themselves an absolute validity with respect to truth. In other words, scepticism has not arrived at a reflective introspection in which thought is directed only to itself and not to its "objects".

If biology, psychology and even anthropology study the function of thought scientifically, they can only examine it as a special aspect of reality, in full relativity with the other aspects of reality. They therefore remain in the realm of "objective thought" *(gegenständliche Denken)*, for which thought itself is a part of "reality", an "object". And so, in all biological, psychological or anthropological thought, the actual "I think", which can never become an "object of thought", remains elusive.

It is precisely the specific task of philosophical thought as reflective thought, according to Litt, to draw attention to this subjective counter-pole (which can never be "objectivised") of all objective reality, and to demonstrate how the validity that the judgements of objectifying scientific thought claim for themselves remains dependent on the absolute validity of the truth of the judgements of reflective thought.

Hence, if it were the case that making the absolute validity of truth dependent on the epistemological relation meant that truth is limited to *real thinking beings*, then, and only then, according to Litt, would his conception of truth have lost its way in a sceptical relativism. But such is not the case at all, he

---

[19] Theodor Litt, *Einleitung in die Philosophie*, Teubner, Leipzig and Berlin 1933, p.29, §3 *(Die Selbstwiderlegung des Skeptizismus)* : [Vernichten : denn das, was sie expressis verbis „Wahrheit" nennen, ist nicht Wahrheit ; voraussetzen : denn dieser Akt der Vernichtung ist ein geistiges Tun, das nur dann sinnvoll ist, wenn „Wahrheit" im ursprünglichen Sinne als möglich und erreichbar angenommen wird.]

says. For, the "cogito", to which the validity of absolute truth is restricted, has to be understand exclusively as "pure thought", that is to say, "the thought of which we have said that it jumps back and forth continually into the counter-pole *(Gegenposition)* of the "object" thought of. This "thought" is no longer at all an aspect of concrete temporal reality. It is the transcendental subject of thought, itself universally valid, the self-consciousness that has reached determinateness in reflective thought, and which is not inherent in individual reality, but "in mere thought" as such. For all temporal and spatial reality, including the *whole concrete self* as individual reality of experience, is in the epistemological relationship only an *objective "counter-pole"* of this transcendental "I think" which, in this transcendental sense, can never be subsumed under it.

According to Litt, the introduction of absolute truth within the epistemological relationship thus conceived does not in any way lead to relativism, because it is not the intention here to *deduce* "truth" from something else: there is merely the acceptance of a strict *correlation* between truth and the (transcendental) "cogito". "There is here, then", he says, "a careful balance between the members united by the relation: just as *truth* is determined with respect to the *thinking being*, so the thinking being is determined with respect to *truth*, and *only* with respect to it."[20] Such a correlation of this absoluteness leaves no room for the least relativism.

15. Criticism of Litt's conception.

We have reproduced Litt's conception of the absoluteness and self-guarantee of theoretical truth in as detailed a manner as possible and often in his own words, not only to do justice to his argument, but also to give our rebuttal the necessary accuracy and sharpness. We shall use our new method of *immanent* criticism.

---

[20] Theodor Litt, *Einleitung in die Philosophie*, Teubner, Leipzig and Berlin, 1933, p.36, §4 (*Die Denk-Korrelation*) : [Hier besteht also ein strenges Gleichgewicht zwischen den Gliedern, die durch die Relation verbunden sind : wie die „Wahrheit" im Hinblick auf das „denkende Wesen", so ist das „denkende Wesen" im Hinblick auf die „Wahrheit" and nur im Hinblick auf sie bestimmt.]

Consider first of all the strict correlation the author posits between theoretical thought and truth. It is clear that the *relativising of the fullness (of meaning) of truth* to a *purely theoretical* truth – which is undoubtedly implied in this relation – will not at all affect the absoluteness and the alleged self-guarantee of truth if the "transcendental cogito" was able to claim the same absoluteness as truth itself. That would mean that "transcendental cogito" and "truth" are one and the same thing and, in a logical sense, identical. Certainly Litt's argument ends in this identification. In truth, every argument for the self-guarantee of "theoretical truth" is intended to safeguard the unconditional and "purely theoretical" character of philosophical thought. For what is beyond question here is *not* the autonomy of "truth", but the *self-guarantee, the autonomy of philosophical thought*. While Litt emphatically rejects the idea that he was trying to *deduce* the "truth" of philosophical thought, he will nevertheless be unable to deny that the supposed absoluteness and autonomy of theoretical truth only exist through philosophical thought, and will disappear with it.

When we attempt, from the philosophical subjective pole of thought, to approximate the meaning of the *correlation* formulated by Litt, we follow him exactly. In his view, it would make no sense to talk about what I cannot grasp in a *concept* when thinking *subjectively*. This also holds good for the "absolute truth". But then, it cannot be denied that a serious danger threatens the absoluteness of truth and if this line of thought is continued, this absoluteness may well be reduced to the absoluteness of philosophical thought. It seems, indeed, that "absolute truth" must, in turn, *be determined* in a theoretical logical manner by philosophical thought. For how else could it be "purely theoretical"? On the other hand, the determination that philosophical thought would have to receive from "absolute truth" appears to be logically *indeterminate* in the extreme.

And if, in the dialectical development of thought, "*absolute truth*" never appears to be identical with the "*absolute cogito*", it immediately falls again – in Litt's line of thought – to the level of an epistemological "object", which has to obtain all its determination from thought itself.

16. First pitfall: The unconditional
character of the transcendental cogito.

However, if we turn to the *subjective pole* of thought, the
transcendental cogito – which in Litt's Kantian view stands in
absolute opposition to all *reality* – then there reappears, in the
conception of the "unconditional character" of this pole of
thought, the pitfall we referred to in our Introduction.

For the *cogito* is nothing other than the selfhood in its
logical activity of thought. It is absolutely impossible to reduce
this *selfhood* to the modal meaning of its *logic function*, without
retaining only a bare *concept*, which is itself merely the product
of the thinking *selfhood*.

This pitfall rightly attracted the attention of Fichte, father
of the dialectical-reflective method, when he stressed the
necessity of a tension between the "absolute selfhood" and
"thinking selfhood".[21] Litt, on the other hand, thinking to
follow Fichte, failed to notice the contradiction of "unconditional thought" because he hypostatises theoretical thought in
the humanist sense of a *value-free* reflection. This is *precisely*
what Fichte, in his Kantian phase, refused to do because he was
not seeking the *root* or the *selfhood* of human existence in
"theoretical reason" but in "practical reason", that is, in Kant's
homo noumenon, the synthetically-hypostatised ethical function
of personality. For Fichte, in other words, theoretical thought
was *ethically determined* from the outset. In Litt, on the contrary,
the *entire selfhood* is identical with the concrete individual complex of *its functions in real space-time*, and as such can now *only* be
determined by absolute transcendental thought. Indeed, in this
"entire concrete selfhood" the *selfhood* that transcends all
thought cannot be found.

Thus, Litt's conception of the absolute self-guarantee of
"purely theoretical truth" is reduced to a hypostatised speculative thought which collapses into internal contradictions,
which no dialectical approach can eliminate for, in the last
analysis, it is by the latter that it declares itself logically

---

[21] Fichte's *absolute ego* has nothing in common with the *total concrete selfhood*, which
Litt made the "object" of thought.

identical (in its opposition) with the "whole self". By accepting the autonomy and unconditional character of philosophical thought, the actual selfhood vanishes. This selfhood, which in its *religious actuality determines all thought,* remains fundamentally distinct from all logical concepts. But with the denial of the actual self or actual personality, there likewise vanishes the possibility of knowledge and the formation of concepts.

Such are the destructive consequences to which Litt should have addressed himself, had he really taken seriously the postulate of the "purity" of philosophical thought. The fact that he could nevertheless develop a philosophical system proves that he was far from thinking in a "purely theoretical" manner.

> 17. Second pitfall: The opposition between transcendental thought and full reality.

The second pitfall in Litt's conception of the transcendental "cogito" is the assumption that, in the antithetic relation of theoretical thought, *the whole of temporal reality recedes* – in opposition to the subjective pole "I think" – to the counter-pole of the *Gegenständlichkeit,* which Litt identifies with *objectivity.*

This assumption is fundamentally flawed and contradictory, because it neglects the temporal coherence of meaning, to which the logical function of thought is subject even in its ultimate actuality which can never be objectivised.

In our transcendental critique of theoretical thought we have shown that the antithetic relation, from which alone the epistemological problem of the "subject" could arise, does not correspond to reality. Therefore the relation itself can never become the "object" of thought in its actual logical function, but can only be a purely intentional abstraction, conducted *within* the real theoretical act of our consciousness. In the absolutisation of the "transcendental-logical subject" the fact is completely lost sight of that theoretical thought is only possible in an intermodal synthesis which presupposes the cosmic coherence of meaning in time and which, consequently, can never be of a purely logical character.

The second error in Litt's argument, which depends on the first, is that the ego or selfhood is determined only by "pure" thought, that is, by dialectical logic.

18. The self-refutation of scepticism restored to its just proportions.

Thus, the self-refutation of scepticism, on which Rickert and Litt concentrate the force of their argument, has actually nothing to do with the pretended self-guarantee of purely theoretical truth. We shall attempt to reduce it to its proper proportions.

The question seems to be that logical thought in its subjectivity is necessarily subject to the laws of logic and, in the case in question, to the principle of contradiction.

Anyone who wants to think theoretically must begin by recognising the validity of this principle, which does not have an absolute and "unconditioned" character, but rather a cosmic-temporal one. Does this mean that other creatures, even God himself, could free themselves from the principle of non-contradiction in their thinking? If this question is to make any sense, we must start from the assumption that God himself, or his angels perhaps, *would have to think* in a temporal cosmic manner. It is true that human thought can be expressed contrary to the principle of non-contradiction, as it does, at least, throughout "dialectical logic". But whoever supposes that this way of thinking could also be attributed to God and his angels would at the same time have to assume that they are part of the cosmic-temporal order and subject to the laws governing it, while being able to violate them insofar as they have a normative character. How absurd, and in respect of the sovereign God, what blasphemy.

Since the time of the Greek *Sophists*, sceptical relativism has been characterised by the initial denial that thought is subject to a norm of truth. It is an *irrationalism* in the epistemological domain.

In fact, this denial must necessarily lead to a contradiction, just like the judgement: "There is no truth", which must itself be tested by the norm of truth. But in its claim to truth, does such a judgement imply the validity of absolute, autonomous theoretical truth? No way. Whoever says: "There is no truth", denies firstly the validity of any norm of truth in the temporal coherence of meaning. In addition, such a judgement is directed in an absolute manner against the supra-temporal *totality* and Origin of truth. Hence, it lands itself in an antinomy, because this judgement has to appeal to a truth that must be the unique truth.

When Litt proclaims the autonomy of *theoretical truth*, he too lands in a sceptical relativism, and so in the same antinomy. To maintain his own consistency, he cannot accept any norm that would dominate the absolutised "transcendental-logical subject". Does he not say that the subjective "cogito" is sovereign, and the Origin of all meaning and order? And how will subjective theoretical thought maintain its autonomy, if it were acknowledged that it is subject to a law *that it has not imposed on itself?*

In line with this thinking, the "transcendental cogito" does not belong to the full temporal reality *in its indissoluble correlation with the law-side and subject-side*. Reality, as given *(Gegebenheitskorrelation)*, is only seen in the absolutised individuality, attributed to the "concrete selfhood". It is as little subjected to law as the "transcendental ego", but it is understood as the irrational absolute that can only be *objectivised* in the epistemological correlation *(Erkenntniskorrelation)*, and conceived by the "transcendental-logical selfhood" in forms of universally valid thought.

Nowhere in Litt's philosophy does the cosmic law really have a place in its original indissoluble correlation with the individual *subjectivity* that is subjected to it. The "pure thinking subject", with its reflective and objectivising forms of thought, is itself the "universally valid" and the origin of all universal validity.

The "universal theoretical validity" that arises from the "autonomous" selfhood (identifying itself with its transcendental logic function in order to be only "pure thought") replaces the cosmic order and its various spheres of law, to which all individual subjectivity is nevertheless subjected under the divine law of creation.

Thus arises a dialectical tension, a truly antinomic relation between *universal validity* and *individuality*, between absolutised theoretical thought, secure in its alleged absolute autonomous truth, and individual subjectivity in its relation to the given *(Gegebenheitskorrelation)*, between the "thinking I" and the "living (experiencing) I", between *philosophy as a universally valid theory* and a *worldview*, the latter conceived as an absolutely individual impression of life, emanating from a sovereign personality *that is not itself subject to any norm of truth*.

In his *dialectical thought*, according to Litt, philosophy must at the end of the day establish this absence of determination, this absolute freedom of *individuality*. In the irrationality of life, it must recognise its dialectical *other* which has no universal validity. It must establish this absence of determination and free personality in its worldview in a "universally valid" way, in order to understand ultimately its dialectical *unity-in-the-opposition* with this worldview. Because in fact, "purely theoretical" dialectical thought, on the one hand, and "worldview" considered as an "individual impression of life" without norms, on the other, are, in the light of Litt's transcendental basic-Idea, two dialectical emanations of the same selfhood, which lives in a humanistic personality-ideal that has been relativistically debased.

The absolutisation of the "transcendental cogito" in an "absolute", "sovereign" and autonomous instance implies that "pure thought" is independent of a *cosmic order*, in which the laws of logical thought, nevertheless, are also founded. Since theoretical reason seeks to create the coherence of meaning between its logical aspect and the other modal aspects of our cosmos, there results a dialectical way of thinking which relativises, in a fundamentally *logical* manner, the fundamental laws of logic as norms and limits for our subjective logical function.

How then could such a "dialectical thought" still be subject to a real norm of truth that is *over* it? The absolutising of theoretical truth, which issues in a dissolution of its *meaning*, is the work of an apostate selfhood that refuses to comply with laws established by the Origin of all creation, and consequently attributes sovereignty to dialectical thought, which elevates itself beyond the limits of the laws. For Litt, the criterion of relativism resides in the denial of the autonomy of "purely theoretical" truth. We have seen how the proclamation of this autonomy is *in truth* nothing but the primary absolutisation of theoretical thought, *which is the source of all relativism*, because it denies the fullness of the meaning of truth and uproots theoretical thought.

The "self-refutation of scepticism" is at the same time the self-refutation of the postulate of neutrality and of the autonomy of theoretical thought.

Nevertheless, the significance of this self-refutation should not be overestimated. Ultimately, it proves nothing more than that, to think theoretically, one has to submit oneself to a theoretical norm of truth that cannot derive from thought itself; because this norm only has meaning in the *coherence of meaning* and in relation to the totality or *fullness* of truth which, precisely as fullness, must *transcend theoretical thought*, and so never be "purely theoretical".

This self-refutation which manifests itself in a contradiction where logical thought destroys itself by turning against its own laws, does not lead us in any way to a positive knowledge of truth. It is only a *logical* criterion (itself governed by law) of truth.

In the conception of the genuine material meaning of truth, philosophy reveals its absolute dependence on its transcendental basic-Idea, the ultimate theoretical expression of its fundamental religious ground-motive.

19. The test of the transcendental basic-Idea.

In applying the test of the transcendental basic-Idea to Litt's philosophy, we reach the surprising result that there is much less a question with him of a genuine rationalist tendency than with Rickert. In his dialectical thought, Litt inclines more towards an irrationalist philosophy of life, which he has simply developed in dialectical forms. The absolutisation of dialectical thought which he considers far superior to a "restricted objective thought" *(borniertes gegenständliches Denken)*, which submits to the principle of non-contradiction, leads him in his conception of individuality to the opposite of a rationalist hypostatisation of universal laws. In this regard, Litt is very similar to Hegel, whose "panlogism" one must be careful not to interpret rationalistically, because it reveals its true intentions only against the Romantic irrationalist trend of the humanist personality-ideal. In general, dialectical thought assumes an anti-rationalist tendency.

Judged by his own criterion, Litt's dialectical philosophy is an "irrationalist worldview" presented in the supposedly universally valid forms of dialectical thought, an *irrationalist logicism*, historically oriented.

As for us, who use a different criterion, we do not recognise any dialectical unity between philosophy and a worldview. Instead, we discover a deep unity between them because of their religious ground-motive. The content of Litt's transcendental basic-Idea is determined by an irrationalist turn in the humanist freedom-motive in its dialectical tension with the scientific domination of nature which, in his philosophy, has undergone a fundamental impairment.

Part 5: The transcendental basic-idea and the meaning of truth.

> 20. A religiously neutral theory of worldviews is not possible. The meaning of the concept of truth is never purely theoretical.

It is the task of philosophy, on account of its own theoretical character, to render a theoretical account of the worldview. We have already noticed that they are both closely united in their religious root. However, philosophy cannot accomplish this task before it has unearthed its own transcendental basic-Idea by a critical self-reflection. Philosophy, which is not in the least religiously neutral, cannot construct a neutral theory of worldviews. No such theory can be neutral, since it cannot be so with respect to the material sense of truth, even when adopting a sceptical relativism that overturns all the foundations of philosophy.

Litt believes that worldviews are bound in a "dialectical unity" with philosophy.[22] They are personal confessions reflecting the individual struggle between person and cosmos. If it wants to be a *universally-valid* science, philosophy must go beyond the content of these "merely concrete" (merely individual and limited) confessions, although the *impulse* of philosophical thought comes from this same concrete view of life. Litt has a secularised, irrationalist and personalist worldview, which depends on the irrationalist humanist personality-ideal that we find at the base of his transcendental Idea.

Litt is certainly entitled to interpret his own worldview in this way, but as soon as he claimed "universal validity" and "absolute truth" for his conception of worldviews in general he abandoned any "theoretical neutrality", and he could not do otherwise without abandoning his own humanist vision of the meaning of truth.

The deification of "pure" dialectical thought only serves to liberate the human person, in his interpretation of life, from any norm of truth and to release his individuality from servitude to law. This is the origin of the conflict against all "universally valid norms and values" by which a rationalist or semi-rationalist humanism tries to bind this individuality in the human person. Rickert's theory is no more neutral than Litt's. According to him, there is a religious unity between the meaning of his theoretical concept of truth and his proclamation of the sovereignty of a personality released from the norm of truth in its choice of a worldview. But he stops halfway along the road to irrationalism, still clinging to universally valid formal values and norms of reason.

By forcefully incorporating worldviews into the theoretical framework of his philosophy of values, he seriously distorts the meaning of every worldview that disagrees with the religious starting point of his philosophy.

Is he serious, for example, when he interprets the Calvinist worldview theoretically (included in his sixth type) as a

---

[22] Theodor Litt, *Einleitung in die Philosophie*, Teubner, Leipzig and Berlin, 1933, p.251ff, §2. *Die dialektische Einheit von Weltanschauung und Philosophie.*

"theistic" worldview with holiness as its "highest value" – to which "piety" responds subjectively – and with the "world of the gods" as its "good"? Who does not see here the insertion, in a religious apriori manner, of an idealist humanist meaning into the theoretical transcendental Idea of truth? Who does not see that any impartial understanding of a worldview with a different religious foundation is now made impossible?

Now the meaning that a philosophy gives to the theoretical concept of truth depends intimately on its *transcendental basic-Idea*. An engagement with the various conceptions of truth developed by immanence-philosophy will provide the evidence.

Compare, for example, Hobbes' *nominalist* conception with Aristotle's *realist metaphysical* conception. For Hobbes, truth and error are attributes of language, not of "things". The exact truth is the internal agreement between concepts, based on conventional definitions[23]. For Aristotle, truth is the agreement of our judgement with the metaphysical *essence* of the things we judge.

Compare similarly Kant's *transcendental-logical idealist* concept of truth with Hume's *psychological* concept, or Descartes' *mathematical* concept with the *dialectical* vision of a Hegel or a Litt, let alone the *pragmatic* concept of scientific truth in modern humanistic philosophy of life, and in existentialism.[24]

It is pure illusion to maintain that the meaning of truth can be determined in a universally valid manner by restricting the validity of truth to pure theory.

In truth, the postulate of neutrality results in giving everyone the right to choose his own concept of truth, in accordance with his own worldview.

Immanence-philosophy does not recognise any norm of truth above its transcendental basic-Idea. The dogma of the

---

[23] Thomas Hobbes, *Leviathan*, Part I, 4.

[24] On the very confusing diversity of ideas of the meaning of truth, just see, for example, Eisler, *Wörterbuch der Philosophischen Begriffe*, vol. III, 4th ed. 1930, on the word *Wahrheit*, pp.450-471, or, Lalande, *Vocabulaire de la philosophie*, on the words *Vérité* and *Vrai*.

autonomy of theoretical reason, especially in its humanistic sense, makes truth dependent on the subjective behaviour of the apostate selfhood. The attempt by transcendental idealism to refute the relativity of truth through *logical* argument is inevitably doomed to failure.

In its fullness of meaning and temporal coherence, truth resists reduction to the theoretical logical sphere. *Its validity necessarily extends as far as the domain of judgements.*

> 21. Theoretical and non-theoretical judgements. The validity of truth cannot be restricted to the former without internal contradiction.

One consequence of Litt's and Rickert's[25] conceptions is the distinction between theoretical judgements and atheoretical value-judgements: only the former can have a claim to universally valid truth[26]. Thus the judgements: "This rose is beautiful" and "This action is immoral" have no claim to universal validity by this criterion.

However, this distinction is untenable and, on reflection, self-destructive. A value judgement may, if it makes sense, lay claim to validity as a *judgement*. With respect to its intention, the aesthetic judgement "This rose is beautiful" means: "This rose is beautiful *in truth*". The same applies to moral judgements, as when one says "This action is *in truth* immoral". These judgements therefore assume that there is a universal standard of aesthetic and moral assessment or evaluation and that, in my judgement, it is with truth that I ascribe to this rose the predicate "beautiful", and to this action that of "immoral",

---

[25] Heinrich Rickert, *System der Philosophie*, J.C.B. Mohr (Paul Siebeck), Tübingen, 1921, p.388, persists nevertheless in calling all judgements *theoretical*. But he cannot escape the consequences we have suggested. There is no denying that "Truth is the highest value" is a judgement which nevertheless, from his standpoint, cannot be called *theoretical*, because it originates in a worldview. In addition, it is well known that for Rickert theoretical judgements have also been oriented towards a (theoretical) *value*.

[26] Here we find the distinction already made by Kant between theoretical knowledge and apriori rational faith, born of his transcendental basic-Idea.

even if I am unable to account theoretically for this assumption.

This arises from the fact that no modal aspect of our temporal cosmos is autonomous, but each of them refers to the *intermodal coherence* of meaning. Whoever denies this denies thereby
the meaning of aesthetic and moral judgements and, having
shattered the coherence that binds the logical, aesthetic and
moral spheres together, finds it impossible to assert the principle of contradiction with respect to those judgements called
"a-theoretical".

A man contemplates Rembrandt's *Night Watch* at the Royal Museum in Amsterdam. If, against the general judgement,
he describes this masterpiece as *un-aesthetic*, and at the same
time says: "There is no universal standard of aesthetic evaluation", he would fall into the same contradiction as the sceptic
who denies the existence of any universal truth. Maybe he will
say to justify himself: "As far as I'm concerned..." However, it
does not make sense to oppose this subjective impression of the
prevailing opinion. If this critic agrees with this and makes no
attempt to impose his opinion on others, his judgement loses
all *meaning* as *aesthetic* judgement. In other words, his judgement, stripped of any aesthetic quality or accuracy, ceases to be
an *aesthetic* judgement.

Every subjective valuation receives its determination from
its dependence on a norm or standard that determines the
subjectivity and defines its *meaning*. There is no *aesthetic* subjectivity outside of a universal aesthetic norm to which it is
subject. [27]

The whole point is, does the judgement: "The *Night Watch*
is beautiful" really have universally valid meaning or not. If it
does not, it makes no sense to say that the *Night Watch* is a
work of art. If it does, this judgement necessarily appeals to
universally valid truth. There is no third term.

---

[27] It cannot be objected here that the beauty of *Night Watch* is at this point so
individual that it is impossible to confer on it a universally valid normative aesthetic
character. For individuality is unique to the *subjective* as such, and the *Night Watch* is,
without question, the objective realisation of a *subjective* aesthetic conception that is
truly individual.

22. Theoretical and non-theoretical judgements. The latter are not a-logical but non-objective.

In our transcendental critique of theoretical thought, we have already shown that theoretical judgements are scientific, analytical and synthetic judgements. They provide a theoretical knowledge that exists in an intermodal synthesis of meaning between the logical aspect of thought and the modal meaning of a non-logical aspect of our experience, which we have made into our "object". These judgements are subject to the norm of theoretical truth, which is valid for scientific knowledge.

In our view, non-theoretical, so-called "practical" judgements are not a-logical – since no judgement can be – they are simply non-objective *(nichtgegenständliche)*, that is, they do not depend on a theoretical approach of knowledge, which sets the logical aspect of thought *over against* the theoretically isolated non-logical aspect of experience. These judgements are subject to the norm of pre-theoretical truth, which is valid for pre-scientific knowledge but which, just like the norm of theoretical truth, possesses *universal validity*. [28]

All truth is based on the temporal coherence of meaning of the logical and non-logical aspects of reality. Hence, it points beyond itself toward the fullness of meaning of truth, which is only given in the religious totality of meaning of our cosmos, in its relation with the Origin. So every judgement also appeals, for its *meaning*, to the fullness of truth, within which no temporal restriction makes any sense. In the *fullness* of *its meaning*, truth has no limitation.

If we relativise the validity of a so-called "pure" theoretical thought, and at the same time acknowledge that scientific theoretical judgements do not exhaust the domain of judgements, we fall into the logical self-refutation of scepticism. For on the one hand, in fact, we would deny the fullness of truth by *relativising* it within the particular domain of *theoretical* truth

---

[28] When we come to deal with the problem of knowledge, we will have occasion to show that theoretical truth is never "parallel" to pre-theoretical truth, but they mutually refer to each other in a very profound way.

as opposed to all non-theoretical truth, and on the other, we would claim full validity of truth without the least restriction for our own conception. [29]

> 23. According to Litt, the distinction between theoretical truth and "general truth" is self-refuting. The non-meaning of judgements that are not subjected to the norm of truth.

Litt makes a clear distinction between truth in the genuine sense of universally valid theoretical truth, and what he calls "*weltanschauliche Wahrheit*", the truth of a worldview that we shall call, for want of anything better, "general truth". This distinction could be relevant if Litt did not deny, in fact, any "general truth". In this sense, the word "truth" is no more to him than a mere predicate referring to the assertions of a worldview, intended to express "the absolute sincerity with which a thinker confesses to himself and others his own interpretation of life, the orderliness and consistency *(Folgerichtigkeit)* with which he develops it, the strength of conviction with which he is able to present it...and the internal harmony between this conception and the conduct of his life"[30].

But when we seek to seriously apply this conception, it dissolves itself in an internal contradiction. If the judgements entailed by a worldview are not subject to a universal norm of truth, they immediately lose all meaning. They are not judgements, and cannot contain an individual "interpretation of life" *(Lebensdeutung)*.

---

[29] This antinomy originates from a fundamental antinomy in the transcendental Idea of the thinker. On the one hand, indeed, he *cannot* reduce the *totality of meaning* to the theoretical, because then the personality-ideal with its a-theoretical "values" would be relegated to a corner. But on the other hand, it implies that he can find his Archimedean point within theoretical thought. We will have occasion to show that a purely logical antinomy does not exist.

[30] Theodor Litt, *Einleitung in die Philosophie*, Teubner, Leipzig and Berlin 1933, p.255, §3. *Weltanschauliche Wahrheit*. [(Es kann bedeuten) die ungeschminkte Aufrichtigkeit, mit der ein Denker sich vor sich selbst und anderen zu seiner Lebensdeutung bekennt, die innere Folgerichtigkeit, mit der er sie entwickelt, die überzeugende Kraft, mit der er sie vorzutragen und zu begründen weiß und...die Übereinstimmung zwischen ihr und seiner tätigen Bewährung im Leben.]

Indeed, a "subjective interpretation of life" that expresses itself in a series of judgements can only be meaningful if the cosmos we live in actually exists as a coherence of meaning. If so, the judgements that reflect this interpretation are necessarily subject to a universal norm of truth, and then my subjective interpretation must be in harmony with the true facts; in other words, the question is whether or not a judgement is true with respect to the meaning of our cosmos. On the other hand, if there is no universal truth within an interpretation of life, I would find it absolutely impossible to have any "subjective interpretation of life", for *I can only interpret what I really regard as having meaning if personally I have to hold in abeyance the question of the truth of my personal interpretation.*

Litt assumed he could escape these destructive consequences by making the universal validity of theoretical truth the judge of the essence, meaning and *limits* of "general truth". Once more, these are the judgements of a worldview subjected to the very mysterious "universally valid theoretical truth", but with the sole purpose of being once again immediately freed from any norm of truth. Universal truth is quite simply the truth that the judgements of a worldview, expressing a purely personal impression of life, are "beyond truth and error".

From the transcendental basic-Idea of his thought, we know that Litt is much more opposed to an intellectualist philosophy than Rickert. Truth must be restricted to the theoretical domain to prevent theoretical thought from once again dominating the worldview of sovereign personality, as did the old intellectualism.

If, however, Litt persists in asserting that judgements such as "God is the Creator of the world, which he created for his glory" and "Religion must make way for science" are located "beyond truth and error" because they only express individual interpretations of life, then we must draw all the consequences, namely, that there can now no longer exist any universal truth about the totality of meaning our temporal world (which, even according to Litt, *is more than purely theoretical*) and its relation with the modal diversity of meaning. If we accept this consequence, at the same time as we deny the meaning of "theoretical truth", we also deny the truth of a worldview as well as that of philosophical theoretical thought. And thus the theoretical thought destroys its own foundations. For, if there is no universal truth about the relations of the totality, speciality and coherence of meaning, then philosophical thought, directed to the totality, no longer has any norm of truth by which it can be judged. So we arrive at the pole of an absolute scepticism and hence at a complete self-refutation. The concept of "purely theoretical absolute truth" dissolves itself in an internal contradiction.

In addition to the *logical* contradictions in which the doctrine of the autonomy of "pure theoretical truth" loses its way, our transcendental critique penetrates to the root of this doctrine, and lays bare the relativist foundation on which it constructs all its theory. This *religious* relativist attitude provides us with the key to the insistence with which this school, in modern times, attempts to at least safeguard theoretical truth against the invasion of a relativism which, for a long time, has undermined its worldviews.

A Christian philosophy does not need to learn from the humanist personality-ideal that theoretical thought can dominate neither religion nor worldview. Instead, humanist philosophy can learn from our transcendental critique that philosophical thought is always dependent on the religious ground-motive of the thinking self.

Part 6: The true relation between philosophy and worldview.
The meaning of the concept of universal validity.

It is time to specify how and in what sense philosophy must account for a worldview.

The task of philosophy is to theoretically bring every worldview to internal clarity, by accounting theoretically for the pre-theoretical picture it is concerned with. Insofar as it studies worldviews based on a religious foundation different from that which is expressed in its own transcendental basic-Idea, philosophy must try to clarify this foundation for the particular basic-Idea to which it leads. Only thus can it really do justice to the various types of worldview.

> 24. Without giving up its very nature, a worldview is not, and cannot possibly become, a system.

Why can philosophy never replace a worldview? For exactly the same reason that theoretical knowledge cannot replace naive experience. Indeed, in any worldview there permanently resides a living immediacy that must always elude theoretical concepts.

An authentic worldview is never a system: not because it would be reduced entirely to faith or *feeling*, but because its thought is always *concentrated* on the entire concrete reality. This is precisely what *systematic theoretical thought*, by definition, can *never* do.

The moment a worldview becomes a system it loses its peculiar universality. It no longer speaks to us out of the fullness of reality, but from across the divide that scientific abstraction has to maintain in opposition to life if it is to provide us with theoretical knowledge.

A worldview does not have the universality of a philosophical system. Far from having a "closed" character, as Litt supposed, it must, on the contrary, always remain *open* to every concrete situation of life in which it is placed. It is only in its religious root that its profound unity can be discovered. Consider some examples.

When, in the Roman Empire, Christianity was persecuted by fire and sword, its attitude towards politics and secular culture could hardly be anything but negative. A positive involvement by Christians could be only considered after it became possible to exert a positive influence in those areas.

Without the concrete influence of Enlightenment rationalist thought in all areas of life, the reaction of the personality-ideal would never have occurred in humanist circles. This reaction represents an important milestone in the development of the humanist worldview. For it is only in this concrete situation that the requirement of the neutrality of science over against the personal commitment of a worldview could have arisen.

A Calvinist worldview, such as the one developed by Dr Abraham Kuyper in the Netherlands in the late nineteenth century, also has a radically Christian view of science. But how does this conception of science come about? Not, as one might think, from a philosophical or systematic train of thought, but in the midst of a concrete situation of life. The pressure of the scholastic notion of science on the one hand and, on the other, the need to respond to the prevailing humanist conception, stimulated neo-Calvinism to consider its religious vocation in the domain of science.

We could multiply examples for this thesis. At every turn we see the development of worldviews taking place in immediate contact with concrete situations in the fullness of life. And it always will be thus, because this immediacy of life is essential to every worldview.

That is why we like to repeat that it would be a profound mistake to see in Christian philosophy no more than the development of a Christian worldview which, by definition, can be constructed only in a succession of immediate concrete situations. It cannot be "developed" in a philosophical manner.

So, is a worldview peculiar to the individual, and thus unable to lay claim to "absolute validity"? This is what we have to consider.

> 25. The concept of "universal validity". The Kantian conception.

To answer this question effectively, we must first define the true meaning of the concept "universal validity", a concept we have up till now only encountered in the dogmatic framework of an alleged "unconditioned pure thought" where it occupied the place of a standard or norm of truth.

Kant, as we know, was the first to give it an apriori epistemological meaning. For him», "universally valid" means: independent of any "empirical subjectivity", valid for the "transcendental consciousness", the "transcendental cogito" which, in its apriori synthesis, is the origin of all universal validity in the domain of experience. So *the synthetic apriori, which makes objective experience possible*, is universally valid. As for perception, its validity is purely "subjective" since it depends on sense impressions, on which no necessary objective validity can be founded.

Kant applies this distinction to *judgements*, distinguishing them by two categories: simple judgements of *perception* and judgements of *experience*. "Insofar as empirical judgements have *objective validity*", he says "they are judgements of *experience*. But those that are only *subjectively valid*, I call mere judgements of *perception*. The latter do not require any pure concept of understanding, but only a logical connection of perceptions in the thinking subject. The former, however, always require, in addition to representations of sensory intuition, *special concepts* originally produced in the understanding, which constitute objectively-valid judgements of experience." [31]

Kant explains this distinction with a few examples. The judgements "The room is warm, sugar is sweet, etc...", on one hand, and "The sun warms the stone" on the other hand, are only subjectively-valid judgements of perception. But the latter becomes a judgement of *experience* and rightly claims universal validity if I say: "The sun is the cause of the heat of the stone", because "perception is then added to the concept of the understanding, that is, causation, which *necessarily* connects the concept of sunlight with the concept of heat; and this synthetic judgement becomes necessarily universally valid and therefore objective, since it is transformed from perception to experience." [32]

---

[31] Immanuel Kant, *Prolegomena zur einer jeden künftigen Metaphysik*, in *Immanuel Kants Werke*, Großherzog Wilhelm Ernst Edition, 4th edition, 1928, Vol. IV, p.422, §18. [Empirische Urteile, so fern sie objektive Gültigkeit haben, sind Erfahrungsurteile ; die aber, so nur subjektiv gültig sind, nenne ich bloße Wahrnehmungsurteile. Die letztern bedürfen keines reinen Verstandesbegriffs, sondern nur der logischen Verknüpfung der Wahrnehmungen in einem denkenden Subjekt. Die ersteren aber erfordern jederzeit über die Vorstellungen der sinnlichen Anschauung noch besondere, im Verstande ursprünglich erzeugte Begriffe, welche es eben machen, daß das Erfahrungsurteil objektiv gültig ist.]

[32] Immanuel Kant, *op. cit.*, p.423 and footnote on p.426, §20. [...Sage ich aber: die Sonne erwärmt den Stein, so kommt über die Wahrnehmung noch der Verstandes-begriff der Ursache hinzu, der mit dem Begriffe des Sonnenscheins den der Wärme

This whole conception of universal validity is consistent with the critical humanist perspective of immanence, and its vision of the structures of experience and of temporal reality. It follows that to break with the immanence viewpoint is, like it or not, to break with this notion of universal validity.

In the light of our transcendental basic-Idea, the universal validity to which a judgement can lay claim can only be an agreement between this judgement and the religious cosmic law that transcends all arbitrariness, that is, the divine law that governs the cosmos in its modal diversity, intermodal coherence and fullness of meaning, apart from the validity of which no judgement has any meaning.

> 26. The possibility of universally valid judgements depends on the supra-subjective universal validity of the structural laws of human experience.

In our view, the possibility of universally valid judgements lies solely and exclusively in the universal validity (beyond any individual subjectivity) of the structural laws of human experience.

"Universal validity" is a normative characterisation that assumes that the subject who judges is subject to laws that do not arise from the transcendental-logical subject, and with which the subject who judges *may come into conflict*. As such, this validity is strictly related to the *structure* of truth. The problem of universal validity depends on the problem of knowledge, which we will address in due course. A few remarks will suffice for our present purposes.

First of all, universal validity cannot be restricted to judgements of theoretical thinking for the simple reason that its laws are not valid "in themselves" but only in the cosmic coherence of meaning and in their dependence on the radical religious unity of the divine law.

Universal validity ought to be attributed to every judgement in which any subject who judges ought to concur, and never to a judgement that would only make sense for the

---

notwendig verknüpft, und das synthetische Urteil wird notwendig allgemeingültig, folglich objektiv, und aus einer Wahrnehmung in Erfahrung verwandelt.]

individual subject who expresses it. The judgements "I do not believe in God" and "I do not think *Night Watch* is beautiful" can never have universal validity because they only express a subjective opinion that, *in the subjective function of the judgement*, is restricted to the individual self.

On the other hand, whether a judgement is expressed regarding a concrete individual state of affairs, *beyond the subjective function of the judgement*, or regarding an abstract theoretical state of affairs, does not affect its validity.

The judgement of naive experience: "This rose, which is on my table, is red", if it is to be taken seriously, claims both a concrete (practical) validity and a universal validity for every human subject who perceives it at that moment in time. In its subjective function, such a judgement is not restricted to the individual self, but rather has a distinctly objective meaning. Indeed, universal validity depends on the structural laws of pre-theoretical experience, in which thought does not bring into play the intentional antithetic relation.

27. The universal validity of a correct judgement of perception.

Certainly, there are structural differences in the universal validity of judgements, and first of all between theoretical and pre-theoretical judgements.

The validity of judgements of perception such as the one above does not depend on the concrete *hic et nunc* (here and now) of the subjective sensory aspect of perception. If it did, then – as Kant thought – a judgement of perception would only have subjective validity, with no claim to universal validity. But, as we have seen, the structural laws of naive experience are laws that guarantee the universal validity of correct judgements of perception. [33]

These laws also govern the subject-object relations of naive experience. We will return to this later. They guarantee the plastic structure of the experience of things, both in terms

---

[33] When we come to deal with the problem of knowledge, we will establish that the structural laws of naive experience are at the same time the structural laws of temporal reality.

of *their subjective-objective sensory and their logical aspects*, and make the universal validity of concrete judgements of perception possible.

That Kant assigns only a subjective validity to such judgements stems first of all from his construction – which denatures the entire structure of naive experience and of its data – of this data as a chaotic sensory material that has to be first *formed* by a transcendental consciousness into a coherent objective reality, ordered in a universally valid manner. Secondly, it stems from the ancient metaphysical dogma that the "secondary" qualities of things, that is, the sensory qualities that can neither be measured nor weighed, are merely subjective, and have no "objective" reality.[34] Finally, it stems from the fact that, from his critical viewpoint, Kant has completely erased the structural differences between theoretical knowledge and naive experience.

> 28. The criterion of the universal validity of a supra-theoretical judgement.

Secondly, there is a fundamental difference between a judgement about a supra-theoretical religious state of affairs such as: "God is the creator of the world" or "All laws are founded in absolute reason" on the one hand and judgements about matters cosmic or cosmological within the temporal boundaries of the universe, on the other.

---

[34] Immanuel Kant, *Prolegomena zur einer jeden künftigen Metaphysik*, in *Immanuel Kants Werke*, Großherzog Wilhelm Ernst edition, 4th edition, 1928, Vol. IV, §19, p.423. In a footnote, Kant comments on the examples of judgements of perception he has given: "I readily confess that these examples do not represent such judgements of perception as could ever become judgements of experience, even if we added a concept of the understanding to them, for they relate only to feeling, which everyone recognises as merely subjective, and which consequently can never be attributed to the object or become objective." [Ich gestehe gern, dass diese Beispiele nicht solche Wahrnehmungsurteile vorstellen, die jemals Erfahrungsurteile werden könnten, wenn man auch einen Verstandesbegriff hinzu täte, weil sie sich bloß auf Gefühl, welches jedermann als bloß subjektiv erkennt und welches also niemals dem Objekt beigelegt werden darf, beziehen und also auch niemals objektiv werden können.]

The universal validity to which the former judgements lay claim is dependent on their agreement or disagreement with the central religious unity of the divine law, as revealed in the Word of God, to whom the self who judges is *subjected* in the heart of its existence, and which is *the religious law of concentration of its temporal existence.*

All universal validity claimed by a judgement depends, ultimately, on the unconditional validity of this religious law of concentration. No modal law, not even the cosmic order of time, is sufficient *by itself* to guarantee the universal validity of a judgement, because the validity of such a law has the creaturely character of *meaning,* and because law divorced from its Origin is *nothing.*

In the light of the Christian law-Idea, it becomes clear that the universal validity of a religious judgement expressed by a worldview never depends on the extent of its reception, and that it cannot be depreciated by the fact that human thought in its apostasy is subjectively separated from the fullness of truth, and that man is now incapable *by himself* of directing his thought toward the absolute truth.

> 29. "Transcendental" consciousness is merely a deification of theoretical thought that has abandoned the fullness of meaning of truth.

The deifying of "transcendental" consciousness and the making of it the Origin of universal validity undermines the validity of truth in its root. In immanence-philosophy, truth is now made dependent on a thought that has renounced the fullness of meaning of truth at every turn.

It makes no sense to suppose that the immanent laws of human consciousness should withdraw theoretical thought from the religious fullness of truth. Indeed, it is the apostate self under the influence of its dialectical religious ground-motive, and nothing else, which tries by every means at its disposal to dissociate these laws from their coherence of meaning and to separate them from their religious root, and thereby subjectively falsify their signification in the judgement. The concept of "normal consciousness" is in no way to be identified with a "norm of consciousness".

The truth and universal validity of a judgement cannot have their criterion in an apostate "normal consciousness".

CℰCℰCℰ

Litt believes he can see in the great diversity of worldviews and their differences the evidence that they are only individual impressions of life, and that they lack any universal standard of truth. However this argument does not render the least service to the opinion that would confer universal truth only on the judgements of theoretical thought. When we become aware of the woeful divisions between philosophical theories – and even special scientific ones – we are very quickly convinced of the need to abandon a path that leads nowhere, at the earliest opportunity.

30. Universal validity and individuality are not in the least contradictory.

When we come to deal with the problem of knowledge, we will show that the opposition between universal validity in theoretical thought and concrete individuality in a worldview is unsustainable. For it is impossible to eliminate the individuality of the one who thinks from theoretical thought. The notion that there should be no place for the individual in theoretical thought is a relic of the rationalist conception of science from the time of the Enlightenment.

We have shown why every worldview is formed independently of any systematic tendency and should remain in close proximity to concrete situations of life, even when it (justifiably) gives a general formulation to its judgements. Embedded in the midst of temporal reality, every worldview – as well as the one who appropriates it – directs the religious vision of totality towards the reality of life in its most concrete structure. It no longer conceives the evolution of history, which it should keep track of, in a scientific way. In its continuing involvement in full reality, it grasps it as an element that is not to be distinguished theoretically.

This will suffice to reduce Litt's exposition of the non-scientific individual character of a worldview to its proper proportions.

> 31. Neither worldview nor philosophy can be understood in an individualistic way.

What shall we say, finally, of the notion that a worldview, unlike philosophy, only moves in the sphere of common convictions?

We readily concede that a worldview has a social, not an individual, origin. It expresses *ex origine* a common conviction, subject to the norm of truth, of a human community united by a central religious ground-motive.

But in our transcendental critique of the theoretical attitude of thought, we have shown that philosophy, too, is necessarily bound to a religious ground-motive around which a particular philosophical community of thought is bound.

Both in philosophy and in a worldview, illegitimate social prejudices appear, associated with a restricted vision of the concrete social context, and that have to be overcome: class prejudices, racial prejudices, the prejudices of narrow church groups, etc. The sociology of modern thought, with Max Scheler, Karl Mannheim, Wilhelm Jerusalem and others, has highlighted this state of affairs with a penetrating analysis. Philosophy is particularly well equipped, on account of the theoretical attitude of thought which it exclusively possesses, to rapidly adopt a critical attitude towards all these illegitimate assumptions. So we may imagine the salutary influence it can and must exercise over pre-theoretical reflection. It is impossible for philosophy and worldview not to mutually influence one other.

Philosophical thought should find in the worldview to which the thinker adheres a real and constant stimulus to religious critical reflection. On the other hand thanks to philosophy a worldview will achieve genuine theoretical clarity.

But if philosophy cannot slip into the concrete style of a worldview with impunity, neither can a worldview with impunity leave behind concrete reality and adopt the ways of theoretical thought.

While one in root, referring mutually to each other and being reciprocally influenced, philosophy and worldview must nevertheless remain strictly separate and accomplish their respective tasks in faithfulness to their respective natures.

C3CBCB

Chapter 5

The Antithetic and Synthetic Viewpoints in Christian Philosophical Thought.

Part 1: Systematic presentation of the antithesis between the structure of the Christian transcendental basic-idea and that of various types of humanism.

> 1. Summary of conclusions regarding the development of the fundamental antinomy in the cosmonomic[1] Idea of humanist immanence-philosophy.

In a sizable section of the first volume of his *Philosophy of the Law-Idea*[2], Herman Dooyeweerd presented a detailed study of "The development of the fundamental antinomy in the cosmonomic idea of humanistic immanence-philosophy". As part of our Prolegomena, we cannot even begin to present the *conclusions* of this detailed study. We can only summarise them as an introduction to the comparison we wish to make between the starting points of the various currents in humanistic philosophy and those of the philosophy of the Law-Idea.

In a very precise manner, with the same acuity we find in his critiques of Kant, Litt and Rickert on the issues we have examined, and quoting the sources and texts that he knows firsthand because of his immense erudition, Herman Dooyeweerd demonstrates how in the transcendental basic-Idea of humanist thought the fundamental antinomy develops into

---

[1] [Marcel rarely uses this word, invented by Dooyeweerd for the English translation of *De Wijsbegeerte der Wetsidee (A New Critique of Theoretical Thought)*. He generally uses the phrase *Law-Idea*, which I have consistently followed throughout.]

[2] Cf. *De Wijsbegeerte der Wetsidee*, Vol. I, pp.139-461, and *A New Critique of Theoretical Thought*, Vol. I, pp.169-495.

polar opposites within the various systems and between these systems themselves.

By referring continuously – with the method of immanent critique – to the common basic structure of this transcendental Idea, Herman Dooyeweerd reveals the profound unity lying at the very foundations of all humanist philosophical thought. The development of this thought, in systems which to all appearances are diametrically opposed, is in fact only the development of an internal dialectic in the same religious ground-motive, that of *nature* and *freedom*, which determines the general framework of the humanist transcendental basic-Idea.

The religious root of this basic-Idea is the freedom-motive which, by its ambiguity, evokes the opposite motive of the domination of nature. Before the appearance of transcendental philosophy, this root was concealed by the primacy of the science-ideal, which itself was evoked by the personality-ideal.

In immanence-philosophy, it was the transcendental current which first succeeded in penetrating to the foundation of the science-ideal, that is, to the ideal of sovereign personality. Fichte deserves the credit for this discovery, which led to a break with the dualistic Kantian transcendental basic-Idea. However, the immanence viewpoint remained a formidable obstacle for humanism, which prevented it from achieving a genuine transcendental critique of philosophical thought.

In its critical self-reflection, transcendental humanist philosophy fails to go beyond the *idea* of the sovereign freedom of personality, which is constantly identified with the religious root of the cosmos. It sought the transcendent root of reality in various immanent normative aspects of the cosmos, separated from others by abstraction then absolutised in a transcendental basic-Idea. It could never imagine that the free personality of man cannot be identified with his moral, aesthetic or historical functions.

For Hegel, it is true, the free personality was a dialectical phase in the logical unfolding of the universally comprehensive metaphysical "idea". But this metaphysical point of view meant the abandonment of the transcendental critical attitude of humanist thought which Fichte, at least in his first period, had retained. In Hegel's absolute idealism, once again, philosophical thought was identified with absolute divine thought. Recognising no critical limit in respect of faith and religion, Hegel sought to resolve the religious antinomy of his ground-motive with a theoretical dialectic. The same may also be said of Schelling's "absolute thought".

The transcendental critical perspective in humanist thought can be maintained only by rejecting all absolutising of theoretical dialectic. In this case, Fichte's critical moralism, which appears to be the highest level of critical self-reflection possible in humanist immanence-philosophy, reached its apogee. Yet even in this very profound system, humanist transcendental critical philosophy fails to grasp the transcendent determination of philosophical thought. Even when it thinks it has made the selfhood its Archimedean point, it does not concentrate its attention or its vision on the religious roots of personality, the focal point of all temporal existence, but rather on a hypostatised function of personal experience.

This is the limit that immanence-philosophy cannot get past. If a philosopher were willing to go beyond these limits, he would discover *his real personal religious root which, in his rebellion, has denied the true Origin as well as any genuine personality*. But this radical religious critique is only possible from the biblical perspective of transcendence; humanism cannot get beyond its own religious starting point.

From the perspective of humanistic immanence philosophy, it is certainly easy to regard the internal dialectic of philosophical thought as an internal necessarily polar process of its development, due to the true nature of all philosophical theory as such.

But when Christian philosophy embraces the humanist perspective and allows it to impose its method of thinking and particular problems, we should not be surprised that the crucial problem of a synthetic Christian philosophy – the conflict between philosophical thought and Christian faith – can never be resolved.

2. Schema of the basic structure and
polar types of the humanist Law-Idea,
compared to the Christian basic-Idea.

In developing our transcendental critique of theoretical thought, we have already highlighted the antithesis between the fundamental structure of the humanist basic-Idea in some of its types and the Christian structure. Our observations have been confirmed and developed by a study of the development of the fundamental antinomy in the cosmonomic-Idea of humanist immanence-philosophy that runs to more than three hundred pages in Herman Dooyeweerd's work, and to which we have only been able to allude in a summary of his findings.

Before undertaking a positive exposition of the philosophy of the Law-Idea, and to facilitate a comparison of the starting points, content and methods of immanence- and Christian philosophy, we now present, schematically, the contents of both basic-Ideas and their respective implications. We will be forgiven if the style of our outline is a little abrupt and somewhat inelegant in its brevity.

A simple glance will be sufficient to make clear that, in our opinion, any compromise between these two philosophies is out of the question.

A. The Archimedean Point.

In humanist philosophy, the Archimedean point is the selfhood which, in and by its apostasy, adopts the immanence-standpoint. Consciously or otherwise, it absolutises the theoretical attitude of thought (the *cogito* in the rationalist and irrationalist conceptions).

The irrationalist conception, where the Archimedean point is not the *cogito* but either the *vivo* or the *ex-sisto*, completely loses sight of the fact that theoretical thought is absolutised.

In the Christian transcendental basic-Idea, the *Archimedean point* is Christ, the new religious root of the temporal cosmos, from whom regenerated humanity receives its spiritual life, in subjection to the religious central meaning of the law: *Love God and your neighbour with all your heart.*

Although in this Archimedean point philosophical thought is freed from the darkening influence of sin, it nevertheless remains immersed in time and continues to be subject to error (on account of its activity not being entirely withdrawn from the apostate root of existence).

Christian *freedom* is indeed only guaranteed in a constant subjection to the Word of God which reveals us to ourselves.

The *heart*, in its deepest biblical sense, is the religious root and centre of all human existence. It should never be identified with the function of feeling or with that of faith. It is not a complex of functions, such as the metaphysical concept of the soul in Greek and humanist metaphysics. It is unrelated to any alleged dualism between the body (as a complex of natural functions) and the soul (as a complex of psychological and normative functions).

The heart is not a blind or mute witness, even when it transcends the limits of cosmic time, its temporal diversity of modal aspects, and the temporal thought that unfolds it. It is the fullness of our selfhood, in which all our temporal functions find their religious concentration of meaning and the fulfilment of their meaning. To Descartes *cogito ergo sum*, and to the irrationalist *vivo in fluxo continuo, etiam cogitans*, we oppose the *Ego, in Christo regeneratus, etiam cogitans ex Christo vivo*.[3]

B. The Religious Ground-Motive of Theoretical Thought.

For humanist philosophy, the religious ground-motive is that of nature and freedom. This dialectical ground-motive has its origin in a secularisation of the Christian Ideas of creation and freedom, and it emancipates the human personality from its religious dependence on God and Revelation.

---

[3] [I, who am regenerated in Christ, live by Christ even in my thinking.]

For us, our religious attitude in philosophical thought depends on the fact that, belonging to Christ, the Christian engages in a daily struggle, even in philosophical thought, against the "flesh" in the biblical sense, against our apostate selfhood that absolutises the temporal and withdraws it from the sovereignty of God.

C. The Fundamental Problem and Polar Tensions.

In humanist philosophy, the fundamental problem is the inherently antinomic relation between the science-ideal and the personality-ideal, with their various common denominators.

Polar tensions manifest themselves within specific types of antinomies. For example:

1. The passion for the domination of reality expressed in the idea of creative scientific thought, versus the concept of practical freedom expressing itself in the idea of an absolute sovereign selfhood.
2. Pessimism versus optimism.
3. Rationalist individualism versus irrationalist transpersonalism.
4. Universal validity versus individuality; form versus matter; theory versus life.
5. The speculative metaphysics of the science- or personality-ideal versus scepticism, which is the culmination of a rapacious extension of the science-ideal beyond its proper foundations; the concept of function versus the concept of substance.

For us, the religious ground-motive is the biblical ground-motive of creation, fall into sin and redemption in Jesus Christ in the communion of the Holy Spirit. It implies the conflict between the Kingdom of God and the Kingdom of darkness at the root, and in the temporal coherence, of our cosmos. It also implies the recognition of the work of *common grace*, which stubbornly resists the degrading activity of sin, for the love of a renewed humanity, which God, in Christ the Head, accepts and sanctifies by his *particular grace*.

This ground-motive does not involve philosophical thought in an antinomy, but in an absolute antithesis to all philosophy dominated by apostate ground-motives. It also leads to a confession of thanksgiving for all the gifts and talents God has given, and still gives, to fallen humanity.

D. The Idea of the Origin.

In humanist philosophy, the Idea of the Origin has two distinct forms.

I. *With the deification of the modal laws.*

This is rationalism in all its forms, from naturalism with the primacy of the science-ideal, to freedom-idealism with the primacy of the personality-ideal and deification of the categorical imperative.

The legislator or law-giver here is "reason".

1. *If the science-ideal is dominant,* it is special scientific thought that is absolutised (mathematical thought, mechanical thought, biological thought, psychological thought, etc.).

2. *If the personality-ideal is dominant,* it is transcendental thought in its apriori syntheses, directed towards the Idea of freedom, which is absolutised.

    a) In the dualistic transcendental type of basic-Idea (Kant). Transcendental thought in its relation to the experience of nature is the formal origin of the laws of nature; this same transcendental thought, as "practical reason" in its direction towards the Idea of autonomous freedom is the origin of the norms of moral freedom.

    b) In the speculative metaphysical conception of the science-ideal or of the personality-ideal, "reason" (in the theoretical or practical sense) is, in a final hypostatisation, identified with the deity.

II. *With the deification of individual subjectivity.*

We have irrationalism in all its forms, from biological vitalism to irrationalist dialectical spiritualism and historicism.

Here, dialectical or hermeneutical thought absolutises the subjective side of reality in one of its modal aspects, and rejects the notion of general laws. In the speculative metaphysical current of this irrationalist Idea of origin, the Origin is called "spirit" *(Geist,* idealistic type*),* or "vital stream", "élan vital" *(Lebenstrom,* naturalist and historical types*).* In general, the "philosophy of life" *(Lebens-Philosophie)* does not recognise the theoretical character of its Idea of the origin.

For us, the Origin of law and of individual subjectivity, in accordance with their religious unity and their temporal diversity in the coherence of meaning, is the sovereign creative will of the holy God. Our cosmos is God's creation, both on its law-side and on its subject-side. The law is the boundary between God and his creation, that is, all creatures are, by nature, subjected to God's law. God alone is *legibus solutus,* though not *exlex* as in nominalism.

E. The Idea of the Totality of Meaning.

In humanist philosophy, this Idea unfolds either through deification of the modal laws or through deification of the modal aspects of individual subjectivity (irrationalism).

I. *With the deification of the modal laws.*

1.   *Under the primacy of the science-ideal:* the natural or mathematical scientific system of functional relations within the absolutised aspect of temporal reality, which gives scientific thought its infinite task. Hence, all other aspects are conceived by theoretical thought as modes of the absolutised aspect (e.g., the mathematical aspect, the mechanical, biological or psychological aspects).

     In the speculative metaphysical current of the science-ideal the Idea of totality of meaning is enclosed within the metaphysical concept of substance (dualistic, pluralistic, and unitary systems have been developed along these lines).

2.   *Under the primacy of the personality-ideal:* the Idea of the totality of meaning is that of the *homo noumenon*, as a categorical imperative (Fichte in the first two periods of his thought).

a) Kant's dualistic transcendental basic-Idea lacks a clear definition of the Idea of totality, which he conceived in a dualistic sense. Kant held to a kind of agnosticism regarding the background of "nature", the *Ding an sich*. He conceived the *theoretical* Idea of totality exclusively in its relation to the science of nature; however it does not refer to the root of reality. The *practical* Idea of totality is conceived in the moralistic sense of moral autonomy and freedom.

b) In the modern idealist philosophy of values, its transcendental trend continues to recognise the primacy of the personality-ideal. The Idea of totality here is that of the "totality of values", uniting theoretical and a-theoretical values in a hierarchical order, established by the autonomous freedom of personality.

II. *With the deification of the modal aspects of individual subjectivity,* and consequently under the primacy of the personality ideal, the Idea of totality of meaning is respectively:

a)   In the vitalist metaphysical trend: the élan vital (vital stream, *Lebenstrom*) with its endless succession of individual forms (Bergson).

b)   In the psychological trend: the totality of feeling (feeling philosophy). Compare this with Goethe's assertion, *Gefühl ist alles.*

c)   In Historicism: the historical stream of experience (Dilthey, Spengler, etc.).

d)   In the absolute idealist trend: the absolute Idea of normative creative individuality. This Idea is developed in a dialectical manner, and all reality is placed under the common denominator of an absolutised aspect (aesthetic, moral, or historical irrationalism, etc.). A formal limitation of it is possible through transcendental thought forms.

For us, the Idea of the totality of meaning is obtained by directing philosophical thought on Christ, the root and fullness of meaning of the cosmos. Christ fulfilled the law. In Him is concentrated the fullness of meaning of all subjective individuality. Nothing that is part of our temporal cosmos can be removed from the sovereignty of Christ. There are no "things indifferent" (*adiaphora*, ἀδιάφορα).

F. The Idea of the Intermodal Coherence of Meaning, Binding Together the Modal Aspects of Reality.

I. *With the deification of the modal laws (rationalism)*.

1. *Under the primacy of the science-ideal:* the continuity of the movement of thought within the absolutised aspect of meaning is the philosophical common denominator of reality. There are, therefore, various types of this Idea of continuity: mathematicism, mechanism, biologism, psychologism. In this continuous coherence of thought, a relative diversity of meaning is accorded to the other aspects of reality

2. *Under the primacy of the personality-ideal:* the continuity of the Idea of freedom, which, using a common denominator chosen in a normative aspect of reality, seeks to establish a strict coherence between the various modal aspects. In the philosophy of values, it is the axiological hierarchy of values, established by autonomous freedom.

II. *With the deification of the modal aspects of individual subjectivity (irrationalism)*, and consequently under the primacy of the personality-ideal:

a) The psychological vitalist metaphysical trend: it is the continuous coherence of creative stream of life, in which all individual moments are interpenetrated in a qualitative duration.

b)   In the relativistic transcendental trend of historicism: it is the dialectical-historical continuous stream of experience (the transcendental "vivo").

c)   In the absolute idealistic current: it is the dialectical-logical continuity in the internal development of the absolute Idea in its dialectical transition through the totality of its individual forms in historical time.

Note: For the whole of this section (F) it should be noted that the humanist Idea of the coherence of the various modal aspects of the cosmos is utterly inconsistent with the acceptance of a divine cosmic order, which would abolish the sovereignty of reason and theoretical knowledge.

For us, the Idea of the coherence that exists in the modal diversity of meaning, on the law-side as much as on the subject-side of temporal reality, cannot be a construction of philosophical thought. It is established by the divine temporal order of the world, an order that is at the same time the condition of theoretical thought.

The modal aspects of meaning, as law-spheres, have an internal sovereignty with respect to one another. Within its own structure, each aspect points toward the temporal coherence of meaning, and expresses this coherence which, in turn, points beyond itself towards the fullness of meaning in Christ. The cosmic order of time guarantees the *integral* coherence of meaning between the modal aspects. A pre-logical reality of nature, in itself *(an sich)* and separated from the normative aspects of reality, does not exist.

G. The Modal Concept of Law and Subject.

I.   *With the deification of the law-side of the cosmos.*

1.   *Under the primacy of the science-ideal.* A law is a general concept of function employed by theoretical thought to create the genetic coherence of reality. Individual

subjectivity is an "exemplary" instance or particular function of this law.

2.   *Under the primacy of the personality-ideal,* in Kant's transcendental idealism: the law, in the sense of universal law of nature, is a transcendental form of thought, which determines the sensory material of experience. In the supra-sensory domain of autonomous freedom, the law is a "categorical imperative" that is identified with the pure will of the selfhood. All the pre-logical functions of reality are objects of consciousness, not subjects; the only subject is the transcendental consciousness, and the *homo noumenon* is the law-giver. Objectivity is identified with a universally-valid conformity-to-law, and both are identified with "antithetical objectivity" (*Gegenständlichkeit*).

a) In the dualist transcendental type of the Idea of law (Kant), there is an unbridgeable gulf between two types of law: the laws of nature and the norms of freedom.

b) In the monistic transcendental type, the law of nature is derived from the ethical norm (Fichte).

II. *With the deification of the modal aspects of individual subjectivity.*

The laws, as mathematical scientific concepts of nature, are technical symbols that denature reality, in order to dominate nature for the benefit of man's biological adaptation (Nietzsche, Bergson, Heidegger, etc.).

The subject is the actual creative individuality, which is not itself subject to a universally valid law. It possesses its individual and irrational law in itself, both in nature and in culture and ethics.

For us, the law, in its modal diversity of meaning, is the universally valid determination and limitation of individual subjectivity which is subjected to it. The subject is *subject,* that is, *subjected* to the law in the modal diversity of the law-spheres. There is no law without subject and vice versa.[4]

Part 2: Attempts to synthesise the Christian faith and immanence-philosophy before and after the Reformation.

> 3. Result of the synthetic viewpoint for Christian doctrine and for the study of philosophy in patristic and scholastic thought.

We have seen how, from its beginnings, Christian philosophy has sought the help of ancient philosophy, even in the formulation its own transcendental basic-Idea.

Patristic thought and, even more, medieval scholastic thought were developed as philosophies of compromise. In the relation between Christian faith and Greek philosophy, both[5] embraced a synthetic point of view. It is however important to distinguish carefully between two different types of synthesis.

The first binds philosophical thought to the revealed Word, the second proclaims the autonomy of "natural reason" in the domain of natural thought. Under the influence of the scholastic nature-grace ground-motive, it was the latter approach that prevailed. Unfortunately, from the moment Scholasticism felt it had found its real starting point in natural reason we have to recognise a progressive decay in Christian philosophy.

Indeed, the Christian religion cannot temporise with any theoretical conception of cosmic reality that ignores the fundamental religious ground-motive of the Bible. Such conceptions are inevitably dominated by ground-motives that are wholly

---

[4] General observation: This schema includes only the most representative types of humanist transcendental basic-Ideas, which present us with a pure basic structure. The synthesis of the ground-motive of this basic-Idea with the fundamental ground-motives of the law-idea of the Greek or scholastic thought, gives rise to new tensions and complications that would require a detailed presentation. The science-ideal and the personality-ideal, as secularisations of the Christian ideas of creation and freedom, are foreign to pre-humanist systems.

[5] [i.e., Patristic and medieval scholastic thought.]

or partially apostate, and their search for an authentic resting place for thought is futile. The Christian religion cannot accept the deifying of heteronomous dependent meaning and the conferring on it of the quality of autonomous independent being, even when such absolutisations are disguised under the cloak of a speculative "natural theology". The Aristotelian speculative Idea of an "unmoved mover" as "pure form" is not at all, as Thomistic scholasticism supposes, the natural pre-amble to the knowledge of God who reveals himself. The revelation that God gives us of himself in Jesus Christ is, in the fullest sense of the term, a fire that consumes all apostate speculation, by which man in his insolence imagines he can create God in his own image.

Neo-Platonic, Aristotelian, Stoic, and other ground-motives penetrated patristic and scholastic thought in the Middle Ages. Immanence-philosophy infected Christian doct-rine and faith, and paved the way for a speculative "natural theology".

All Christian theology has been profoundly influenced by the synthetic point of view, whose devastating consequences have made themselves felt particularly in opposition to the biblical conceptions of *soul*, *heart*, *flesh* and *spirit*, which were simply replaced by the abstract concepts of Greek metaphysics, subjected to the dualist religious ground-motive of *form-matter*.

> 4. The conflict between "faith" and "thought" is rather the conflict bet-ween Christian faith and immanence-philosophy.

As soon as Christian philosophy, under the influence of this metaphysics, began to search for the focal point of human existence in "reason", it prevented the biblical ground-motive from undertaking any intrinsic and fruitful penetration of philosophical thought. An abyss, that rapidly became un-bridgeable, deepened between speculative philosophy and authentic Christian faith. Questions completely foreign to the domain of biblical thought, and charged with Greek meta-physics, invaded theology. Scholasticism offers us the sad spectacle of those sterile controversies that have nothing in common with the spirit of Christianity. Does a really biblical theology have any interest in raising such questions as the conflict between the primacy of the will or the intellect in God's essence? Is it its business to defend the individual immortality of the soul with philosophical reasoning based on an Aristotelian realist conception that seeks the "principle of individuation" in matter? What importance could there be for it in the controversy over which "parts" of the soul are immortal? – a question that Calvin himself took seriously in his *Institutes of the Christian Religion*. What interest could biblical theology take in the problems of "psycho-creationism", that is, in a scholastic transformation of the Platonic doctrine outlined in his *Timaeus*, and of the Aristotelian doctrine of the origin of the active intellect (νοῦς ποιητικός) in the human soul? According to Aristotle, the intellect does not come from nature but from outside; according to Plato the divine Demiurge himself formed only the immortal human νοῦς.

Such problems are only pseudo-problems and have no meaning in a biblical theology.

> 5. The erroneous conception of the relation between science and Christian revelation. Philosophy is neither the servant nor the mistress of theology.

The scholastic attempt at accommodation of immanence-philosophy to biblical Revelation prompted a contrary movement which defended the equally false idea that Holy Scripture could provide solutions to scientific problems, at least those that scholastic theology discussed on the basis of Aristotelian metaphysics, physics and psychology. Theories and so-called biblical solutions were then advanced with all the authority of divine Revelation against any scientific enquiry that departed from traditional conceptions.

Suffice it to recall the Church's position with respect to Copernicus' astronomical theory. Though understandable in terms of history, this attitude was nonetheless reprehensible.

This attempt at synthesis between Christianity and immanence philosophy led to inextricable confusion and countless internal contradictions. It was equally oppressive to Christian faith and honest scientific enquiry.

Nothing better characterises the scholastic point of view than this attempt to use Scripture as a scientific *deus ex machina*. Without a reform of theoretical thought in a radically Christian sense, scholastic theology – promoted by its own concerns to the rank of "queen of sciences" – felt entitled to control "secular science". Once it had accepted and accommodated the Aristotelian philosophy, theology had no option but to interpret the Scriptures in an Aristotelian sense and, in turn, to employ it to confirm Aristotelian responses to Copernicus', and later Descartes', conceptions.

In truth, it was all the outcome of the scholastic notion of philosophy as "handmaid of theology" *(ancilla theologiae)*: but the handmaid was soon to be emancipated and become a demanding mistress.

> 6. Consequences of the Reformation for scientific thought. The failure to reform philosophy.

It was the Reformation that first drew together the conditions necessary for developing a conception of the relations between the Christian religion and scientific thought in a way radically different from scholasticism.

We have had occasion to note that late scholastic nominalism had severed Christian faith from Greek metaphysics. A new worldview preceded the Reformation. This modern humanist conception posed an inescapable dilemma for the Reformers. They would have to choose one of two things: either the antithesis[6] between Christian religion and temporal life, or a secularisation of the Christian attitude in the humanist personality-ideal. A return to the medieval synthesis, appealing to scholastic philosophy in order to make headway against

---

[6] [But see *A New Critique of Theoretical Thought*, I, p.511 where Dooyeweerd describes the dilemma as the antithesis between (a) the attitude of the Christian religion with respect to temporal life on the one hand and (b) the secularisation of that attitude in the humanist personality-ideal on the other. There is no antithesis between the Christian religion and temporal life.]

humanism, was too glaring a contradiction of the true nature and spirit of the Reformation.

In fact, the Reformation could not appeal to anything other than a purely biblical conception of Christian doctrine, which meant a return to the radical integral ground-motive of Holy Scripture, the only possible religious ground-motive for its theological and philosophical thought and also for its worldview. Under this religious ground-motive, the Reformation should also have resulted in the internal reformation of philosophical thought.

However, we make the disturbing discovery that, after a very promising beginning, Protestantism returned, against logic and against all the odds, to the scholastic viewpoint of "compromise". How do we explain this fact? Herman Dooyeweerd maintains that it can only be explained by the legacy of a very old tradition that had profoundly influenced the Christian faith, namely the dialectical scholastic ground-motive of *nature and grace*. This traditional ground-motive found fertile soil in Lutheranism especially, and under the influence of Melanchthon managed to triumph over even the Calvinist ideal of science, and to influence the philosophical standpoint of orthodox Protestantism for a long time.

> 7. Luther's spiritual distinction between Law and Gospel was the result of a nominalist dualism.

In a very elegant way Luther confessed the central meaning of the sovereignty of God in the biblical sense. He recognised that divine grace given in Jesus Christ should penetrate every area of temporal life. And yet he never managed to shake off the nominalist influence of the Occamist University of Erfurt or the study in which he had engaged in an Augustinian monastery. "I am of Ockham's school", he proclaimed.

This influence is very evident in his dualistic conception of the relationship between Law and Gospel. Luther believed that a person who is in a state of sin is bound to temporal ordinances. A Christian in a state of grace, however, is no longer intrinsically subject to the divine Law, but lives in an evangelical liberty under the norm of love. If, in this earthly vale of tears, the Christian submits to the commandments in order to obey the will of God, this can only be because of the sinfulness of his nature, and because he seeks to permeate the commandments with the spirit of Christian love. But intrinsically, this spirit contradicts the strictness of the Law.

This dualism between Law and Gospel was to have serious consequences. In the relationship between Christian religion and philosophy, it had to lead once more to a nominalist separation of faith and science, with the inevitable depreciation of science that Occamist thought implies. Plainly visible here is the influence of the scholastic nature-grace ground-motive in its antithetical Occamist conception. Certainly, Luther fulminated against Aristotle and medieval scholasticism; he stands vehemently against a biblical humanism that, in Germany and with Erasmus in the Netherlands, sought a new synthesis between the Christian faith and the spirit of Graeco-Roman antiquity. But nowhere do we find in him the conviction that the religious root of the Reformation also demanded a radical reform of philosophy as such.

Luther never really got on with the humanistic spirit. In his attitude to human knowledge, he remained a prisoner of the medieval Occamist mentality. The spiritualist inclination of his temperament was strongly influenced by the Germanic mysticism of Eckhart, and the Franciscan Augustinian spirit. If his broad "open-mindedness" towards the world allowed him to reject the monastic ideal, it nevertheless remained fractured by a dualism that is absolutely impossible to explain by the biblical doctrine of the corruption of "nature" by the fall. Luther never became free from nominalist dualism, either in his conception of the Church, or in the regulation of the "visible church" – which he saw as a relatively indifferent matter, in particular handing over to the prince the duty of ecclesiastical reform – or in the distinction, later abandoned, between personal and official morality. It is therefore not surprising that his attitude towards scientific thought was obliterated by the same dualist apriori found in his conception of the relationship between faith and natural reason.

All this we can recognise in him without failing to love or esteem this great reformer. That Luther made some mistakes does not alter the fact that his genuinely biblical faith was for him the source of a continuous reformation of thought, and which later on made him abandon many former errors.

8. Melanchthon's scholastic philosophy.

Melanchthon, the *praeceptor Germanicae*, had close literary contact with German and Dutch humanism, without ever having been tempted by the new personality-ideal. He grew up in a circle of German humanists. He admired Agricola and benefited early from the friendship of Erasmus and Willibald Pirkheimer because of his affinity with his nephew[7] Reuchlin.

In August 1518, at the age of twenty-one, he was appointed professor of Greek at the University of Wittenberg. In his inaugural lecture, *De corrigendis adolescentiae studiis (On the Reformation of the Education of the Young)*, he vigorously attacked the barbarisms of the prevailing Scholasticism and, in general, the mutilation of the Greek and Latin languages as well as philosophy among the "seraphic and cherubic doctors". All in all, this dramatic declaration of war against the scholastic corruption of the classics was no more than the expression of a philosophical humanism[8] and did not mean a break with the starting point of scholastic thought.

The reformation of academic studies that Melanchthon advocated remained within the Scholastic framework. The ancient *trivium* – grammar, dialectic and rhetoric – was the preparatory foundation. Its real aim was the reformation of dialectic, by making it an art of reasoning in the nominalist style of Agricola. He also wanted to give youth a first-class

---

[7] [Marcel is mistaken here. Johannes Reuchlin (1455-1522) was Melanchthon's grandmother's brother. Phillip Melanchthon (1497-1560) was thus Reuchlin's *great-nephew* or, alternatively, they were *second cousins* (having the same great-grandparents).]

[8] *Humanism* here is not to be understood in the religious meaning of the word, which we discussed in our transcendental critique. It refers to the study of the *humanities*. However we will have occasion to see that the humanist spirit was no stranger to this conception of the *humanities*.

humanist philological education, so they could read the original texts of the ancient philosophers and poets. It was the spirit of Agricola and Erasmus that animated the young Melanchthon. His programme intended only philological reform matched with one of moral and ecclesiastical reform, in line with the wishes of his mentors. Although tinged with Christian stoicism, his reform programme was nonetheless charged with a nominalist spirit. These men wanted an accommodation of the humanistic personality-ideal to the programme of a "simple biblical Christianity". In fact, their synthesis between Christianity and humanism, by emphasising the moral aspect, only results in a "humanisation" of authentic Christian doctrine.

By nature and disposition, Luther was very different from Melanchthon. In an electrifying contact with this impassioned champion of the faith, Melanchthon became animated with the antithetical spirit of the Reformation. But a careful study of his thought clearly shows that even during this period of his life, Melanchthon did not radically break with immanence-philosophy. His opposition was in fact directed only against speculative realist metaphysics, its doctrine of "universals", its *formalitates*, its theory of infinity, etc. He never abandoned the nominalist dialectics. However, his rejection of the ideals of humanism led to a break with his patron Reuchlin, and Erasmus turned away from him disappointed. After this break, the old love for antiquity awoke again in Melanchthon, inaugurating a new phase in his development.

This period begins in 1536, when he developed a definitive synthesis between the Lutheran faith and a nominalist Aristotelian current of philosophy. Even during his brief antithetical period, he never denied Agricola's nominalist dialectic. And it is, alas, this method – which was the cause of his return to the old immanence-philosophy – which he applied to the Lutheran doctrine. The unsuspecting testimony of Heinrich Maier, in his important study of Melanchthon's philosophy, is sufficient to justify the strict impartiality of our assertion.[9]

It is highly regrettable that in undertaking the enormous task of establishing a relationship between the Reformation and modern science, Melanchthon adopted the scholastic standpoint of accommodation. The influence he exerted in succeeding centuries actually prevented the development of a philosophy truly in harmony with the spirit of the Reformation. His influence dominated the teaching of philosophy in the Protestant universities of Germany and the Netherlands, right up to the time when the Enlightenment infiltrated them. Protestant theology was one of the victims of this alliance with scholastic philosophy.

Leibniz himself, the genius of the Enlightenment, grew up in these schools of philosophy and his own thought is indebted to a number of its features[10] which, however, he transformed in a rationalist humanist sense.

The scholastic tradition has certainly not been a blessing to the Reformation. An immanence-philosophy accommodated to Christian taste and for a while adorned in pious finery could very quickly be stripped of its pastoral robe to reveal its true character.

---

[9] Heinrich Maier, *Philipp Melanchthon als Philosoph*, in *An der Grenze der Philosophie*, J.C.B. Mohr (Paul Siebeck), Tübingen, 1909, p.47. "In this period also", he says of Melanchthon, "the humanistic erudition remains the ideal of education. And also the new Ideas of faith were clothed in the garments of eloquence. The didactic elaboration of the religious material occurs in the forms and with the means of humanistic methodology. But it is evident, that these forms are closely connected with the world- and life-view on which the material philosophy (*Realphilosophie*) rests...So the development with an inner necessity leads to the restitution of" (the nominalistically-interpreted Aristotelian) "physics, metaphysics and ethics." [Die humanistische Erudition bleibt auch damals Bildungsideal. Und in das Gewand der Eloquenz werden auch die neuen Glaubensgedanken gekleidet. Die lehrhafte Bearbeitung des religiösen Stoffs erfolgt in den Formen und mit den Mitteln der humanistischen Methodik. Aber es ist klar, daß diese Formen aufs engste mit der Weltanschauung verbunden sind, auf der die Realphilosophie ruht...So treibt die Entwicklung mit immanenter Notwendigkeit zur Restitution der Physik, Metaphysik und Ethik.]

[10] Cf. Emil Weber, 'Die philosophische Scholastik des deutschen Protestantismus im Zeitalter der Orthodoxie', in *Abhandlungen zur Philosophie und ihrer Geschichte*, Robert Falckenberg (ed.), Quelle and Meyer, Leipzig, Issue 1, 1907.

9. A radically Christian philosophy ~~~
only be developed from Calvin's religious starting point.

Calvin, too, had a brief humanist period in which he wrote
his famous commentary on Seneca's *De Clementis*. But after his
conversion, he broke completely with the nominalist dualism
that continued to some degree to inspire Luther's thought and
that dominated the scholastic nature-grace ground-motive.

In Calvin's biblical perspective, this Scholastic ground-
motive is eliminated. For Calvin, man's true nature cannot be
opposed to grace. Nature, corrupted at its root by the fall, is
only restored or – a far more apt term – *renewed* by the grace of
God in Jesus Christ.[11] Never does the Bible conceive of *nature*
apart from grace, so that natural reason could, having rebelled
against God or separated from him, become the springboard
for a natural philosophy or a natural theology. The Bible
teaching is opposed to every conception in which the νοῦς τῆς
σαρκὸς – the intellect which, "thinking according to the flesh",
denied Christ – would be declared sovereign.

For us to "abide in the truth", to use a biblical expression,
divine Revelation must seize our heart, the root of our entire
existence. It was rationalist scholasticism in its entirety which
rejected a Christian attitude towards knowledge that Calvin
aimed at the heart of when he wrote: *"Nor were it sufficient for
the mind to be illumined by the Spirit of God unless the heart also were
strengthened and supported by his power. Here the Schoolmen* (scholastici) *go completely astray, dwelling entirely in their consideration of
faith, on the bare simple assent of the understanding, and altogether
overlooking confidence and security of heart"*.[12]

---

[11] John Calvin, *Institutes of the Christian Religion*, II. i. 9: "Hence it follows, that that
part in which the dignity and excellence of the soul are most conspicuous, has not
only been wounded, but so corrupted, that mere cure is not sufficient. There must
be a new nature." Trans. Henry Beveridge, Edinburgh, Calvin Translation Society,
1845. [Unde sequitur, partem illam, in qua maxime refulget animae praestantia et
nobilitas, non modo vulneratam, esse, sed ita corruptam, ut non modo sanari, sed
novam prope naturam induere opus habeat.] See also II. i. 6, where the radical
nature of sin is stressed.

[12] John Calvin, *Institutes of the Christian Religion*, III, ii, 33. (Beveridge translation).
[Nec satis fuerit, mentem esse Dei spiritu illuminatam, nisi et eius virtute cor

Calvin categorically rejected every speculative natural theology. It is an "audacious curiosity" *(audaci curiositate)*[13] of "wanting to dissect God and peer into his heart"[14] and of seeking to intrude upon his "essence", which we can never penetrate but only worship[15]. Tirelessly, he warns against a

---

affirmetur ac fulciatur. In quo tota terra Scholastici aberrant, qui in fidei consideratione nudum ac simplicem ex notitia assensum arripiunt, praeterita cordis fiducia et securitate.] This statement simply expresses the pure biblical conception that regards knowledge – and in the first place the knowledge that comes from faith – rooted in the heart "from which proceed the sources of life". In characterising this attitude as "sentimentalism", Roman Catholics make a big mistake. In 1931, for example, A. J. M. Cornelissen in a comparative study, not without merit, on the doctrine of the State in Calvin and Rousseau, *La doctrine de l'Etat chez Calvin et Rousseau* (a thesis defended at the Catholic University of Nijmegen), said: "If faith does not require any preamble provided by reason, but rather rational knowledge is fortified by faith, then it is impossible not to draw the conclusion that the act of supernatural *knowledge* is only an act of feeling. Calvin did not hesitate to draw this conclusion which led him into sentimentalism." (p.25). – Under the influence of Aristotelian epistemology, the biblical concept of "heart" as the religious centre of life is so completely lost sight of that nothing better can be imagined than to identify it with the temporal function of feeling, by opposing it to theoretical thought.

[13] John Calvin, *Institutes of the Christian Religion,* I, v, 9.

[14] John Calvin, *Treize sermons traitant de l'élection gratuite de Dieu en Jacob*, Opera Calvini, LVIII, Sermon iii, p.50. [...et puis quand il dit: En soy-mesme: c'est pour nous advertir que si nous voulons savoir la cause pourquoy, c'est autant comme si nous voulions faire une anathomie de Dieu, et aller iusques en son coeur, et sonder tous ses secrets.]

[15] John Calvin, *Institutes of the Christian Religion*, I, v, 9: "Hence it is obvious, that in seeking God, the most direct path and the fittest method is, not to attempt with presumptuous curiosity to pry into his essence, which is rather to be adored than minutely discussed, but to contemplate him in his works, by which he draws near, becomes familiar, and in a manner communicates himself to us.(Beveridge translation)" [Unde intelligimus hanc esse rectissimam Dei quaerendi viam et aptissimum ordinem: non ut audaci curiositate penetrare tentemus ad excutiendam eius essentiam, quae adoranda potius est quam scrupulosius disquirenda, sed ut illum in suis operibus contemplemur, quibus se propinquum nobis familiaremque reddit, ac quodammodo communicat.]

– *Sermons sur le Deutéronome*, Opera Calvini, XXV, Sermon vi, p.668 : « Ne nous enquerrons point de la vérité de Dieu, sinon en tant qu'elle nous est manifestée en l'Ecriture sainte ? car Dieu ne veut pas que nous lui allions arracher les entrailles, par manière de dire, comme font ceux qui veulent s'enquérir outre mesure, et plus qu'il n'aurait permis...Apprenons donc d'écouter Dieu quand il nous parle, et de ne vouloir point savoir plus que ce qu'il nous a enseigné, et que journellement il nous propose en l'Ecriture sainte. »

vacua et meteorica speculatio on the essence of God, apart from his revelation in his Word.[16]

Calvin expresses the most genuine religious critical attitude to the knowledge of God – that based on the humble vision of the absolute limits established between the Creator and the creation and which, with all due consideration, bows restrained and respectful before the unfathomable mystery of the majesty of God. "A believing ignorance is far better than a reckless science."[17]

The scholastic nature-grace ground-motive is nowhere to be found in Calvin's thought, and we look in vain for the slightest sign of the spiritual opposition between the Divine Law and the Gospel that we encounter in Luther. In the presence of the majesty of God, who will not tolerate man crossing the boundary line between Creator and creation, we cannot accept, with Luther, that Christian liberty is elevated above the divine law.

10. Calvin's Law-Idea is opposed to
the Aristotelian Thomist Idea.

We have had occasion to quote one of the claims Calvin expressed repeatedly: *Deus legibus solutus est (God is not subject to laws)*. Although there is no question here of the nominalist *exlex (without law, arbitrary)*, this statement necessarily implies that all creation is subject to the law.[18]

---

[16] John Calvin, *Institutes of the Christian Religion*, I, x, 2: "...and, secondly, that in the enumeration of his perfections, he is described not as he is in himself, but in relation to us, in order that our acknowledgement of him may be more a vivid actual impression than empty visionary speculation.(Beveridge translation)" [...deinde commemorari eius virtutes, quibus nobis describitur non quis sit apud se, sed qualis erga nos, ut ista eius agnitio vivo magis sensu, quam *vacua et meteorica speculatione* constet.]

[17] John Calvin, *De la prédestination éternelle de Dieu*, Geneva, 1552, p.126. [Vne ignorance conioincte auecques la foy est beaucoup meilleure qu'vne science temeraire] This statement of St Augustine occurs several times in the *Institutes of the Christian Religion*.

[18] John Calvin, *Treize sermons traitant de l'élection gratuite de Dieu en Jacob*. Opera Calvini, LVIII, 187 : [Dieu n'est sujet à nulle loi]. p.37-38 : [Il refuse d'être astreint à quelque loi...mais le conseil de Dieu nous doit être pour toute règle de justice, sagesse et équité].

Christ has freed us from "the law of sin" and the Jewish ceremonial law. But in its religious fullness and its temporal diversity of meaning, the *cosmic* law is not a heavy yoke that is imposed on us because of sin: on the contrary, this law is, in Christ, a priceless blessing. A subject not determined by this law would sink into chaos immediately.

Therefore Calvin recognised the Christian's inherent subjection to the Decalogue, and did not see the least internal contradiction between the Summary of the Law — the central command of love and religious root of the ordinances of God — and the spheres of juridical or economic laws or even the internal structural law of the State. It is because they lost sight of the religious root of the temporal laws that the Anabaptists opposed the Sermon on the Mount, with its teaching of love, to the civil ordinances. Calvin energetically fought this error. Starting from the radical religious unity of all divine temporal ordinances, he very effectively opposed both the absolutisation of any temporal aspect of the Law of God (itself indivisible), and every spiritualised revolution against the state and legal order: "His purpose was, neither to relax nor to curtail the Law, but to restore the true and genuine meaning, which had been greatly corrupted by the false glosses of the Scribes and Pharisees (Beveridge translation)."[19]

   — *De la prédestination éternelle de Dieu*, Geneva, 1552, p.239f : [Je ne reçois point aussi cette glose, mais la reprouve, que quoi que Dieu face, il n'est point à reprendre, d'autant qu'il n'est sujet à nulle loi. Car celui qui fait Dieu sans loi, la dépouille de la plus grande partie de sa gloire mettant sous le pied sa justice et droiture. Non pas que Dieu soit sujet à loi aucune, sinon d'autant qu'il est loi à soi-même.]

   — *Commentaire sur l'Exode*, III, 22 : [Neque tamen hoc modo eum facio exlegem, etsi supra omnes leges eminet ejus potestas, quia tamen voluntas ejus certissima est perfectae aequitatis regula, rectissimum est quidquid facit ? atque ideo *legibus solutus est, quia ipse sibi et omnibus lex est.*]

   — *Commentaire sur l'Exode*, XI, 2 : [*...supra omnes leges* est ejus imperium, . . . quia *ejus voluntas perfectissima est legum omnium norma*]. God has an internal "government". Cf. *Treize Sermons*. Opera Calvini, LVIII, Sermon I, 23 and *Sermons sur le Livre de Job*, Opera Calvini, XXXIII, Sermon XLVII, 584.

[19] John Calvin, *Institutes of the Christian Religion*, II, viii, 26. [Christo non est institutum legem aut laxare aut restringere, sed ad veram ac germanicam intelligentiam reducere, quae falsis scribarum et Pharisaeorum commentis valde depravata fuerant.]

This fundamental Idea of the divine Law has nothing in common with the Aristotelian Thomistic conception of natural law. The latter comes from the religious form-matter ground-motive of Greek thought, and is necessarily opposed to the biblical conception. The speculative Idea of Eternal Law has as a corollary the no less speculative "natural law" with its teleological order of "substantial forms". In this construction, human reason imagines it can define what is a law for God. In the Idea of Eternal Law, the Aristotelian conception of universal order is identified with the "rational essence" of God, and ultimately deified.

The Reformation was forced to oppose this conception by preaching the doctrine of Christian freedom. Calvin and Luther employed it in a remarkable way, but Calvin succeeded in formulating a purer version than Luther, without losing anything of the biblical concept of freedom in Christ in his conception of the Law. Luther did not succeed in ridding himself of a spiritualist antinomianism, to which he had to oppose the biblical concept of divine Law, based on the confession of the sovereignty of God the Creator. This was necessary to maintain the biblical ground-motive of the Reformation.

> 11. Calvin's Law-Idea is opposed to Emil Brunner's dualist irrationalist viewpoint.

Emil Brunner rejects the biblical conception of the Law and seeks to replace it with a rationalistic ethics of love, which he regards as more evangelical and which he places above the divine temporal ordinances. The latter, he says, do not express the true will of God.[20] In a typically spiritualist manner, Brunner fulminated against the idea of a Christian science, a Christian philosophy, a Christian culture, a Christian politics,

---

[20] Emil Brunner, *Das Gebot und die Ordnungen*, J.C.B. Mohr (Paul Siebeck), Tübingen, 1932, p.108ff, and "Das Einmalige und der Existenzcharakter", in *Blätter für deutsche Philosophie* (1929). The commandment of love, as *Gebot des Stunde* or *Gebot des Augenblickes* (*the need of the hour/what is called for now*...a characteristically irrationalist term), is opposed to the temporal ordinances of the Law. [English trans.: Emil Brunner, *The Divine Imperative.*, trans. Olive Wyon, Cambridge, Lutterworth Press, 2002 (1941).]

etc. From a philosophical point of view, we have here the indication of yet another attempt to compromise with the immanence-standpoint, in particular with Kantianism and modern irrationalist existentialism. This compromise, which owes nothing to Calvin but harks back to Luther's dualism, cannot have a bright future in Dooyeweerd's opinion.

Brunner seeks to accommodate Luther's nominalist dualism between "nature" and "grace" to the Calvinist conception of the Law. But this dualism is incompatible with the fundamental biblical ground-motive and, for that reason, with Calvin's standpoint. For the Word of God, which reveals to us the root of our temporal existence and, in that root, the unbridgeable gulf between the Kingdom of Christ and the kingdom of darkness, forces upon us an inescapable choice.

If a Christian philosophy, a Christian idea of law or State, a Christian art, etc., are impossible, then all these temporal spheres of life are removed from under the lordship of Christ. Like it or not, we are once again compelled to accept the unbiblical dualism between "nature" and "grace", or between the Law and the Gospel, and then – as we have to try and overcome this dualism – to surrender to scholastic accommodation. But if we, rightly, reject the synthesis of the Christian faith with Aristotle's rationalist cosmonomic-Idea, or with that of the Stoics, why should modern humanist irrationalism or Criticism be regarded as any more Christian?

If, with Brunner, we follow this path we will end up depreciating certain aspects of reality. His irrationalism requires him to give the central religious command of love a highly questionable interpretation. He inordinately qualified love and the notion of Christian ethics at the expense of the Idea of justice, which his dialectical viewpoint requires him to devalue in a neo-Kantian manner to a "purely formal value".[21]

---

[21] Emil Brunner, *Das Gebot und die Ordnungen*, J.C.B. Mohr (Paul Siebeck), Tübingen, 1932, p.675, where he says of the critical Kantian conception of the Idea of legal order "that, based on experience and for good reasons, it is understood only by those lawyers who have ties of kinship with the tradition of faith of the Reformation" (e.g. Stammler and Burckhardt). [...erfahrungsgemäß und aus guten Gründen nur von solchen Juristen verstanden wird, die mit der reformatorischen

Brunner defends a thesis that, in our view, violates the fullness of meaning of the Cross: he believes that "perfect justice" is in itself a contradiction, and that though love has to go through "formal justice" it must abolish it in the end.[22] If we follow Brunner's synthesis we will fall into the same trap. Christian philosophy has no more choice here than does immanence-philosophy.

The synthesis with ancient immanence-philosophy entangled Christian thought in complex antinomies; and it is the same with every synthesis of humanistic immanence philosophy. Not only does it shackle Christian thought in the fundamental antinomy between "nature" and "freedom", but above all it leads inevitably to the clash of two irreconcilable ground-motives: the apostate ground-motive that lurks in humanist thought and the central biblical ground-motive of

---

Glaubenstradition in Zusammenhang stehen.] And so the synthesis with Kantian immanence-philosophy is complete.

[22] Emil Brunner, ibid., p.436 : "For the Christian faith as such there is no conceivable idea of perfect justice. Because justice is in itself flawed." [Gerade vom Christlichen Glauben aus gibt es keine irgendwie faßbare Idee der vollkommenen Gerechtigkeit. Denn Gerechtigkeit ist an sich unvollkommen.] For Dooyeweerd, it is justice "in itself" which actually doesn't exist, because it can only be an absolutisation devoid of all meaning. And we can say the same about love "in itself". "Love", says Brunner (p.437) "is concrete, personal, unpredictable; it is neither general nor legal. Justice, by contrast, is general, legal, predictable, impersonal, abstract and rational."– From a biblical standpoint, we simply say that Brunner's opinion is not compatible with the biblical understanding of the Law, but stems from a semi-humanist perspective. A Christian must learn to bow to the majesty and justice of God, which is no different from his love. God is *the origin and original unity* of all the modal aspects of human experience, which cannot be separated from each other in the temporal order, but overlap in their religious root and *a fortiori* in their divine origin. In his later work, *Gerechtigkeit* (1943), Brunner does not substantially alter his previous position. Again, he speaks of the "justice of faith" by opposing it to the justice of ordinances (*Ordnungen*), and the former has no internal connection with the latter. This "justice of faith" is identified with love in the Gospel, and it abrogates justice in any retributive sense. This is also true of divine justice, which is diametrically opposed to earthly justice in the sphere of ordinances. Although earthly ordinances and justice are opposed to *the command of love*, the former come to the aid of a life of love. This conception is characteristically Lutheran. Cf. Reinhold Niebuhr, *The Principles of Ethics*, ch. V and VI, and *Nature and Destiny of Man*, II, ch. IX. If earthly justice is *diametrically opposed* to divine justice, and if nevertheless the former belongs to the realm of divine ordinances, then we introduce a dialectical dualism into the divine Will that betrays the influence of the dialectical nature-grace ground-motive.

the Christian religion. Dialectical theology is merely an expression of the religious dialectic that emerges from this clash.

With a grasp of the whole issue, and noting that Calvin was the first to develop a truly biblical conception of the Law in its origin, its radical religious unity and its temporal diversity, we conclude that a genuine reformation of philosophical thought cannot be historically inspired by Luther, but only by Calvin's starting point.

But it is important nonetheless that there be no misunderstanding about this conclusion. When we speak of a reformation of philosophy in the Christian sense, there can be no question of starting a new school similar to Thomism, and championing the authority of a system or a man. We do not in any way imagine that Calvin should be elevated to the rank of the *pater angelicus* of Reformed philosophical thought; any more than we imagine we could find in his work a philosophy that is not there. Our only ambition is to lay the foundation, the starting point and transcendental direction of philosophical inquiry in the new root of our cosmos, Jesus Christ. We cannot accommodate any philosophical conception that takes "natural reason" as an autonomous Archimedean point. What we desire is an *internal reformation* of thought, one that originates in the life-giving power of the Word of God and not in an abstract static principle of reason. Therefore, the development of a Christian philosophy must be constantly and in a very effective manner stimulated by the fundamental biblical ground-motive of the Reformation, which implies the desire for a continual and uninterrupted reformation of philosophical thought. So there can never be any question of *canonising* a philosophical system.

Christian philosophical thought does not find its inspiration in a spiritualistic mysticism that regards itself as beyond God's Law. It can only be driven by the quickening spirit of the Word of God. That Word, despite the interference of sin in our temporal world, maintains the richness and diversity of its structural meaning and, because it is impossible to find in time the fullness of its meaning, leads Christian philosophical thought and calls it to look upon the world as God's creation concentrated in its new religious root: Jesus Christ.

The only antithesis[23] accepted by the Christian transcendental basic-Idea is the religious antithesis between the *apostasy* of creation and its *restoration* by grace. Christian philosophy, therefore, does not seek any dialectical *synthesis* in the style of a *natura praeambula gratiae*. Rather, it recognises in common grace a divine force that opposes the destructive effect of sin in the world, for the *antithesis* between sin and creation is *really* destroyed by redemption in Jesus Christ.

> 13. No dualism between *common* and
> *particular* grace.

We must beware of opposing common grace to particular grace dualistically. If this is done, the dualistic nature-grace ground-motive, under another name, reappears in Reformed thought. Calvin was always anxious to subordinate common grace to particular grace, and to God's honour and glory.[24]

---

[23] We will have occasion later to note that this is not a kind of "cult of contradictions" here as Cornelissen, no doubt under the influence of dialectical theology, quite wrongly imagined the state of affairs in Calvin's thought.

[24] Cf. John Calvin, *Institutes of the Christian Religion*, I, xvii, 7: "Thus, for the good and safety of his people, he overrules all the creatures, even the devil himself who, we see, durst not attempt anything against Job without his permission and command.(Beveridge translation)" [Sic et creaturas omnes in suorum bonum ac salutem moderari, ei curae est; ac diabolum etiam ipsum, quem conspicimus, nihil ausum fuisse tentare adversum Iob, sine permissu eius ac mandato.]
  – I, xvii, 11: "When they call to mind that the devil, and the whole train of the ungodly, are, in all directions, held in by the hand of God as with a bridle, so that they can neither conceive any mischief, nor plan what they have conceived, nor how much soever they may have planned, move a single finger to perpetrate, unless in so far as he permits, nay, unless in so far as he commands; that they are not only bound by his fetters, but are even forced to do him service, – when the godly think of all these things they have ample sources of consolation. For, as it belongs to the Lord to arm the fury of such foes and turn and destine it at pleasure, so it is his also to determine the measure and the end, so as to prevent them from breaking loose and wantoning as they list (Beveridge translation)." [Iam si vel a diabolo, vel a sceleratis hominibus impetitur eorum salus: hic vero, nisi providentiae recordatione ac meditatione confirmentur, protinus concidere necesse sit. Verum ubi in memoriam revocant, diabolum totamque improborum cohortem sic omnibus partibus

It is Christ, root and Head of regenerated humanity, who gives common grace its meaning. Without him, it is devoid of all meaning, because it manifests itself only *in the temporal cosmos*, which in turn is necessarily related to its religious root without which it has absolutely no existence. Common grace is the grace manifested to humanity taken as a whole, regenerated in Christ its new root, but not yet been delivered from its old apostate root. This is the meaning of the parable of the wheat and the tares: both must grow side by side until the harvest.[25]

---

manu Dei, tanquam freno, cohiberi, ut nec concipere ullum adversus nos maleficium, nec conceptum moliri, nec ad perpetrandum, si maxime moliantur, digitum movere queant, nisi quantum ille permiserit, imo nisi quantum mandarit: nec compedibus tantum eius teneri ligatos, sed etiam ad obsequia praestanda freno cogi: habet unde se prolixe consolentur. Nam ut Domini est, eorum furorum armare, et convertere destinareque quo libuerit: ita et modum finemque statuere, ne pro sua libidine licentiose exsultent.]

– III, iii, 25: "...there cannot be the least doubt that God will be ready to pardon those who turn to him truly and with the heart, seeing his mercy extends even to the unworthy though they bear marks of his displeasure...he gives some examples of his inclination to pardon, that the pious may thereby be stimulated to amend their lives, and the pride of those who petulantly kick against the pricks be more severely condemned (Beveridge translation)." [...quia minime dubitandum est, vere et ex animo conversis Deum fore ad ignoscendum facilem, cuius clementia se ad indignos usque extendit, dum aliquid displicentiae pare se ferunt. ..Se quaedam (ut iam dixi) exempla profert suae ad dandam veniam propensionis, ex quibus pii animentur ad vitae correctionem, et gravius damnetur eorum superbia, qui proterve adversus stimulum calcitrant.]

– III, xx, 15: "...to stimulate his true worshippers to more urgent prayer, when they see that sometimes even the wailings of the ungodly are not without avail (Beveridge translation)." [...deinde ut probos suos cultores ad orandum magis exstimulet, dum vident profanos eiulatus non carer interdum profectu.]

– III, xxiv, 2: "When he first shines with the light of his word on the undeserving, he gives a sufficiently clear proof of his free goodness. Here, therefore, boundless goodness is displayed, but not so as to bring all to salvation, since a heavier judgement awaits the reprobate for rejecting the evidence of his love. God also, to display his own glory, withholds from them the effectual agency of his Spirit (Beveridge translation)." [Verbi sui luce dum immerentibus primum affulget, eo gratuitae bonitatis suae specimen satis luculentum exhibet. Hic ergo iam se exserit immensa Dei bonitas, sed non omnibus in salutem: quia reprobos manet gravius iudicium, quod testimonium amoris Dei repudient. Atque etiam Deus, illustrandae gloriae suae causa, Spiritus sui efficaciam ab illis subducit.]

– Cf. *Institutes of the Christian Religion*, I, v, 14 ; II, ii, 16.

[25] Matthew 13:24-30. We will have occasion to develop this point when we examine the *opening-process* in the General Theory of the Law-Spheres.

14. Why we reject the expression *Calvinist philosophy*. Importance of the *Philosophy of the Law-Idea* for Christian thought.

Herman Dooyeweerd has pointed out that the birth and systematic expression of the *Philosophy of the Law-Idea*, as he explains in the first three volumes of *De Wijsbegeerte der Wetsidee,* is a fruit of the Calvinist revival in the Netherlands during the second half of the nineteenth century, the movement of which Abraham Kuyper was the undisputed leader.

However, the *Philosophy of the Law-Idea* is not to be understood as the exclusive thought of a small "clique" of Calvinists. Its importance and significance, on account of its foundation and its transcendental basic-Idea, far exceed the limited circles of "Calvinists". It is addressed to all those who seek to think in a truly Christian manner. Indeed, no Christian can evade the dilemma it presents, if he really takes seriously the universality of the Kingdom of Christ and confesses the sovereignty of God, the Creator of the cosmos. Unless one hides behind such sterile words as "Christian freedom" under the pretext of its being the corollary of "freedom of thought", the clash is unavoidable. Besides, could "Christian freedom" ever mean for thought a being freed to be guided by an antichristian ground-motive?

It is in this general sense that Abraham Kuyper spoke of a religious antithesis in life and thought. Countless *Christians*, animated by irenic sentiments, have seriously misunderstood the meaning of this antithesis. They think it refers to a *personal* line of demarcation between individuals, when it is really a matter of a dividing line between *fundamental principles* in the world, cutting across and through the existence of every Christian. This antithesis is not a human invention, but an innate gift of God, by which he preserves his fallen creation from ruin. To deny it is to deny Christ and his work in the world.

Therefore, though he called it *Calvinist* to begin with and regards it as a fruit of the Calvinist revival, Herman Dooyeweerd now categorically rejects the term *Calvinist* as a description of the *Philosophy of the Law-Idea*, and he regrets that the philosophical society that was founded in the Netherlands has taken the name "The Association for Calvinistic Philosophy".

However, Herman Dooyeweerd believes that, on account of its fundamental religious ground-motive and transcendental basic-Idea, his philosophy deserves the name of *Christian* philosophy, without further qualification, because it appears impossible for an intrinsically Christian philosophy to be based on *any another* ground-motive than the one we have defined, a really integral and radical scriptural ground-motive that does not depend in any way on man.

It is true that Thomistic philosophy has always rejected the term *Christian*. It is also true that some neo-Thomists such as Gilson and Maritain have distanced themselves somewhat from this tradition, for reasons that seem to stem from an Augustinian rather than a Thomist influence.

However, it appears that it is still possible to speak of a *Reformed* Christian philosophy, as opposed to a *neo-scholastic* Christian philosophy which may have abandoned the dogma of the autonomy of philosophical thought. But we can only do so if we believe that the fundamental scriptural ground-motive of the Christian religion is at work in the former to promote an internal reformation of philosophical thought and that the latter remains bound to the scholastic nature-grace ground-motive and, within this framework, looks only to break down the line of demarcation between the natural and the supernatural realms in order to show the inadequacy of natural philosophical thought for the Christian faith.

15. The *Philosophy of the Law-Idea* and Blondelism.

One neo-Scholastic current, which has embarked on the path we have just alluded to and which has broken radically with Thomism, had its origins in the French spiritualism of Maine de Biran, and has been developed in an increasingly anti-rationalist manner by Ravaison, Lachelier, Boutroux, and others. Its aim is to continue the Augustinian tradition in Christian thought. But by taking over the nature-grace ground-motive, this current has definitively cut itself off from an authentically Augustinian conception that radically rejects the autonomy of philosophical thought and makes philosophy no more than the handmaiden of theology.

The principal representative of this neo-scholastic philosophy is Christian Maurice Blondel, a disciple of the neo-Scholastic philosopher Ollé-Laprune. Beginning from the standpoint of immanence-philosophy, he strives to demonstrate the deficiency of philosophical thought, through an irrational and activist metaphysical interpretation of thought and being. This interpretation is strongly influenced by the Leibnizian Idea of the immanence of the universe in the representations of all metaphysical being, and by the irrationalist and universalist turn that it had taken in Schelling's "absolute concrete thought", and much later in Bergson's philosophy of life. It was also inspired by Malebranche's Idea of the *visio omnium rerum in Deo*.

On no account, however, can Blondel's Christian philosophy be considered intrinsically *re-formed* thought. From the start it lacked a transcendental critique of philosophical thought as such. Its dialectical character is clearly evident in the fact that this Catholic thinker intended to break through the immanence standpoint and arrive at a Christian conception by means of an irrationalist, universalist and activist metaphysics, dominated from the start by the humanist ground-motive accommodated to the scholastic nature-grace ground-motive.[26]

---

[26] This dialectical synthesis of the humanist and scholastic ground-motives in Blondel's thought is very clearly explained by his disciple Henry Dumery in his work: *Blondel et la philosophie contemporaine*, Etudes Blondélienne 2, Paris, Presses Universitaires de France 1952, p.71ff. Cf. H. Dooyeweerd, *Le problème de la philosophie chrétienne. Une confrontation de la philosophie blondélienne avec la nouvelle philosophie reformée en Hollande.* [*The Problem of Christian Philosophy : A comparison between Blondel's philosophy and the new reformed philosophy in Holland*] Two public lectures delivered at the University of Aix-en-Provence-Marseille, in May 1953, and in *Philosophia Reformata*, 1953, pp.49-76. – Ferdinand Sassen, in his *Wijsbegeerte van onzen tijd* (Antwerp, Uitgeverij De Standaard, 1940) felt entitled to say that there was a connection between Dooyeweerd and Blondel's voluntarist philosophy. This observation could only have been an unfortunate misunderstanding.

16. The significance of the *Philosophy of the Law-Idea* for contact between the different schools of philosophy.

The significance of the *Philosophy of the Law-Idea* cannot be confined to Christian thought. Indeed, by its transcendental critique, this philosophy has identified new problems that must be taken into account by every philosophy, whatever their starting point. In addition, it implements an internal critique that can approach each system from within, from the standpoint of its own fundamental ground-motive and its own real concerns. We have already pointed out that from the beginning this philosophy permitted a better understanding between different philosophical schools, which remained otherwise isolated in a dogmatic exclusivism due to the prejudice of the autonomy of theoretical thought, mere supra-theoretical prejudices having been elevated to the rank of theoretical axioms.

In addition, the Philosophy of the Law-Idea is not at all restricted in its significance for other schools to negative matters. It gives them an overwhelmingly positive contribution. Herman Dooyeweerd's theory of the modal structures of the meaning-aspects, his theory of individuality-structures and their interlacements, which will be the object of a future exposition, reveal facts which hitherto had escaped philosophical examination. These new issues come into play even within the structure of empirical reality, and we have seen that, as with the laws of theoretical thought, the facts are the same whatever viewpoint one takes. Since no philosophy can claim a monopoly, especially ours, the question is which philosophy will be able to provide a satisfying theoretical explanation of the new facts. Every philosopher must work with a spirit of healthy competition in a common task. But such cooperation is possible only on one condition: that the schools of immanence-philosophy must be willing to abandon their theoretical dogmatism, and to consider with the utmost seriousness the transcendental critique of philosophical thought we have put forward.

This applies first and foremost to our theoretical conception of empirical reality. We know that because of the internal structure of theoretical thought our view of empirical reality depends on the transcendental basic-Idea that directs all our enquiries. This content is itself determined by supra-theoretical ground-motives. If we do not acknowledge this, then all exchange of ideas is doomed to failure even before it starts. Between schools which differ in their starting point, a philosophical discussion is possible if, and only if, a clear distinction is made between genuinely theoretical judgements (about which discussion is always possible) and the indispensable *pre-theoretical apriori's* that are the basis for these judgements.

Every philosophical discussion about theoretical judgements, to be successful, must be based on indisputable facts relating to the structure of theoretical thought and empirical reality, which *precede every theoretical interpretation*. These facts must be established independently of, and be applicable to, every theoretical interpretation. They must then be confronted with the various philosophical conceptions, to discover which of them, from their own supra-theoretical starting point, is able to account for the facts in the most satisfactory manner.

CႽCႽCႽ

Chapter 6

General Outline of the *Philosophy of the Law-Idea*.
The Relation between our Philosophy and the Special
Sciences.

Part 1: The divisions of systematic philosophy and the
transcendental basic-idea.

> 1. The different *divisions* of philosophy
> depend on the transcendental basic-
> Idea.

With the previous chapter, we reached the end of our
critical examination into the meaning of the transcendental
basic-Idea for all philosophical thought. Before developing the
positive content of the *Philosophy of the Law-Idea*, we shall
outline the general plan we intend to follow.

Could we adopt as a method of exposition one of the
fundamental divisions of problems that immanence-philosophy
created? It would not succeed, because the classification and
formulation of philosophical problems depends intrinsically on
the transcendental basic-Idea at the root of each philosophy.
For example, in the systematic development of humanist
philosophy, the division of problems into various categories or
sections depends on the two terms of the humanist basic-Idea:
the science-ideal and the personality-ideal, and the postulate of
continuity inherent in each.

All humanist philosophy since the Renaissance has been
dominated by these two terms of the humanist basic-Idea.

Pre-Kantian rationalist humanist philosophy was powerfully dominated by the Cartesian programme of a universal
mathematics *(mathesis universalis)*. In the natural sciences
(Hobbes) this programme could only lead to an encyclopaedic
systematisation of the sciences as a continuous progression

from the more elementary to the more complex spheres of knowledge. This systematisation, called first philosophy *(prima philosophia)*, was built on mathematical logic. The mathematical method was applied to all areas of philosophical enquiry, in accordance with the postulate of continuity of the science-ideal. The same might be said of Auguste Comte's positivism.

The primacy of the science-ideal in the dualist types of pre-Kantian metaphysics led to a fundamental metaphysical separation between natural philosophy on the one hand, and ethical and metaphysical psychology, on the other.

Christian Wolff divided philosophy into two main areas: *theoretical* philosophy or metaphysics – which included natural theology, psychology and physics – and *practical* philosophy.

Pre-Kantian empirical philosophy was likewise divided into theoretical and practical sections. John Locke, for example, believed that philosophy, as a scientific system, consisted of three main sections: *physica* or natural philosophy, *practica*, with ethics as the essential element, and *semiotica*, with nominalist logic as its main constituent.

It is to Kant that is due the merit of having discerned the importance of the ideals of science and personality as regulative principles for a systematic classification of philosophical problems. The *Critique of Pure Reason* delimited a primary domain of enquiry: that of the foundation of knowledge, and the limitation of the classical science-ideal, oriented towards the domination of nature. The *Critique of Practical Reason* delimited a second: that of the critical foundation of an autonomous ethics, in accordance with the humanistic personality-ideal. Kant also discussed issues of law *(Metaphysische Anfangsgründe der Rechtslehre)*, and theology. In his *Critique of Teleological Judgement*, he investigated the philosophical problems of biology, history and aesthetics, and sketched a subjective synthesis of the two Critiques.

Fichte takes over this fundamental division. His *Wissenschaftslehre* includes a theoretical section and a practical section, which he crowns with a pantheistic metaphysics of Absolute Being.

Hegel makes a dialectical division of philosophy into logic, natural philosophy and philosophy of mind, in which we detect the influence of the same humanist basic-Idea.

CʒCʒCʒ

In the philosophy of the twentieth century, the pursuit of a systematic division continues to be made in conformity with the fundamental structure of the humanist transcendental basic-Idea.

Cohen, for example, the founder of the neo-Kantian school of Marburg, divides philosophy into three main areas: *Logic of pure knowledge, Ethics of pure will, Aesthetics of pure feeling*. It is obvious that such a classification is influenced by Kant.

Neo-Kantian philosophy of values, with Rickert, for example, makes a division between the domains of real nature and ideal values. As we have seen, it seeks a subjective synthesis between these in the intermediate domain of culture. This system of values, to which philosophy should conduct us, is founded on the fundamental distinction between theoretical and practical values. Once again, we recognise the dualism of the science-ideal and the personality-ideal. Theoretical philosophy becomes a transcendental critique of natural science, and practical philosophy becomes a theory of worldviews.

The division of philosophy into theoretical and practical is an authentic feature of all Western immanence-philosophy. The tension between the science-ideal and personality-ideal within the structure of the humanist basic-Idea always gives this division its particularly humanist meaning.[1]

---

[1] On Windelband's opinion in his *Einleitung in die Philosophie*, 2nd ed., J.C.B. Mohr (Paul Siebeck), Tübingen, 1920, p.19-20, see H. Dooyeweerd, *De Wijsbegeerte der Wetsidee*, Vol. I, p.497-498, and *A New Critique of Theoretical Thought*, Vol. I, p.531-532. [English trans. : Wilhelm Windelband, *An Introduction to Philosophy*, trans. Joseph McCabe, London, T. Fisher Unwin, 1921.] Herman Dooyeweerd undertakes a detailed study here of the distinction between theoretical and practical philosophy in Greek thought, under the influence of the dialectical form-matter ground-motive. But this would take us too far beyond our current purpose. Cf. *De Wijsbegeerte der Wetsidee,* Vol. I, p.498-503; *A New Critique of Theoretical Thought,* Vol. I, p.532-540.

2. We cannot divide philosophy into
the theoretical and the practical.

The division of philosophy into two sections – theoretical
and practical, or natural philosophy and philosophy of mind –
is only possible on the immanence standpoint and is due to its
conception of the human selfhood. The division is the result of
an internal conflict in the Archimedean point, and it inevitably
leads to the primacy being given at one moment to natural
philosophy and the next to practical philosophy.

From our perspective, and because of the transcendental
basic-Idea of our philosophy, we cannot endorse such a distinction, in whatever form it presents itself; not in any way for
the sake of originality or a desire to denigrate immanence-
philosophy, but because it is incompatible with the biblical
ground-motive of our philosophical thought.

We know that our human selfhood, as religious root and
heart of our entire existence, transcends the temporal boundaries of our cosmos, and of all its modal aspects. Directed in all its
activity towards the totality of meaning, philosophy must be
of a theoretical nature.

From the Christian perspective which we adopt, it would
thus not make any sense – and it would be very dangerous – to
adopt a classification which, in immanence-philosophy, is the
outcome of an internal conflict at the heart of its Archimedean
point. In addition, "practical reason" is unable to control the
underlying diversity of the normative aspects of our cosmos.
Finally, neither theoretical nor practical reason, in the sense of
immanence-philosophy, is identical with our true transcendental selfhood.

Part 2: General outline of the *Philosophy of the Law-Idea.*
The internal coherence of its themes.

3. General outline of the *Philosophy of
the Law-Idea.*

Under the guidance of our transcendental basic-Idea, our
investigation will be conducted in accordance with a number

of fundamental themes that are inextricably linked. They may
be summarised under the following five heads:

1. *The transcendental critique of philosophy*, which implies an
    enquiry into the religious ground-motives that deter-
    mine the content of the transcendental basic-Ideas.

2. *The analysis* of the various modal aspects of temporal
    reality to define their functional structure. This is the
    General Theory of Law-Spheres.

3. *The theory of knowledge*, taking into account naive exp-
    erience, the special sciences and philosophy – in other
    words, the transcendental reflexive critique of the
    universally-valid conditions of naive experience, the
    theoretical analysis and synthesis of modal meaning,
    under the direction of the transcendental basic-Idea.

4. A study of the data of naive experience, in an attempt
    to identify and understand the *typical structures of indiv-
    iduality* of temporal reality, and their various structural
    interlacements.

5. A study of the *structural unity of human existence* within
    cosmic time, in the light of the transcendental idea of
    human selfhood. Only after the previous themes have
    been developed will it be possible to address this
    philosophical anthropology.

In our philosophy, the problem of time is not the topic of
any particular theme. Time has a universal and transcendental
character and is found to be implied in each particular philosophical question, of which it forms the transcendental underpinning.

The *transcendental critique of philosophical thought* has been the
subject of these Prolegomena. It now remains for us to apply
ourselves to the other four issues.[2]

---

[2] Dooyeweerd dealt with themes 2, 3, and 4 in the second and third volumes of *De
Wijsbegeerte der Wetsidee* and *A New Critique of Theoretical Thought*. He intends dealing
with anthropology in the third volume of *Reformation and Scholasticism in Philosophy*.

4. The internal unity of our various
themes.

The enumeration of the five themes of our philosophy
does not mean a division of the different areas of philosophical
research into as many spheres of autonomous problems. Theoretical thought is directed to the totality of meaning and such a
division would be in conflict with the essence of philosophical
thought. At all stages in the development of our philosophy,
we are engaged in a religious self-reflection carried through by
philosophical thought. It is therefore impossible for any problem to be separated out from the others and considered in
isolation.

This is particularly true of the problem of knowledge.
Psychological epistemology, as well as the so-called critical
epistemology, treats the problem of knowledge as a fundamental, independent and isolated problem. In our view, such
an absolutisation of epistemological questions (regarded as
merely theoretical) is impossible, because a truly critical transcendental epistemology depends on religious self-knowledge
and on knowledge of God, which transcend the theoretical
domain. Epistemology is itself a theory directed to the totality
of meaning of human knowledge, a theory in which our
selfhood reaches the limits of philosophical thought, returns to
itself and in so doing reflects on the limits and supra-theoretical
presuppositions of temporal knowledge. What, then, is philosophy if not an epistemology?

But in thus situating the problem of knowledge, we must
at the same time say: "What is philosophy, if not a philosophy
of the structures of temporal reality and of time?" In all its
dimensions, philosophical enquiry is directed toward a structural theory of temporal reality, led by a religious self-reflecting
critique of the totality of meaning and its Origin. Without this
religious self-reflection on the meaning of our cosmos, a truly
critical theory of knowledge would be impossible for philosophy, because our temporal knowledge, both in theory and in
naive experience, only makes sense in the coherence of meaning of reality.

So when we proceed to develop our thought using the
remaining four themes we enumerated, it is merely a question

of giving a systematic exposition of a single basic problem viewed from different perspectives. These themes develop this single problem in its relationship with the various structures of cosmic time and reality, in accordance with the moments inherent in our transcendental basic-Idea – the transcendental Ideas of Origin, supra-theoretical totality and temporal diversity of meaning in its modal aspects (which the theoretical antithetic relation[3] opposes to one another, even though they remain united in cosmic time) – and in its temporal individuality structures.

Only the transcendental basic-Idea can account for an explanatory method used in philosophy.

> 5. No one particular philosophical science constitutes the theoretical foundation of philosophy. Only our transcendental critique can fill this role.

Immanence-philosophy often assumes that some particular philosophical science might be considered a sufficient basis for scientific and philosophical enquiry in certain special branches. Our transcendental basic-Idea does not allow us to accept any other theoretical foundation for philosophy than the transcendental critique of philosophical thought as such. Husserl and Scheler's *phenomenology*, a *first philosophy* promoted by speculative metaphysics, Lask's *logic of philosophy*, Hume and Kant's *critique of knowledge*, Nicolai Hartmann's *critical ontology*, the *symbolic logic* of the Vienna Circle, are not a genuine basis for philosophical inquiry because they all lack a really critical foundation.

Neither do we believe that a philosophy of values or a philosophy of mind can provide an adequate basis for the cultural[5] sciences, whereas epistemology could form a basis for

---

[3] [i.e. the *Gegenstand*-relation.]

[4] [The Vienna Circle (German: *der Wiener Kreis*) was an association of philosophers gathered around the University of Vienna in 1922, chaired by Moritz Schlick, also known as the Ernst Mach Society (*Verein Ernst Mach*).]

[5] [Marcel always refers to what we call *cultural science* as *sociological science* (*science sociologique*). We shall use the term *cultural* throughout.]

the natural sciences. That philosophy can be based on some such autonomous science is a notion that is only possible or acceptable on the immanence standpoint, whether we take philosophy as a coherent whole or – in the case a dualistic partitioning of its field of enquiry – consider it in its various parts. Immanence-philosophy withdraws thought from every truly transcendental critique.

The transcendental critique of theoretical thought we propose is, without doubt, the ultimate theoretical foundation of philosophy. But it is by no means a fundamental, philosophical and autonomous science in the sense of immanence philosophy, because it sets out to account for the *supra-philosophical conditions and foundations* of all philosophy.

Because of its immanent limitations, philosophical thought remains immersed in the temporal diversity of meaning, in which no specific synthesis may become the common denominator of others or of a complex of others. The philosophies of mathematics, physics, biology, psychology, logic, history, language, sociology, economics, aesthetics, law, ethics and theology, as special philosophies, will be explored during the development of our third and fourth themes. They therefore belong to the particular theory of the modal aspects and the theory of individuality-structures, insofar as they express themselves within the modal aspects of reality, which delimit the specific domain of enquiry of each branch of science.

Thus, no *special* philosophy, as we understand it, can serve as a basic philosophical science. We will have occasion to show in detail that the particular philosophical presuppositions of a special science exert their apriori influence in the most concrete problems of each particular science. But the particular philosophy of a special science can only exist, *as a philosophy*, insofar as it examines its own basis in the light of a total theoretical vision of temporal reality, a vision ruled by the transcendental basic-Idea and the fundamental religious ground-motive.

A special *philosophy* exists only to formulate the basic problems of the special sciences in the universal coherence of all of reality, and to relate these problems to the supra-temporal fullness of meaning and its Origin. An isolated special philosophy is a contradiction.

Part 3: The relation between philosophy and the sciences.

6. The sciences want to be independent of philosophy.

Once again the question arises as to whether science can be independent of philosophy. We recall that in our transcendental critique of theoretical thought this question has already been answered in the negative. But a detailed examination of this problem will not be superfluous, for the presupposition of the independence of science with respect to philosophy seems almost invincible.

We note at what cost and with what a struggle, during the Renaissance and the period that followed, the sciences managed to free themselves from philosophy. Mathematical physics had to struggle to free itself from the tutelage of the Aristotelian philosophy of nature which, with its doctrine of substantial forms and especially its non-mathematical conception of natural events, obstructed any genuine enquiry. In the nineteenth century, the science of law had to fight against the rationalist philosophy of natural law (Wolff and his school). Even today, especially in the natural sciences, Hegelianism demonstrates the dangers of a philosophy that tries to intrude on the problems of the special sciences.

Our transcendental critique has undoubtedly shown that the autonomy of philosophical thought with respect to faith and religion is impossible. But our contention that the sciences also, from the beginning, lack such autonomy because they are necessarily based on philosophical presuppositions, will arouse express reservations, especially from the exact sciences. But we have no reason to suppose that this attitude comes from any contempt for philosophical reflection as such.

Logic, ethics and aesthetics are usually considered part of philosophy.[6] In addition, we readily concede that there must be room for a philosophy of the special sciences and a general epistemology. But it is a very common notion that the "object-ivity" of science requires it to be separate from philosophy, and to remain so. That the sciences are dedicated to their own sphere and employ their own scientific methods is sufficient for them to be independent of philosophy.

> 7. The separation of philosophy and the sciences according to modern humanism.

Up till now, humanism has generally conceded that the special sciences are autonomous with respect to philosophy. However, in modern humanistic metaphysical philosophy, we notice a reaction against the tendency of science to consider philosophy as a negligible quantity for empirical research.[7]

In the positivist period of the second half of the nineteenth century, speculative philosophy was completely discredited, and philosophy had great difficulty in regaining its prestige, which is why humanist thought now seeks to avoid its former mistakes by granting the sciences complete autonomy in their own field.[8]

---

[6] Dooyeweerd does not share this view. Only the special *philosophies* of logic, ethics and aesthetics have this character. But philosophy penetrates these sciences too.

[7] Hans A. E. Driesch, for example. *Zwei Vorträge zur Naturphilosophie*, Leipzig, Verlag von Wilhelm Engelmann, 1910, p.21f: "(The philosophy of nature) will not only be a guide for the natural sciences, telling them which road to take and which to avoid, but for philosophy it will be one of those crossroads where all possible ways of thinking about the data meet, and from where pathways lead towards the domain that is the goal of all philosophy: a theory of reality, of *being-that-exists-not-just-for-me (Nicht-bloß-für-mich-sein)*: in a word, a metaphysics." [(Die Naturphilosophie) will nicht nur den Naturwissenschaften eine Lenkerin sein, die ihnen sagt, welche Wege sie gehen müssen, und welche Wege sie nicht gehen dürfen, sondern sie will auch für die Philosophie den einen von jenen Sammelpunkten bedeuten, in welche alle möglichen Wege des Denkens über Gegebenes zusammenlaufen, und welche ihrerseits Wege ausstrahlen lassen in jenes Gebiet, das das Ziel aller Philosophie ist, in die Lehre vom Wirklichen, vom Nicht-bloß-für-mich-Sein: in die Metaphysik.] Driesch acknowledged that his conception differed from that generally received.

[8] In this school of thought it is assumed that *empirical* reality has no normative aspects. Consequently there can be no *normative sciences*.

Even many supporters of "critical" epistemology have now changed their mind on this point. Kant in his critical period[9] claimed that three-dimensional space, as a form of intuition, was the transcendental condition of geometry, and some of his followers (L. Ripke Kühn, etc.) opposed Einstein's theory of relativity. But the neo-Kantian school of Marburg was quick to accommodate the Kantian theory of knowledge to non-Euclidean geometries (Gauss, Lobatschewsky, Riemann, Bolyai, etc.). The same applies to the Kantian apriori conception of the causal law of nature, oriented to Newton's classical physics, which is refuted by modern quantum physics.

But when the epistemology is exclusively oriented to the *Factum* or, in the words of the Marburg School, the *Fieri* of the mathematical sciences, the fact remains that any philosophical critique of the methodology of these sciences and their theoretical constructs is impossible and we are obliged to accept them as they are. The universal validity and self-sufficiency of a scientific theory must be accepted apriori, since in rationalist immanence-philosophy, thought which refers to the natural aspects actually occupies the same position in the field of "natural reality" that the divine cosmic order does in Christian philosophy. By simply following in the footsteps of science, epistemology avoids any conflict with scientific progress. Philosophy is neither a guide nor a counsellor; it is content to just reflect on the course of the sciences, and is thereby assured of their good graces. For their part, the sciences do not need to know how philosophy seeks to explain their actions: they can and should remain philosophically and religiously neutral. What science could be more neutral than mathematics and physics? When the other sciences follow the same method, they will not need any help from philosophy.

---

[9] In his pre-critical period, Kant did regard non-Euclidian space as conceivable. Cf. *Gedanken von der Wahren Schätzung der lebendigen Kräfte* (1747, §9ff) and *Allgemeine Naturgeschichte und Theorie des Himmels* (1755, ch.III). [Why Dooyeweerd and Marcel referred to these old editions is a mystery. These two books may be found in: Immanuel Kant, *Immanuel Kants Werke*, Großherzog Wilhelm Ernst Edition, 4th edition, 1928, Vol. II.]

Even when the methodological monism of the humanist classical science-ideal is called into question, the neutrality of science is generally regarded as beyond doubt. Recall Rickert and Litt's conceptions of the relations between philosophy and science.

These conceptions are still so deeply rooted in philosophical and scientific circles that even the slightest divergence of opinion is generally seen as an unscientific return to an outdated notion of the role of philosophy. But we should not be intimidated by general opinion, however imposing it is. And if it is true, as we have shown it is, that the classical distinction between philosophical and scientific thought is incompatible with a truly critical perspective, we must not hesitate to say so and explain why.

Certainly, we are well aware of the danger of an apriori speculative metaphysics, when it intrudes upon issues within science. There is no need to portray the pathetic spectacle of yesteryear. But since we reject all speculative metaphysics and advocate a *comprehensive empirical* research in philosophical enquiries, far from leaving us open to the same criticisms, our critique will instead bring about a valuable contribution to the solution of this problem and to the future of science.

> 8. The separation of science from philosophy is inherently untenable, even for mathematics.

We maintain that it is impossible to draw a dividing line between philosophy and science with the intent of *freeing* the latter from the former. Science cannot be isolated in an absolutely independent field of enquiry. Any attempt to do so would call forth a very serious critique.

We could talk about the autonomy of science only if a special science could actually study a particular aspect of temporal reality without theoretically considering its coherence with all other aspects of reality. But no scientific thought is possible if it withdraws into itself "with all the shutters up". Whether it likes it or not, it is constantly confronted with the temporal coherence of the modal aspects of reality and cannot avoid following the transcendental Idea that concerns it. Even the sciences of the first two modal aspects of experience – the numerical and the spatial – cannot, as we have shown, avoid philosophical presuppositions.

Can modern mathematics really succeed in avoiding philosophical presuppositions about the relations between and the coherence of the arithmetical aspect and the spatial, analytical, linguistic and sensory aspects? Is it permissible, with Dedekind, to include in our concept of number the original moments of continuity and dimensionality? Is mathematics only an axiomatic symbolic logic, whose criterion of truth rests only on the *principle of contradiction*[10] and that of the *excluded middle?*[11] Do the "transfinite" numbers have actual numerical value? Can the subject-side of the numerical sphere be reduced, in a rationalist manner, to a function of the principle of progression – which is a numerical law – and is it then permissible to speak of actual infinitesimal numbers? Are we right to conceive of space as a continuum of points, or to regard real numbers as spatial points? Is movement possible in the original (mathematical) sense of the spatial aspect?

No one would deny that these are fundamental philosophical questions that go to the heart of mathematical thought, and about which no mathematician can remain neutral. Whether we reflect on its necessary presuppositions or not, we are forced to choose. It is precisely in "pure" mathematics, not applied, that a complete separation between philosophy and science proves to be the most problematic, because here we have an *apriori*[12] science, one whose results cannot be subjected

---

[10] [Latin: *principium contradictionis.* That is, two contradictory statements cannot both be true at the same time, e.g. the two propositions "A is B" and "A is not B" are mutually exclusive.]

[11] [Latin: *principium exclusi tertii.* Known as the *Principle of the Excluded Third* or the *Law of the Excluded Middle.* That is, all statements are true or false; there is no third option. The intuitionist school of mathematics under L. E. J. Brouwer denies this however.]

[12] The view that pure mathematics is *apriori,* that is, it starts from entirely arbitrary axioms, is incompatible with the Christian concept of divine order of the world, which is the ultimate foundation of all scientific enquiry. In our view, the apriori character of pure mathematics cannot mean that it is freed from the modal structures of the mathematical aspects in the temporal order of experience. The study of these

to the test of scientific experiment. Is not the real task of the philosophy of mathematics, then, that of studying the modal structures of the mathematical aspects, on which all well-founded judgements in pure mathematics depend?

Is it legitimate to separate the tasks of mathematical science and philosophy of mathematics by saying that the latter is merely trying to explain the epistemological possibility of an apriori mathematical knowledge, whose methods and content should be accepted without question? But this would be to consider mathematics a *fait accompli*, and any possibility of a truly philosophical critique of it would be excluded.

Such an attitude toward the sciences might be acceptable in the framework of a transcendental basic-Idea where the humanist science-ideal has a foundational function. But in the light of our transcendental critique of theoretical thought, it must be rejected as erroneous and dogmatic.

While philosophy can only explain the *foundations* of mathematics, this does not justify the ascription of autonomy to mathematical thought, which is largely taken up with the techniques of calculation, construction and deduction. Philosophy cannot confer this autonomy on it, because the mathematician must necessarily work with subjective philosophical presuppositions whose consequences are evident in mathematical theory itself, as we have already explained.

> 9. The positivist-nominalist conception of the purely technical character of constructive scientific concepts and methods.

The truce between philosophy and science, which may be summarised by the axiom: "Each man is master in his own home", has the effect of sanctioning the positivist-nominalist

---

structures can only be carried through *empirically*, since they are neither creations of human thought, nor apriori "forms of thought"; they are, on the contrary, part of the "modal horizon" of our experience, as an apriori *datum*. They must be *discovered* through reflection on our experience of the mathematical aspects. The Kantian conception of apriori empirical moments in human knowledge identifies the "empirical" with sensory impressions. This conception of "empirical" is incompatible with our integral conception of human experience.

conception of the sciences. Here, at least in respect of his constructive work, the theorist claims he is operating only with technical concepts and methods that are independent of philosophical presuppositions and, a fortiori, of religious presuppositions.

In our profession, says the mathematician, when we use the concept of the actual continuity of the series of real numbers, we do so without any philosophical prejudice. We use such concepts only because we find them practical and because they lead to the acquisition of satisfactory results.

We use the concept of "legal person", says the lawyer, as a construct of thought, by which we understand a whole complex of legal phenomena. We use it for purely technical legal reasons, because it is advantageous and conforms to the principle of logical economy.[13] Behind this technical construct, we grant philosophy complete freedom to find a social reality, a collection of individuals or a supra-individual "person". Furthermore, when we formally reduce all positive law to the will of the state and declare that the lawmaker is legally omnipotent, we remain entirely independent of every viewpoint that depends on a philosophy of law or of the political absolutism of the state. We use this concept of the source of law in a purely formal sense, and thereby we do but express the fact that all positive law receives its formal validity from the state. We do not thereby accord to the philosophy of law any the less freedom to criticise specific statutes as wrong or detrimental to justice, and there is nothing to prevent it from opposing an absolutist state by insisting on the freedom of the individual.

---

[13] [Marcel generally uses the phrase *Principe de l'économie des pensées* (principle of economy of thought) – an almost literal translation of Dooyeweerd's Dutch phrase *het denk-economisch principe* found in *De Wijsbegeerte der Wetsidee*. In the English translation – *A New Critique of Theoretical Thought* – this became the *Principle of logical economy* (in one instance, the German term *denkökonomische* was used: NC, I, p.551). Marcel also uses *le principe de l'économie logique* and other variants. We have translated it *logical economy* throughout.]

10. The positivist conception of reality
versus the juridical facts.

Despite these assertions, the fact remains that behind these concepts that aspire to be technical there lurk some very positive philosophical presuppositions. In particular, this applies to the principle of *logical economy*, which legitimises the use of theoretical fictions that do not correspond at all to the true state of affairs within the modal aspect of reality that forms the specific field of theoretical enquiry. In the general theory of the law-spheres, we will show that the *principle of logical economy* only makes sense logically in close association with the *principle of sufficient reason,* which requires that we *genuinely* and validly account for the theoretical facts. This principle can never condone theoretical fictions, whose intervention only serves to obscure the antinomies that arise from a false theoretical conception of empirical reality.

The positivist conception of law, now dominant, identifies empirical reality with its physical-psychical aspects, that is, with an absolutised theoretical abstraction. In this naturalistic representation of reality, there is no longer any place for modal aspects of an inherently normative character. If, with modern so-called "realist" jurisprudence, the juridical or legal aspect is reduced to physical-psychical phenomena, it loses all its (what is nevertheless *irreducible*) modal meaning. But the juridical *facts* are the *juridical aspect* of *real* facts; within this aspect, these real facts cannot be established apart from the juridical norms to which they are subjected. In theoretical jurisprudence which maintains the normative nature of legal rules, once these structural facts are lost sight of and these "facts" are understood in the juridical aspect as "physical-psychical facts", we witness the springing up of countless theoretical antinomies that are generally concealed by the introduction of "theoretical fictions". The principle of *logical economy* is called upon simply to justify this. We will have occasion to come back to this.

For now we shall only remark that behind this positivist conception of law, supposedly "non-philosophical", there lies concealed in fact a *philosophical conception of reality* that is far from neutral with respect to faith and religion.

Under the mask of the neutrality of philosophy or of a worldview, the technical pragmatic conception of scientific thought has done considerable damage, particularly in the areas of theoretical enquiry that have the normative modal aspects of reality for their "object".

To clarify this we shall note the essential difference between the *typical* concept of an individuality-structure and the *modal* concept of function.

In each modal aspect, we distinguish:

1.   A general *functional* coherence. Its role is to maintain a correspondence between the individual functions of things, events or social relations within a given law-sphere. This coherence is independent of the typical differences between these things, events or social relations, each of which functions on its own account within the given modal aspect.

2.   *Typical* structural differences that manifest themselves within this modal aspect, but which can be understood only in terms of the individual structures of reality, considered in its integral intermodal coherence.

We have already drawn attention to the fact that an individuality-structure embraces all the modal aspects without exception, and that each individuality-structure groups together, typically and in its own way, all the modal aspects into an individual whole. In addition, each individuality-structure expresses itself in every aspect by typicalising the general modal relationships and functions.

To clarify this distinction, here are some examples from the juridical and physical aspects.

In the juridical aspect of reality, all phenomena are linked by a *functional* juridical coherence. From the perspective of this normative aspect, this means that constitutional law and civil law, internal ecclesiastical law, domestic commercial law, the domestic law of trade unions and other organisations, international law, etc., are not independent of each other, but are united by a horizontal functional coherence that guarantees the modal structure of the juridical aspect. In considering only this universal functional coherence between the different types of laws, we abstract it from the internal structural differences, which entail the different laws and distinguish them from each other.

This general functional viewpoint is absolutely abstract. It merely serves to distinguish the modal functions within the juridical aspect, regardless of the typical individuality structures which are inherent in the integral character of reality. But with a general juridical concept of function alone, it is absolutely impossible to identify the internal structural differences of the various kinds of law. So it is obvious that the general modal concept of law can never contain the typical characteristics of State law, for example.

Now consider the general functional coherence between the phenomena in the physical aspect. We can conceive it abstractly without regard to the differences that characterise the individual structures of reality. To discover the general laws of physical interaction, physics considers all the physical phenomena under the modal functional denominator of energy. The physical modal concept of function is a systematic concept par excellence, because it is able to grasp the universal horizontal coherence of all possible physical phenomena in this modality.

But insofar as we are only concerned with this functional view, scientific thought cannot take into account the internal individual structure of the concrete things of nature. A tree, an animal, etc., as well as an atom, a molecule or a cell, has physical and chemical functions, both in its internal structure and as a natural thing. But a purely functional view of the physical aspect reality will not tell us anything about the energy relations of the universe, as we encounter them in the typical structure of an individual whole; a tree or an animal, for example. This functional view merely discloses the external relations of abstract "energy" or "matter", relations that dominate every internal structural difference, and are only grasped in terms of the functional aspect of the physical laws. This functional view is apparent in Newton's law of gravitation. This law is independent of the typical structures of "things", and indeed dominates the entire physical universe. A feather falling to the ground and the motions of the planets are equally subject to the law of gravitation.

Every science, with the exception of pure mathematics, is confronted with the typical individual structures of reality. Though chemistry investigates the same law-sphere as physics, it would only obtain meagre results with no more than a general concept of function. The same applies to physics since the discovery of the internal structures of atoms. Freely-flitting electrons only make us aware of the purely functional properties of mass, charge, movement, attraction and repulsion; but when they function within the structure of an atom or molecule, they are specific properties at the root of the internal structural differences.

The distinction between the functional modal structure and the typical structure of reality, which we have just demonstrated in the juridical and physical modalities, can also be found in all other modal aspects. We will demonstrate this in detail.

> 12. The absolutisation of the concept of function and the illegitimate introduction of a specific structural concept of individuality, conceived as functional.

What happens, then, under the influence of the positivist conception of the task of science? The postulate of continuity in the humanist science-ideal led to the absolutising of the concept of function and the destruction of the modal diversity of meaning in the various modal aspects. As a result, the attempt was made to completely erase the typical individuality-structures that reality displays within the modalities investigated. Especially in the "pure theory of law" *(reine Rechtslehre)* and in "pure economics" we frequently observe a curious confusion between the functional modal and the typical structural viewpoints. Often without noticing it, and under cover of a general concept of function, a specific concept of individuality-structure is surreptitiously introduced here, which levels all the other typical structural differences within the investigated aspect of reality.

Consequently, a modal concept of function that is supposed to be merely general is actually transposed into a typical structural concept. In the guise of a purely functional abstraction, the Austrian school of "pure economics", for example, absolutises free-market relations at the expense of other societal structures that the economic aspect of reality equally displays.

Similarly, the "pure theory of law " developed by Hans Kelsen and his neo-Kantian school, seeks to construct a purely logical-functional coherence between the various typical domains of positive law, by assuming either the sovereignty of constitutional law, rather than State law, or that of international law. In a pseudo-logical manner, all other typically legal spheres are thus reduced in the former case to State law, and in the latter to the law of a supposedly-international Super-state *(civitas maxima)*. The confusion between the functional modal and the typical structural viewpoints is completed by a pseudo-logical identification of law and State, or of law and Super-state.

But if State and law are identical, it no longer makes any sense to speak of a *State* law. And if, from a purely legal point of view, as Kelsen supposes, all positive legal norms have *the same formal nature* and all material typical differences have to be considered *meta*-juridical, then it is contradictory to introduce the typical characteristics of *State* law or of *Super-state* law into this modal functional concept of law.

Like all other spheres of human society, the State has an internal individuality-structure that functions in all the modal aspects of reality. And that is precisely why it is impossible to grasp the true nature of the State in an abstract concept of function, any more than in its typical juridical sphere.

The modal concept of function is falsified when, under the guise of a merely functional view of law, the entire question of the sources of law is referred to the State or to an international community of States.[14]

Such errors indicate that the absolutisation of a functionalist viewpoint by scientific thought is never neutral with respect to philosophy or religion. Such an attitude can only be the result of a nominalist view of science, based on the humanist science-ideal. This ideal, it is true, is currently losing ground due to the fact that it is conceived in a merely technical manner, especially by the positivist School of Ernst Mach and the more recent logical positivism of the Vienna Circle. In modern times, psychology and the cultural sciences have begun to react against the intrusive domination of this functionalist science-ideal. This reaction stems from the pole opposed to this functionalism: irrationalism.

> 13. The empirical sciences depend on individual typical structures. The revolution in physics in the 20th century.

Herman Dooyeweerd does not deny that the descriptive and experimental sciences are closely related to the functional modal structures and the typical structures of empirical reality. And so the discovery of indisputable facts in the course of empirical enquiry can reveal the inadequacy or incorrectness of rationalist levelling methods. In the twentieth century, for example, physics has undergone a profound revolution and has had to abandon its classical functionalist concepts of causality, matter, and physical space and time. The theory of relativity and quantum theory have reduced Newton's physical conception of the world to a mere special case.

In keeping with the humanist science-ideal, the classical mechanistic concept of causality led to an absolute function-

---

[14] In a special treatise: *Het substantiebegrip in de moderne natuur-philosophie en de theorie van het enkaptisch structuurgeheel* (The concept of substance in modern natural philosophy and the theory of the enkaptic structural whole), *Philosophia Reformata*, 15th year, 1950, pp.66-139, Dooyeweerd shows that very often in biology there is confusion between the modal functional concept of organic life and a concept of substance relating to a living entity conceived as a totality. Cf. Driesch's conception of "organic life" as an entelechy; Woltereck's conception of organic life as a living material "substance" (matrix), etc.

alisation of reality in a strictly deterministic sense. This concept was unable to explain the microstructure of the physical aspect of reality that was brought to light by countless investigations. Planck's discovery of the quantum structure of energy and the Heisenberg uncertainty relations have now made the reduction of physical processes to a simple continuous causal coherence impossible. On the basis of experiment, quantum theory and relativity theory have radically broken with the Newtonian conception of matter, considered as a static substance occupying an absolute space and subject to radically determined causal processes in an "absolute time". The discovery of radioactivity forced the physicist to recognise an autonomous physical change, which takes place entirely within the internal structure of the atom, and cannot be explained by any external functional cause.

But the discovery of phenomena that cannot be grasped by a classical concept of function, does not assure us that they will be interpreted correctly and in a manner that is philosophically and religiously neutral. On the contrary, it is obvious that the scientific attitude of the best investigators is profoundly influenced by their theoretical conception of reality. It is evident, for example, that Mach and Ostwald denied the existence of real atoms and light waves, and sought to reduce the physical concept of causality to a purely mathematical concept of function, because of their positivist and sensualist philosophical viewpoint. Bernhard Bavink has drawn attention to the fact that the modern trend in physics which, with Heisenberg and Jordan, advocates abandoning the concept of causality, can only make good their claim on the strength of philosophical considerations taken from Mach and Avenarius.[15]

[15] Bernhard Bavink, *Ergebnisse und Probleme der Naturwissenschaften*, Leipzig, S. Hirzel Verlag, 9th edition, 1948, p.233ff. Dooyeweerd believes that this fundamental concept should not be identified with the deterministic concept of the classical mechanistic picture of reality. The concept of causality has an *analogical* character. Every empirical science must conceive it in the special modal sense of its own field of enquiry. The mechanistic determinist conception proves to be incompatible with the true nature of physical phenomena. But this does not mean that every physical concept of causality is without meaning. [English trans.: Bernhard Bavink, *The Natural Sciences: an introduction to the scientific philosophy of today*, New York, Century

The conflict we observe in the philosophical foundations penetrates also to the heart of the special sciences. The physicist is in great danger of uncritically accepting the positivist and nominalist presuppositions. By blindly pursuing only the "technical" aspect of his own field, he will very quickly pick up a nominalist view of philosophical problems without realising their philosophical implications, and a purely technical-constructive view of the methods and concepts of physics.

From the standpoint of science alone, can a physicist accept the thesis that a theory formulated in mathematical terms must be considered correct, if it explains all known phenomena in the simplest possible way by uniting them into a functional coherence? In other words, is the principle of logical economy, in the positivist and empirical-critical sense given it by Mach and Avenarius, the sole criterion of truth in physics?

Recall the conflict caused by Einstein's theory of relativity, not only in philosophical circles, but also in natural science. Think of the controversy between Max Planck, von Laue, Lenard and other physicists on the one hand, and Schrödinger, Heisenberg, Jordan, etc., on the other, about whether or not the physical concept of causality was still admissible, in the classical sense, in the new quantum theory.

Was the former position of classical physics a matter of indifference to the Christian student of nature? Was it no consequence to him that it adopted a fundamentally rationalist conception of empirical reality, in which the entire subject-side of the physical sphere is reduced to the law-side conceived in a merely functionalist manner? In other words, should we accept physical determinism as true, given the state of physics in the nineteenth century, because it could coordinate most of the phenomena then known into a systematic functional coherence?

Is it a matter of indifference to the Christian physicist whether or not physics is identified with the conventional understanding of the Vienna Circle? If it really was immaterial

---

Company, 4th edition, 1932 (reprinted 1975, New York, Arno Press). A later edition does not appear to have been translated.]

whether physics took a position on this issue, the term "science" would lose all its meaning, because science presupposes a theoretical view of reality[16], since it must constantly appeal to it.

14. Defence of the autonomy of the special sciences from a "critical" realist perspective.

From the perspective of critical realism[17], Bernhard Bavink, the famous German philosopher of nature, has sought to show that natural science is autonomous with respect to philosophy: "The main point", he says, "is not knowing what methods or ways of thinking we need in order to investigate things, but rather what results – and probably will result again – from this investigation that, for centuries, we have managed with the greatest success without the help of any epistemology. The issue is not one of epistemology but of ontology, that is, it is absolutely irrelevant to know how I ought to think about the world, or how I can think about it, but how it really is."[18]

---

[16] Bernhard Bavink, *Op. cit.*, p.271, remarks: "For physics, molecules, light waves, electromagnetic fields and their tensors, etc.. have exactly the same kind of reality as rocks, trees, plant cells, or fixed stars." [Für die Physik sind vielmehr die Moleküle und die Lichtwellen, die Felder und ihre „Tensoren" u.s.w. von genau derselber Wirklichkeitsart wie Steine und Bäume, Pflanzenzellen oder Fixsterne.] But he ignores the fact that physics has eliminated the entire naive view of reality.

[17] "Critical" realism (Eduard von Hartmann, Erich Becker, Alois Riehl, August Messer, Oswald Kulpe, etc.) originates in the critical Kantian conception of knowledge. But unlike Kant, it supposes that the categories of thought are related to "things in themselves". It does not accept the Kantian view that a "thing in itself" is unknowable. In doing so, it returned to the metaphysics of the humanist science-ideal which, in Bavink, is accommodated to scholastic realism (*universalia in re et ante rem*). Cf. Bavink, op. cit. p.264. In opposition to Kant's transcendental idealism, it accepts the metaphysical conception of categories. Bavink thinks that the categories can only be deduced *aposteriori* from a scientific investigation of nature. He rejects the Kantian categories of relation as being in conflict with the present state of physics. Rather, he attributes to Kant's teleological view of nature a real not fictional meaning, regarding "nature in itself". Because of its starting point, "critical realism" can only underestimate and reject the naive experience of reality. We will return to this.

[18] Bernhard Bavink, op. cit., 5th edition, 1933, p.204. [Es handelt sich gar nicht zuerst darum, mit welchen Denkmethoden und Denkmitteln wir an die Dinge

Such a statement appears philosophically neutral. Nevertheless, it depends on a very particular presupposed view of the cosmos. Actually, it only makes sense if we adopt a representation of reality in which the universe is opposed to thought as a "world in itself" and in which reality is reduced to its pre-sensory aspects.[19] There is a connection between this view of the cosmos and Bavink's agreement with the epistemological conception of purely subjective characteristics or "secondary qualities": the objective sensory properties of colour, smell, taste, etc.[20]

Since cosmic reality, as universal and temporal coherence of meaning, cannot be reduced to its pre-sensory aspects, Bavink's vision of reality and his conception of the autonomy of science are false. In other words, if the physical aspect of the cosmos is not separated from the psychical sensory aspect and the logical aspect, and if the subject-object relations really exist, it makes no sense to speak of a "nature in itself".

---

heran zu gehen hatten, sondern darum, was bei diesem Herangehen, das wir ohne alle Erkenntnistheorie seit Jahrhunderten mit größtem Erfolge ausgeübt haben, herausgekommen ist und mutmaßlich weiter herauskommen wird. Die ganze Frage ist gar keine Frage der Erkenntnistheorie, sondern eine Frage der Ontologie, d.h. es kommt nicht darauf an, wie ich mir die Welt denken soll oder kann oder muß, sondern wie sie wirklich ist.] In the 9th edition (p.236), the first sentence is omitted, but the viewpoint itself is not changed in the least.

[19] Bavink does not think of "nature" and "reason" as two entirely distinct spheres which have nothing in common; he regards "nature" as "rational" in its ultimate foundation (op. cit., p.273ff). This is consistent with critical realism, particularly in its scholastic accommodation to the Augustinian doctrine of the divine Logos. It does not conflict with the metaphysical conception of the physical world "in itself", independent of the internal coherence of all its modal aspects in cosmic time. It requires only that in this physical world "in itself" the "divine Reason" – which is also the origin of human reason – must be expressed. According to this view, "nature in itself" should be "rational" in an absolute objective sense. This objective rationality of the physical order is completely independent of man's subjective logical function, and is not related to it. But the latter is related to the former.

[20] Bavink, *op. cit.*, p.59. Dooyeweerd is here speaking about "objective" characteristics insofar as they depend on a possible subjectively adequate perception or sensation. But Bavink does not discern the modal difference between electromagnetic physical waves with their different frequencies, and the objective sensory qualities which are founded on them. His opinion conforms to the current psycho-physiological and psychological conception which has lost sight of the modal structures of the different aspects.

The physical aspect of reality cannot be understood by scientific thought apart from a subjective notion of the relation between and the coherence of the different modalities within the cosmic order of time.

> 15. Experiments do not disclose a static reality that is independent of logical thought. The opening-process.

The physical aspect of reality does not present itself in sense-perception like the film in a camera: nor is it ordered "in itself" in accordance with theoretical categories. But because of the intermodal coherence of the meaning-aspects, physical phenomena have an objective function in the sensory aspect; in addition, they must be interpreted subjectively by scientific thought, which thereby logically opens them up. The question of how the physical aspect is to be understood in its relation to the other aspects of reality is thus very important.

The experimental method is essentially a method of isolation and abstraction. Experiments do not reveal the physical aspect of phenomena as something fixed and static in itself, and independent of theoretical thought; instead, they present us with an opening up of the meaning of this aspect which, in its cosmic coherence with the logical aspect, is enriched and unfolds all its meaning in the opening up of its logical anticipations under the direction of scientific thought. We have observed on numerous occasions already that every modal aspect of reality expresses its cosmic coherence with all the other aspects in its modal structure.

Hence, experiments are always the solution to theoretical problems that the scientist himself has raised and formulated.

The views expressed by Bavink that, over the course of the centuries, physics has been able to achieve significant results without the aid of any epistemology, is unworthy of such a thinker, who is well aware of the history of science and philosophy. The truth is that modern physics is based on epistemological presuppositions that have had to fight a fierce battle against the old Aristotelian conception, and these presuppositions have only been very gradually accepted since the days of Galileo and Newton. But many physicists conduct their enquiries without being aware of their philosophical implications, and they accept the foundations of their science as axioms. This kind of philosophical naiveté is extremely dangerous for a Christian scholar.

As for the acquisitions made by physics, the epistemology of Galileo and Newton implied a merely quantitative and functionalist view of reality. This view was not simply restricted to physics; it had to inject its content into the rationalistic humanist science-ideal.

Bavink's arguments in favour of the philosophical neutrality of physics, which at first sight seem conclusive, appear on reflection to be not wholly free of presuppositions that transcend the limits of science. Although he rejects apriori rationalism and the nominalist conventionalism of the Vienna Circle, his personal opinion regarding the philosophical neutrality of science depends on a specific philosophical view of reality that, from beginning to end, is dependent on an absolutisation of a functionalist view of natural science that leaves no room for naive experience.

> 16. The appeal to reality in scientific enquiry is never philosophically or religiously neutral. Historicism in science.

In scientific enquiry, the appeal to "reality" is never without a philosophical and religious apriori or presupposition. Take for now the example of *historical science*.

Ranke believes that the sole task of history is to establish how the events actually took place: *Wie es wirklich gewesen ist (What really happened?)*. But is there not a formidable obstacle in this little word *really (wirklich)?* A special science cannot grasp an event in its full reality. And history, like all the other sciences, can only examine one particular aspect of reality. That is why it groups and disposes the historical material by means of a theoretical modal analysis of temporal reality, without which it could not focus its attention on the historical aspect.[21] The science of history presupposes a theoretical view of reality – one that has a philosophical character – because its enquiry marks out the historical aspect in its theoretical coherence with the other aspects. Now, historicism is a view of reality that erases the boundaries between the different modalities and places all the other aspects of temporal reality under a common historical denominator. It has exercised a considerable influence on the foundations of scientific thought.[22]

In jurisprudence, the historical school has proclaimed that all positive law is an "historical phenomenon". This school has had a great influence on the idea of society and the theory of the State. But when the State is considered historically, it is its modal aspect of *power* the commands attention.[23] Hence comes to pass the idea that the State, in its *full reality*, is only an organisation of power. The empirical reality of the State is thus identified theoretically with its historical aspect. But it is obvious that the typical integral structure of the State, which cannot be reduced to its historical aspect of power, is then misconstrued. Neither can the State be understood as a purely juridical or economic or psychological phenomenon; its typical structure embraces all the modal aspects, and cannot be identified with any of them.

The attempt to consider the State only under its historical aspect of power, tied to a claim of philosophical and religious neutrality, resulted in a view that promoted an erroneous theoretical abstraction in place of the State as it actually exists.

17. The conflict between the mechanistic-functional, the neo-vitalist and the holist currents in modern biology.

Biology also presents numerous examples of a functionalist view of reality, in which a specific modal aspect is absolutised.

---

[21] The modal structure of the historical aspect was made the subject of an extensive study in *De Wijsbegeerte der Wetsidee*, Volume II.

[22] This is demonstrated by Dooyeweerd in Part 2 of the first volume of *De Wijsbegeerte der Wetsidee*.

[23] Dooyeweerd demonstrates in Volume II of *De Wijsbegeerte der Wetsidee* that *power* is the central moment of the modal structure of the *historical* aspect.

The theory of evolution has created a genetic mechanistic concept of space, which destroys the internal structural principles of individuality. It did so in all good conscience, maintaining that this in no way exceeded the limits of biological thought.

Modern biology is currently the theatre for an extremely intense controversy, resulting from different theoretical views of empirical reality. The *holistic* school has tried to reconcile the conflict between the *mechanistic* and *neo-vitalist* schools. The mechanistic school operated with a mechanistic concept of function, and has tried to reduce the modal aspect of organic life to the physical-chemical aspect, conceived in an obsolete mechanistic sense.

The *neo-vitalists*, with Driesch, saw that this method was incapable of dealing with all the materials examined by biology. Driesch, however, did not attack the mechanistic conception of matter, which was conceived as a purely physical-chemical entity enclosed in itself and completely determined by mechanical causality. He simply denied that organic life could be reduced to a physical-chemical material entity. But he did not see that organic life was nothing but a modal aspect of reality. He therefore maintained that organic life was reality in itself: an immaterial entelechy, a substance that would direct the material process without derogating from the principle of conservation of energy. He was trying to correct an absolutised concept of function by means of a concept of substance, in the pseudo-Aristotelian sense. But this "immaterial substance" was in turn only a new absolutism that blocked every genuine theoretical investigation of the typical temporal coherence of the biotic and physical-chemical aspects within the individuality-structure of a living organism.

Holism tried to overcome the antinomic dualism of Driesch's conception with a notion of structural totality. But the typical structures of individual totalities cannot be grasped by theoretical thought apart from a correct theoretical notion of the relations between their various modal aspects. The holistic school was devoid of such a notion. Therefore it could not help falling into the functionalist rut, and it developed a conception of the whole of a living organism, by erasing the modal boundaries of its various aspects. While the mechanistic school tried to reduce the biotic aspect to the physical-chemical aspect, holism went in the opposite direction.

The philosophical conflict we find down at the foundations of biology is encountered at the very heart of scientific problems.[24] Until now, it has been fought exclusively in the context of the humanistic conception of science. Can the Christian biologist take over a mechanistic, a vitalist or a holist conception of a living organism? Would he consider it more prudent to shelter behind the positivistic mask of neutrality? In fact, it is a quite naive[25] positivism that would allow the idea of philosophical neutrality to dominate the special sciences. Our conclusion is that the positivist conception of science is incompatible with the Christian cosmonomic-Idea.

18. Conclusion.

The moment a special science was born, it is forced to confront philosophical problems to do with the modal structure of the special aspect of reality that defines its field of enquiry. To say that science can ignore these issues, under the pretext that it is only engaged in the study of empirical phenomena, can have no meaning. Empirical phenomena have as many aspects as human experience itself. Thus, it cannot be the phenomena as such that constitute the scientific field of a particular enquiry. It must necessarily resort to the theoretical antithetic relation between the logical aspect of our thought and the non-logical aspects of experience in order to carry out the basic division of these fields of enquiry and to define the philosophical problems they entail.

For its part, philosophy cannot ignore the results of the scientific study of empirical phenomena, because it is precisely in these phenomena that the intermodal coherence between the

---

[24] Cf. Richard Woltereck, *Grundzüge einer allgemeinen Biologie*, Stuttgart, Ferdinand Enke Verlag, 1932. [Volume 1 of *Philosophie der lebendigen Wirklichkeit*. Dooyeweerd says that anyone who wants to acquire a sharp view of this state of affairs should read this work. I cannot find an English translation (2011).]

[25] [*naive*: in the sense that the thinker is ignorant of his own philosophical presuppositions.]

modal structures of the aspects of reality is *realised*. The typical individuality-structures can only be studied in their *empirical realisation*, provided that their modal aspects are properly distinguished.

Therefore, an interpenetration of philosophy and the sciences is inevitable. The task of philosophy is both to focus on the philosophical problems of the special sciences, and to account for the content of naive experience.

Such is our provisional assessment of the relationship between science and Christian philosophy, which we have only considered here in the framework of our transcendental critique of scientific thought.

Our purpose was to show that in light of the biblical ground-motive of the Christian religion, the humanist division between science and philosophy is inadmissible and that, in fact, even from the humanist point of view, this division was incapable of withstanding a serious immanent critique.[26]

CßCßCß

---

[26] The interdependence of Christian philosophy and science can only be explained in a truly concrete manner after the development of the General Theory of the Law-Spheres and the Typical Individuality-Structure. For law and sociology, Herman Dooyeweerd has demonstrated this interdependence in his *Encyclopedia of the Science of Law* (5 vols. projected), trans. Alan M. Cameron, Lewiston, NY, The Edwin Mellen Press, 2002.For biological problems, refer to the *Reformation and Scholasticism in Philosophy*, Volume II, trans. Lynn Bolik et al, Grand Rapids, Paideia Press, 2011. In addition, numerous specialist researches on various sciences have been written by scholars and specialists who adhere to the Philosophy of the Law-Idea.

Conclusion

A Reformed philosophy. . . is it either useful or necessary?

We could have asked this question in our Introduction, and tried to answer it in general terms. But is not the best answer to that question (oft-asked and debated in our Protestant circles) already provided by the development of the various chapters of the transcendental critique of theoretical thought that we have just described? If we were to follow Herman Dooyeweerd's thought-processes step by step, who in Protestant circles – and in Catholic and immanence-philosophy circles, for that matter – would not understand its potential, its usefulness, and its necessity? The positive exposition of the Philosophy of the Law-Idea will also, where necessary, provide it with countless proofs.

In fact, the question of a *Reformed* philosophy is not viewed in the same way by all of Protestantism.

For the section of Protestantism regarded as "independent" in its liberal and rationalist forms, which elevates the religious consciousness of the individual to the supreme norm, the question of a philosophy does not even arise. There is only a completely philosophical religion or a completely religious philosophy, which receives its impetus from the Jesus of history, and sometimes (but not always) the prophets and apostles. "Its dogmatics", said Auguste Lecerf, "will only be the intellectual and synthetic translation of religious or mystical emotions of the individual soul. If it is rationalist, philosophy will be what it is for scholastic Catholics. If it is intuitionist, it will be what it is for some independents, Bergson for example. If it is critical, it will be what it was for Kant or Renouvier, and so on. If it wants to be thinking itself, and we do not see by what principle it could be denied the right to think, independent or liberal Protestantism can hardly do other than philosophise."[1]

The proponents of dialectical theology are not unanimous: some firmly reject any possibility of a Christian philosophy; others accept the idea, but only in a negative and critical sense, as a philosophical form of *transcendent* "religious criticism". This is precisely what Etienne Gilson quite wrongly attributed to "Calvinism" when he wrote: "The essence of Calvinism, on this point, can be considered, in a sense, as analogous to that of Kantianism, in that at least it is essentially critical. Calvinism is a religious disqualification of the fallen natural order as the criticism of Kant is a scientific disqualification of the meta-physical order."[2] Still others restrict its positive significance to the problems of ethics and anthropology.

In addition, while not all can be fitted into the category of "evangelical" or one of those sects who, for reasons we do not want to consider at present, are vigorously hostile to the whole idea of a Christian philosophy, a Christian science, etc., many Christians – and even Christian scholars – can see no use for or need of a Christian philosophy. They believe that the Word of God ought to be sufficient, that God gives us in Scripture a sufficiently general cosmological view of the totality and unity of created reality. How could philosophy sit comfortably alongside Scripture? Do not philosophical systems occupy the place among unbelievers that Revelation does among us? Is not what is being sought in philosophical systems already available to us in Reformed dogmatic theology? Does not the development of a Reformed philosophy lead to the construction of a new dogmatics under other forms?

---

[1] Cf. Auguste Lecerf, *Le Protestantisme et la philosophie*, Bulletin de la Société calviniste, No. 20, June 1932, and in *Etudes calvinistes*, p.108, Delachaux et Niestlé, 1949. [Also in : Auguste Lecerf, *Etudes calvinistes*, Aix-en-Provence, Editions Kerygma, 1999, p.108. This is a digital reprint of the 1949 edition. The wording in this edition is slightly different from that quoted above from the 1932 Bulletin.]

[2] Etienne Gilson, *Christianisme et Philosophie*, Paris, J. Vrin, p.71. [English trans.: Etienne Gilson, *Christianity and Philosophy,* trans. Illtyd Trethowan and F. J. Sheed, London, Sheed & Ward (for Institute of Mediaeval Studies, Toronto), 1939].

To answer these questions, it is not enough simply to draw attention to the fact that, down through the centuries, renowned Christian thinkers have actually attempted to develop a philosophy, especially a philosophy of religion.[3] In our view, the above groups ignore facts which otherwise impose themselves on the Reformed Calvinist religious consciousness with the force of a veritable divine injunction. This is because the Word of God is "like fire, like a hammer that breaks the rock in pieces" (Jer. 23: 29). The Word of God frees us, in principle, from the tyranny of the prejudices and presuppositions of unregenerate apostate man, and protects us against the uncertainties, contradictions, antinomies, and intellectual anarchy with which both immanence-philosophy and an "independent" Protestantism that depends on it wrestle. It does this by changing our hearts of stone into hearts of flesh, when it implants in them the incorruptible seed it contains and regenerates us; it does it by subduing us to its sovereign authority in Jesus Christ, the new Root of humanity and cosmos, and Supreme Judge and touchstone of all thought and wisdom; it does it by redirecting all the "sources of life" that spring from our renewed heart. It also frees us from all those prejudices and their consequences that do not comport with the Word of God, taken in its entirety and unity, and from all those that appeal to the Bible while maintaining a dualistic conception of the world.

Our situation as Christians – the diverse callings we receive from God to glorify him in every domain – imposes upon us, whether we like it or not, and short of exempting a number of areas of reality and life from the Lordship of

---

[3] Recently, the Dutch professor Herman Bavinck in his *Wijsbegeerte der Openbaringen*, Kampen, J. H. Kok, 1908 [English trans.: *Philosophy of Revelation*, trans. Geerhardus Vos et al, London, Longmans Green, 1909, later reprinted by Eerdmans (1953) and Baker Book House (1980)]; Auguste Lecerf in his *Introduction à la Dogmatique réformée*, Paris, Editions Je Sers, which devotes two volumes to the exposition of a philosophy of religion (Vol. I : *De la nature de la connaissance religieuse*, 1931 ; Vol. II : *Du fondement et de la spécification de la connaissance religieuse*, 1938). [English trans.: Auguste Lecerf, *An Introduction to Reformed Dogmatics*, trans. S. L-H., London, Lutterworth Press, 1949. Both volumes of the French edition are included in this translation.]

Christ – a genuine and original labour of thought, putting to work every human resource and the gifts we receive through common and special grace. It is our responsibility to be good thinkers, good philosophers, good scientists and good scholars, reflecting, each in his own way, on the unity and meaning of temporal reality, and seeking to achieve a scientific vision of totality that honours the Lord of the world.

Holy Scripture does not obviate the need to develop a philosophy, let alone a science. The Word of God, taken as it stands, is not itself a science; it is *above* every science; it is *valid* for every science that seeks the truth; and it is the *standard*, the divine *measuring rod*, whose task it is to give scientific thought also its direction. This *normative* directing does not nullify the task; quite the opposite, it evokes it. In his Word, God does not bar the way to the scientific study of his works.

The Word of God acting within imposes religious aspirations on me that make philosophy a *vital* necessity. To admire, to love, to glorify God in his work, the Calvinist both desires and seeks to understand the *meaning* of the universe and of God's *works*. He cannot escape from this psychologically binding necessity: "Thou shalt love the Lord the God *with all thy mind*" (Matt. 22: 37). To promote faith in God's sovereignty over every sphere of thought; to overthrow, in apostolic parlance, every fortress that stands against God and to bring every thought captive to the feet of Christ; to purge philosophy and science of their apostate and pagan elements, just as the Reformation purified that part of the Church that is lined up behind the principle it proclaimed; these demand that the practice of thinking philosophically be not only a right but a *religious duty*.[4]

However, the results of a Christian philosophy are not explicitly stated in Scripture. The Calvinist is in the position of a student who, whilst having a worldview and knowing roughly the solution to the problem, still has work to do if he

---

[4] Auguste Lecerf, *Etudes calvinistes*, Aix-en-Provence, Editions Kerygma, 1999, p.111.

is to reach this solution intellectually and scientifically and to justify it, that is, if he is to have a philosophy. The solution to actual philosophical problems will only be found in struggle and hard work. So God also calls his children to devote their whole mind and thinking to science and philosophy. He also wants to receive the homage due to him from a philosophy which, having the scientific study of the world for its task, is *guided* His Word alone. Christian philosophy seeks to achieve even greater light by scientifically searching the wisdom of God as manifested in his works by the cosmic order of law; it also seeks to better understand the truth of the meaning of created reality. But it also wields a sword to fight – on its own ground and with its own weapons – the spirit of the world which, powerfully entrenched behind its scientific apparatus and despite being a "carnal mind", increasingly tries to impose itself on the Church of Jesus Christ; and in doing so it will unmask the lie into which it has strayed.

"*No genuine self-knowledge* – and hence no real philosophy – *is possible unless our heart is enlightened by divine revelation*", we have said. Such an assertion raises the question of the relation between divine Revelation or Holy Scripture, on the one hand, and philosophy on the other.

To be Christian and Reformed, philosophy must first of all keep in close contact with Holy Scripture. Calvin explicitly taught that Scripture, as the Word of God, has authority over all of human life and no area, not even philosophy, either ought to be or can be withdrawn from it; God's Revelation cannot be rejected with impunity. The Calvinist believes in the Fall and the total depravity of human nature (taking "total" in the broader sense of the term) and so also of reason; he is an *abnormalist*. "If the light that is in thee be darkness, how great is that darkness" (Matt. 6: 23). It is hence impossible to think scientifically about the works of God in the universe of which He is Creator and in which He reveals His wisdom, or to "contemplate the heavens and the earth, to consider all that is found therein, and to understand that God made man from nothing and created the whole human race likewise" (II Macc.

7: 28), other than by the light of the Word of God, which illuminates or regenerates the mind. "In thy light shall we see light." (Ps. 36: 9).

It is quite certain, on the other hand, that Scripture is not a textbook of philosophy, nor does it purport to be the textbook of any science. The Word of God is not a science; it is the revelation of His promised grace in Jesus Christ, addressed to mankind so that mankind could know him in Jesus Christ, and could love and serve Him. For its part, science is always *the result of human activity*. It is therefore fallible and prone to error; which means that neither science nor philosophy can be based solely on Scripture.

For these two reasons, at least, divine revelation can never solve on our behalf an essentially *immanent* philosophical problem. It addresses itself to the *religious root* of our existence as a whole; and so also to the root of philosophical thinking, which then reflects on created reality. But since divine revelation in its religious fullness *transcends* philosophical thought, it can *never* solve any *immanent* philosophical or scientific problem. The task of Revelation in Jesus Christ will be to direct our philosophical thought towards the true totality of meaning and the true Origin. It will give us guiding principles, key ideas, and standards that have to be positivised and explained, in every sphere of temporal reality, by means of a logic that operates with a new principle, that of the excluded antinomy. In doing so, it will resolve the drama of philosophical thought which, as *philosophical* thought, must have this direction, which it can *never* find *by* itself or *in* itself. The Christian religion does not penetrate philosophical thought from outside, like a *deus ex machina*, using Revelation to impose authoritarian solutions to philosophical problems on it; rather, because it regenerates the heart, the focal point of our selfhood, it is not without influence on thought, which is naturally separated by sin from the fullness of meaning. *From within*, via the heart, *it awakens this thought to a new* life full of elation and to a new blossoming in harmony with all our other activities. Though philosophical thought *as such* can never account for it, the movement towards the totality of meaning and the Origin which divine

Revelation stamps on our philosophical thinking penetrates this thinking inwardly in all its thought-processes, in the way it poses its problems, in its notions of subjectivity, law, and the structure of reality, in the way its forms concepts, in its explanation of the meaning of naive experience and of theoretical synthesis, in its philosophical notion of the problem of time, etc.

Finally, philosophy must not be confused with dogmatics. Dogmatics is a science that can never be changed into Christian philosophy. It is only the branch of a special science: theology. It develops the dogma of the Church scientifically, it meditates on its Confession of Faith scientifically, and it coordinates revealed Truth – as the Church understands it – systematically. It forms a synthesis of the mysteries of Revelation, carried out by a regenerated reason which acknowledges that faith is the condition of intelligence. Dogmatics is the science of faith by faith. The Christian religion has as its primary purpose to inform us how we are to serve and glorify God by our faith and our works, and as its subordinate purpose to teach us the way of salvation. Dogmatics has as its subject God, man and the world: God, as one who ought to be worshipped and glorified; man and the world, as religiously dependent on Him to bring them to their final destiny, whether lost or saved.

The other sciences and philosophy set out to understand creaturely reality in order to master it, in accordance with the royal vocation man received at the time of his creation. God and his sovereignty come under scrutiny only insofar as they can help us to understand the cosmic order it is concerned with: the meaning of the aspects of reality and the totality of meaning of the universe. As Auguste Lecerf said: "God is the first cause, the logical cement of reality, and the ultimate driving force of the totality of the real."[5]

Through its biblical doctrine of the eternal and immutable pre-ordination of all things, of the creation and preservation of

---

[5] Auguste Lecerf, *Etudes calvinistes*, Aix-en-Provence, Editions Kerygma, 1999, p.111.

the world, and of the royal calling for the world, Calvinism affirms a cosmos and a cosmic order of law, and gives philosophy a field of its own distinct from dogmatics, namely that of being theoretical thought applied to the totality of meaning of our temporal cosmos.

Dogmatics must not overstep its boundaries by taking on the task of philosophy, or throw itself headlong into the study of the relationships and groups that exist in the temporal world and that are outside its purview. The theologian applies his regenerated and illuminated reason to the scientific interpretation of his text, which is positive Revelation. The dogma of the Church is founded only on the Divine Truth that is revealed in Scripture. Philosophy applies believing reason to the study of his text, which is the totality of temporal reality. Hence, philosophy cannot provide a foundation for religion, as central sphere of human existence, or for theology. "Man, with all his acuteness, is as stupid for obtaining of himself a knowledge of the mysteries of God, as an ass is unqualified for understanding musical harmonies". [6]

Ultimately, philosophy cannot *found* anything; it *draws conclusions*, or tries to do so. He whom Revelation has stimulated with a need to understand will philosophise not in order to found his faith but to glorify God before man, not in order to save himself (he is already saved), or to know (for he already knows, by faith), but in order to understand and glorify God with his intellect as he does with his faith. *Ego, in Christo regeneratus, ETIAM COGITANS ex Christo vivo.* [7]

Though the domain of dogmatics is quite different from the domain of philosophy, neither of these sciences can ever do without the other. Reformed philosophy which, in all its fundamental conceptions, continually takes account of Holy Scripture, will never give up being faithful to Scripture or reflecting on the Church's Creed. Hence, it cannot be indiff-

---

[6] John Calvin, *Commentary on I Corinthians* 1:20. Opera Calvini, XLIX, 325. [...et homo cum toto suo acumine perinde est stupidus ad intelligenda per se Dei mysteria atque asinus ineptus est ad symphoniam.]

[7] [I, who am regenerated in Christ, live by Christ even in my thinking.]

erent to the scientific development of this Confession of Faith in its dogmatics. And dogmatics, for its part, can function successfully only if it does not take its presuppositions from immanence-philosophy, but from a philosophy that is itself specifically Reformed.

A radical Christian philosophy will not be an immanence-philosophy adorned with biblical texts. Neither will it be a theology under the guise of a science. It will be none other than a radical reformation of philosophical thought.

It is actually the kind of reformation that the Christian religion – which reveals to us the transcendent religious roots of human existence in all its functions – must take on board; thereby, it exposes the *proton pseudos* (πϱοτον ψευδος), the principal lie of immanence-philosophy. The biblical statement: "Out of the *heart* are the issues of life" (Prov. 4: 23) should, if properly understood, bring about a radical revolution in the religious starting point of philosophical thought.

Because immanence-philosophy in actual fact seeks transcendence in the immanence of theoretical thought, because it is normalist[8] and autonomist[9], and because such an attitude of thought can arise only from the rebellious religious root of human existence, the Christian religion (abnormalist[10] and theonomist[11]) and thus reformed philosophy find themselves forced to engage in a relentless battle against the principles of immanence-philosophy.

Based on the little we now know of Herman Dooye-weerd's thought through our overview of his transcendental criticism, we can offer some provisional remarks.

---

[8] [*normalist*: one who does not believe in the Fall and especially not in the noetic effects of sin.]

[9] [*autonomist*: one who holds that there is no law-giver outside the universe, which is a law unto itself.]

[10] [*abnormalist*: one who believes in the Fall and especially in the noetic effects of sin.]

[11] [*theonomist*: one who hold that all genuine laws, including structural laws, are imposed from outside the universe, generally by a God.]

No one can deny the amazing acuity or the singular penetration of thought of the Master of Amsterdam. He at once
gets to the heart of the matter. Whether we like it or not, we
have been constrained to walk with him and, however un-
familiar we might be with his principles and method, we are
astonished at how far we have travelled and the powerful
investigative tools he has equipped us with in his reflexive
critique. This becomes clear when we read a particular book or
study, dealing with the same problem, and which had formerly
been a joy to read. When we now come back to it, we find
ourselves surprised at how superficial and disappointing the
thinking of otherwise thoroughgoing Christian men is, including those whose calling it is to philosophise. I refer here only
those who move in Calvinist Reformed circles. To give a few
examples: there are the studies published in *Foi chrétienne et
Université (Christian Faith and the University)*[12]; Roger Mehl's
book, *La condition du philosophe chrétien (The Condition of the
Christian Philosopher)*[13], some recent studies published by the
*Institut Œcuménique de Bossey (The Ecumenical Institute at Bossey,
Switzerland)*[14], etc. We find that beneath a sometimes brilliant
appearance and a remarkable display of erudition, and *despite a
multitude of penetrating observations and clear-sighted intuitions* that
reveal with what seriousness and meticulous concern many
thinkers have addressed this problem, their thinking remains
"on the surface" and never gets to the heart of the problems.
Without a robust method, this type of thinking is unable to
give a philosophical and scientific development to some
evident demands on it that the Christian faith is content to
accept as inescapable. It eventually dissolves itself by refusing
to consider the problem of a philosophy having a Christian
structure, which it regards as without substance, in order to
simply fall back on a philosophy of *intent*, on the requirement
of the philosopher, not of philosophy. In the best case, we have
a transcendent critique but no transcendental thought.

---

[12] *Cahiers de Foi et Vie et du Semeur*, 1939.

[13] *Série théologique de l'actualité protestante.* Delachaux et Niestlé, 1947.

[14] *Revue de Théologie et de Philosophie*, Lausanne, 1955, II.

There are, more often than not, very serious and sometimes very painful reasons for this, which our transcendental critique has already partially unmasked, but which we are not concerned with investigating right now. We cannot help thinking that the *Philosophy of the Law-Idea* is highly suitable for extricating from their difficulties those thinkers who, though their thought currently lacks consistency, want to be constructive but have not yet got the means to raise awareness among others that they still have a long way to go if they are to consider in a really serious way what the Word of God demands, namely, the Lordship of Jesus Christ over all areas of life, a Christian attitude, a Christian thought, a Christian method, and a Christian logic.

In his analysis of immanence-philosophy's features and in his insight into its supra-theoretical religious presuppositions and the implications of the transcendental guiding Ideas of philosophical and scientific thought, Herman Dooyeweerd has drawn our attention, in a really impressive way and with poignant intensity, to the extent of the corruption of human reason by sin. He has also made us aware of the tragic struggle within immanence-philosophy that has locked itself in a passionate and titanic, but alas unsuccessful and disappointing, effort to justify its "autonomy" and "neutrality", and to discover and attain the meaning of this life and everything so that it can find a solution, however tenuous and weak, to the anxiety of the human heart that is "without God and without hope in the world" (Ephes. 2: 12). For those who read him in the light of the Word of God, there is a tragic beauty and grandeur at the heart of Herman Dooyeweerd's exposition, because he unmasks the last hiding place, the wealth of ingenuity, and the most subtle evasions of a futile thinking that is prisoner of its own dogmas and autonomy which, far from liberating it, actually crush it and keep bringing it back helpless to its starting point. But there is also the bright hope of a path opened up: the total dedication of our selfhood and all our functions and their activities to the service of God the Creator and Christ the Saviour in the communion of the Holy Spirit, and the possibility of freeing Christian thought from all accommodation and compromise.

In our view, Herman Dooyeweerd's work is in the most authentic style of the spirit of Calvinism, or just Christianity. When we consider:

a.   the notion of time that restores the boundary lines of creation;

b.   the place of God's law and the cosmic order of time;

c.   the rejection of every substantialist notion of being;

d.   the focus so strongly marked on the creaturely mode of being as dependent and heteronomous of all temporal reality, including our personality and human selfhood;

e.   the serious consideration of the fall and sin, but also of redemption in Jesus Christ, the prominent place given to our Lord, the new root and fullness of meaning of humanity and cosmos;

f.   the sovereignty that nothing escapes;

g.   the honour paid to the intelligence and creative wisdom of God Almighty who created and "ordered all things in measure, number, and weight" (Wisdom of Solomon 11:20)[15], and that leads Christian theoretical thought to apply so fruitfully the principle of the excluded antinomy;

h.   the principles of internal sovereignty and internal universality that so amply confirm the cosmic order of law and the interdependence of the various modalities of meaning as heteronomous refractions of a totality;

---

[15] [ἀλλὰ πάντα μέτρῳ καὶ ἀριθμῷ καὶ σταθμῷ διέταξας. A pivotal feature of the medieval worldview, this verse was often quoted, even by St Augustine. Cf. Nicholas Cusanus (1401-1464), *De docta ignorantia* (Of Learned Ignorance) II.13. Admirabili itaque ordine elementa constituta sunt per Deum, qui omnia in numero, pondere et mensura creavit. Numerus pertinet ad arithmeticam, pondus ad musicam, mensura ad geometriam: "And so, God, who created all things in number, weight, and measure, arranged the elements in an admirable order. Number applies to arithmetic, weight to music, and measure to geometry."]

i.   the restoration of a genuine notion of subject that doesn't strip reality of the wealth of subject-object relations it deploys;

j.   the respect accorded to naive thought and experience, and the real rehabilitation of man this entails to the same status before God and in life as the thinker and scientist, as being placed in and living in the same universe;

k.   the denial of an axiological hierarchy of worldview and philosophy or science;

l.   the place accorded to the sciences, which also must serve and glorify God who gives them their meaning, etc.;

all this seems to us authentically Christian and Calvinist, and translates into scientific terms the spirit of the Reformation, which pursues its work tirelessly.[16]

It is fashionable in France, where almost nothing is known of the Calvinist literature, to consider "Calvinism" and "Calvinists" as reactionary and unable to fit into the context of contemporary life or cope with the "demands" and "aspirations" of modern man. It flits around after novelties of all kinds, but actually goes nowhere. For accommodation and compromise – which is all these "novelties" are, that claim to refloat a sinking Christianity – don't unfortunately point the way forward. The superficial judgements here brought against Calvinism are possible only on account of the considerable ignorance and misunderstanding of its impressive literature that many, because of their preconceived opinions, don't seek out, while it remains inaccessible to all those who, with no eye to God's glory, refuse to make an effort to read what is in foreign languages, especially in Dutch.

We believe the *relevance* of Calvinism, in the broadest sense, as well as of its worldview and for philosophy and science, is greater now than at any time since the Reformation.

---

[16] [This long sentence, which in the original begins with the words "The notion of time...", has been broken up into a list and the introductory "When we consider..." has been added to make it readable in English. It still contains around 380 words!]

Some of its principles, which have been labelled as "backward", are now seen, after a humiliating defeat for the supporters of immanence-philosophy, to be in the vanguard of progress, both in the natural sciences and in philosophy, logic, and the other cultural sciences, including theology.

The *Philosophy of the Law-Idea* is expected to play a prominent role in the development of Reformed thought in all fields of activity, reflection and human enquiry. It is not simply a matter of reforming philosophy as such, but of actually reforming the philosophy of sciences and the sciences themselves, including theology.

The latter is too often invaded by false problems and questions that are quite foreign to the spirit of Christianity and to the Word of God. They come from the rise of a way of thinking, and of concepts, issues and problems that appertain to immanence-philosophy, and they arise as often as not as the crippling, regressive and nimble elements of a schismatic power of which the history of Christianity affords us regrettable proof. It is true that Protestant theology has sometimes been in such a sorry state because of its dependence on immanence-philosophy that it could appear to be relatively healthy at such a time of change of influence: for example, under the influence of existentialism – which, by the way, is often regarded as being itself due to the influence of Christian thinkers.

We have alluded to the enormous effort our Reformers made to free theology from Scholastic problems and ways of thinking. But in their references to the Fathers, they were not always watchful that the latter had not, in the systematic expression of their thought, engaged in accommodation and consciously or otherwise accepted the path of compromise. Secondly, we have highlighted the failure, at the time of the Reformation and during the seventeenth century, of a reformation of philosophical thought, which to some degree returned Reformed theology to the ways and methods of scholasticism and accommodation.

We are convinced that the Philosophy of the Law-Idea can and should render outstanding service to all disciplines in theology. A purification of its vocabulary is needed, even in

Reformed dogmatics; it must also bring about a change in the way problems are raised, even the simplification or elimination of several of them, and this in the greatest fidelity to the message the Word of God alone. It must also do this for the greater good of ecumenism. For, divisions and sects have more often than not emerged in the course of history on issues that have no bearing on Revelation itself or on religious matters. Rather they were the consequence of doctrines whose development was only possible as a result of the intrusion of unbiblical, meta-theological, supra-theoretical and immanent grounds, endowed from the start with all the authority of the Word of God, and finally identified with it. The Word of God, for example, reveals every "Why?" we need to ask, with all their answers. But when theologians start using reason to discover the "How?" they usually cease to be theologians who respect the limits imposed by the revelation on human knowledge and become philosophers, with all the pitfalls and dangers of the philosophies they espouse.

When a start is made by means of a transcendental self-reflecting critique, based on the religious ground-motive of Christianity we have described, to expunge from theology issues not relevant to it – because they depend on religious ground-motives alien to the spirit of Christianity – much will already have been done to promote a *Christian* ecumenism. And while this self-reflecting critique will also lead some detractors to recognise the supra-theoretical and non-Christian prejudices which underpin their *dogmatic* positions, it will undoubtedly not always persuade them to abandon them (because other interests are at stake) but it will finally allow everyone to share things and to recognise countless differences that are not attributable to the Word of God which is nothing less than a nose of wax, let alone the angle from which it is considered. Fruitful discussions will then be possible. The authority of the Word of God, if possible, will triumph; the unbiblical dogmatism of the theologies will lose ground; but our hearts will gain in honesty, clarity and objectivity, as well as in mutual respect, because we no longer confuse *supra-*

theoretical and extra-biblical prejudices with *revealed doctrines*. There will be no more anathemas.

This leads us in concluding to stress the social and ecclesiastical value of Calvinism, which Herman Dooyeweerd so brilliantly brings to light in the field of philosophy. In our opinion, the position of Calvinism is always that of a rallying point. With its remarkable soundness, it is always and in everything as far removed from the extreme right as from the extreme left, because in it truth is still a real living equilibrium, an *et tamen* (and yet) in the fight of faith that is constantly subjected to the Word on the principle of the analogy of faith. Therein lies the greatness of Calvinism, but therein too lies what makes it so difficult to be and remain genuinely Calvinist or simply Christian. From a merely human perspective, in respect of intelligence, sensibility and reason – even when regenerated and enlightened – I firmly believe that true Calvinism is the most uncomfortable position possible. It demands unremittingly the struggle and victory of faith. Both come with the signal grace of God, and we can neither abandon the fight nor fail to accept the victory with thanksgiving and according to God's irrevocable promise.

The deep, charitable and irenic distinction highlighted by Herman Dooyeweerd – which is necessarily part of the structure of thought – between *philosophical* judgements and *apriori supra-theoretical* judgements calls for the mutual understanding and cooperation of all men of goodwill who are unperturbed by the unmasking of their religious starting point and who are filled with a rich future. On the other hand, it has the merit, or according to others the disadvantage, of making the opposition between religious ground-motives more acute, and probably irrevocable. But this irreducible character comes not from us, but from the religious choice of men and from the Word of God. It is also this distinction which, by stripping us of any dogmatic exclusivism, and because we have a genuine theology of sin, enables us to understand the sinner and love him though a sinner, and pushes us to a fruitful cooperation with all men of good will. But this it is also which defines the boundaries we cannot cross, by remitting every judgement to God.

Herman Dooyeweerd deserves our unbounded gratitude for opening up for us a new path.

To work, then, so that every *thought,* and above all our own thought, might be brought into captivity to the obedience of Christ, the Alpha and the Omega, the Beginning and the End of all creation which, with ourselves and all our faculties, subsist only in Him, through Him and *for* Him.

CℨCℨCℨ

Appendix 1

Schematic Table of the Law-Spheres in the Cosmic Order of Time

Boundary between God and the cosmos
■■■■■■■■■■■■■■■■■■■■■■■■■■■■■■■

15	Pistic or faith sphere
14	Ethical, moral
13	Juridical, legal
12	Aesthetic; harmony
11	Economic; frugality
10	Social
9	Symbolic; lingual
8	Historical; cultural
7	Logical; analytical
6	Psychical; sensory; feeling
5	Biotic; organic
4	Physical; energy
3	Kinematic; movement
2	Spatial; continuous extension
1	Numerical; discrete quantity

What we have here is neither a hierarchical order nor an order of greater or lesser complexity, but only an architectonic order of before and after, similar to the colours of white light refracted through a prism.

Appendix 2

Glossary of Dooyeweerdian Terms

The following glossary of Dooyeweerd's technical terms and neologisms is reproduced and edited by Colin Wright, with the kind permission of its author, Dr Daniel F.M. Strauss, General Editor, *The Collected Works of Herman Dooyeweerd*. It is taken from H. Dooyeweerd, *Christian Philosophy and the Meaning of History* (Edwin Mellen Press, NY, 1996).

⊰⊱⊰⊱⊰⊱

The following glossary of Dooyeweerd's technical terms and neologisms is reproduced and edited by Daniel F. M. Strauss, with the permission of its author, Albert M. Wolters, from C. T. McIntire, ed., *The Legacy of Herman Dooyeweerd: Reflections on Critical Philosophy in the Christian Tradition* (Lanham, MD, 1985), pp.167-171.

This glossary of Herman Dooyeweerd's terms is an adapted version of the one published in L. Kalsbeek, *Contours of a Christian Philosophy* (Toronto: Wedge, 1975). It does not provide exhaustive technical definitions but gives hints and pointers for a better understanding. Entries marked with an asterisk are those terms which are used by Dooyeweerd in a way which is unusual in English-speaking philosophical contexts and are, therefore, a potential source of misunderstanding. Words or phrases in small caps and beginning with a capital letter refer to other entries in this glossary.

⋆ Analogy (see **Law-Sphere**) – Collective name for a **Retrocipation** or an **Anticipation**.

⋆ Anticipation – An **Analogy** within one **Modality** referring to a later modality. An example is "efficiency", a meaning-moment which is found within the historical modality, but which points forward to the later economic modality. Contrast with **Retrocipation**.

⋆ Antinomy – Literally "conflict of laws" (from Greek *anti*, "against", and *nomos*, "law"). A logical contradiction arising out of a failure to distinguish the different kinds of law valid in different **Modalities**. Since ontic laws do not conflict (Principium Exclusae Antinomiae), an antinomy is always a logical sign of ontological reductionism.

⋆ Antithesis – Used by Dooyeweerd (following Abraham Kuyper) in a specifically religious sense to refer to the fundamental spiritual opposition between the kingdom of God and the kingdom of darkness. See Galatians 5: 17. Since this is an opposition between regimes, not realms, it runs through every department of human life and culture, including philosophy and the academic enterprise as a whole, and through the heart of every believer as he or she struggles to live a life of undivided allegiance to God.

Aspect – A synonym for **Modality**.

Cosmonomic idea – Dooyeweerd's own English rendering of the Dutch term *wetsidee*. Occasionally equivalents are "transcendental ground idea" or "transcendental basic idea". The intention of this new term is to bring to expression that there exists an unbreakable coherence between God's *law* (*nomos*) and created reality (*cosmos*) factually subjected to God's law.

Dialectic – In Dooyeweerd's usage: an unresolvable tension, within a system or line of thought, between two logically irreconcilable polar positions. Such a dialectical tension is characteristic of each of the three non-Christian **Ground-motives** which Dooyeweerd sees as having dominated Western thought.

* Enkapsis (enkaptic) – A neologism borrowed by Dooye-weerd from the Swiss biologist Heidenhain, and derived from the Greek *enkaptein*, "to swallow up". The term refers to the structural interlacements which can exist between things, plants, animals, and societal structures which have their own internal structural principle and independent qualifying funct-ion. As such, enkapsis is to be clearly distinguished from the part-whole relation, in which there is a common internal structure and qualifying function.

Factual Side – General designation of whatever is *subjected* to the **Law-side** of creation (see **Subject-side**).

Founding function – The earlier of the two modalities which characterise certain types of structural wholes. The other is called the **Guiding-function**. For example, the founding function of the family is the biotic modality.

* Gegenstand – A German word for "object", used by Dooy-eweerd as a technical term for a modality when abstracted from the coherence of time and opposed to the analytical function in the theoretical attitude of thought, thereby estab-lishing the Gegenstand-relation. Gegenstand is therefore the technically precise word for the object of **Science**, while "object" itself is reserved for the objects of **Naive Experience**.

Ground-motive – The Dutch term *grondmotief*, used by Dooyeweerd in the sense of fundamental motivation, driving force. He distinguished four basic ground-motives in the hist-ory of Western civilisation: (1) form and matter, which domin-ated pagan Greek philosophy; (2) nature and grace, which underlay medieval Christian synthesis thought (3) nature and freedom, which has shaped the philosophies of modern times; and (4) creation, fall, and redemption, which lies at the root of a radical and integrally scriptural philosophy.

Guiding function – The highest subject function of a struct-ural whole (e.g. stone, animal, business enterprise, or state). Except in the case of humans, this function is also said to **qualify** the structural whole. It is called the guiding function because it "guides" or "leads" its earlier functions. For example, the guiding function of a plant is the biotic. The physical function of a plant (as studied, e.g. by biochemistry) is different from physical functioning elsewhere because of its being "guided" by the biotic. Also called "leading function".

* **Heart** – The concentration point of human existence; the supratemporal focus of all human temporal functions; the religious root unity of humans. Dooyeweerd says that it was his rediscovery of the biblical idea of the heart as the central religious depth dimension of human multifaceted life which enabled him to wrestle free from neo-Kantianism and phenomenology. The Scriptures speak of this focal point also as "soul", "spirit", and "inner man". Philosophical equivalents are Ego, I, I-ness, and Selfhood. It is the heart in this sense which survives death, and it is by the religious redirection of the heart in regeneration that all human temporal functions are renewed.

* **Immanence Philosophy** – A name for all non-Christian philosophy, which tries to find the ground and integration of reality *within* the created order. Unlike Christianity, which acknowledges a transcendent Creator above all things, immanence philosophy of necessity absolutises some feature or aspect of creation itself.

* **Individuality-structure** – This term represents arguably one of the most difficult concepts in Dooyeweerd's philosophy. Coined in both Dutch and English by Dooyeweerd himself it has led sometimes to serious misunderstandings amongst scholars. Over the years there have been various attempts to come up with an alternate term, some of which are described below, but in the absence of a consensus it was decided to leave the term the way it is.

It is the general name or the characteristic law (order) of concrete things, as given by virtue of creation. Individuality-structures belong to the law-side of reality. Dooyeweerd uses the term individuality-structure to indicate the applicability of a structural order *for* the existence of *individual* entities. Thus the *structural laws* for the state, for marriage, for works of art, for mosquitoes, for sodium chloride, and so forth are called individuality-structures. The idea of an individual whole is determined by an individuality-structure which precedes the theoretical analysis of its modal functions. The identity of an individual whole is a relative unity in a multiplicity of functions. (See **Modality**.) Van Riessen prefers to call this law for entities an *identity-structure*, since as such it guarantees the persistent identity of all entities (*Wijsbegeerte*, Kampen 1970, p.158). In his work (*Alive, An Enquiry into the Origin and Meaning of Life*, 1984, Ross House Books, Vallecito, California), Magnus Verbrugge introduces his own distinct systematic account concerning the nature of (what he calls) *functors*, a word first introduced by Hendrik Hart for the dimension of individuality-structures (cf. Hart: *Understanding Our World, Towards an Integral Ontology*, New York, 1984, cf. pp.445-446). As a substitute for the notion of an individuality-structure, Verbrugge advances the term: *idionomy* (cf. *Alive*, pp.42, 81ff, 91ff.). Of course this term may also cause misunderstanding if it is taken to mean that each individual creature (subject) has its *own unique* law. What is intended is that every *type of law* (*nomos*) is meant to delimit and determine unique subjects. In other words, however specified the universality of the law may be, it can never, in its bearing upon unique individual creatures, itself become something *uniquely individual*. Another way of grasping the meaning of Dooyeweerd's notion of an *individuality-structure* is, in following an oral suggestion by Roy Clouser (Zeist, August 1986), to call it a *type-law* (from Greek: *typonomy*). This simply means that all entities of a certain type conform to this law. The following perspective given by M. D. Stafleu elucidates this terminology in a *systematic way* (*Time and Again, A Systematic Analysis of the Foundations of Physics*, Wedge Publishing Foundation, Toronto 1980, p.6, 11): *typical laws* (type-laws/typonomies, such as the Coulomb law – applicable only to charged entities and the Pauli principle – applicable only to fermions) are special laws which apply to a limited class of entities only, whereas *modal laws* hold universally for all possible entities. D. F. M. Strauss ('Inleiding tot die Kosmologie', SACUM, Bloemfontein 1980) introduces the expression *entity structures*. The term *entity* comprises both the *individuality* and the *identity* of the thing concerned – therefore it accounts for the respective emphases found in Dooyeweerd's notion of *individuality-structures* and in Van Riessen's notion of *identity structures*. The following words of Dooyeweerd show that both the *individuality* and *identity* of an entity is determined by its 'individuality-structure': "In general we can establish that the factual temporal duration of a thing as an individual and identical whole is dependent on the preservation of its structure of individuality" *(A New Critique of Theoretical Thought, III:79)*.

Irreducibility (irreducible) – Incapability of theoretical reduction. This is the negative way of referring to the unique distinctiveness of things and aspects which we find everywhere in creation and which theoretical thought must respect. Insofar as everything has its own peculiar created nature and character, it cannot be understood in terms of categories foreign to itself.

* Law – The notion of creational law is central to Dooyeweerd's philosophy. Everything in creation is subject to God's law for it, and accordingly law is the boundary between God and creation. Scriptural synonyms for law are "ordinance", "decree", "commandment", "word", and so on. Dooyeweerd stresses that law is not in opposition to but the condition for true freedom. See also **Norm** and **Law-side**.

Law-Side – The created cosmos, for Dooyeweerd, has two correlative "sides": a law-side and a factual side (initially called: **Subject-side**). The former is simply the coherence of God's laws or ordinances for creation; the latter is the totality of created reality which is subject to those laws. It is important to note that the law-side always holds universally.

Law-Sphere (see **Modal Structure** and **Modality**) – The circle of laws qualified by a unique, irreducible and indefinable meaning-nucleus is known as a law-sphere. Within every law-sphere temporal reality has a modal function and in this function is subjected (French: *sujet*) to the laws of the modal spheres. Therefore every law-sphere has a law-side and a subject-side that are given only in unbreakable correlation with each other.

* **Meaning** – Dooyeweerd uses the word "meaning" in an unusual sense. By it he means the referential, non-self-sufficient character of created reality in that it points beyond itself to God as Origin. Dooyeweerd stresses that reality *is* meaning in this sense and that, therefore, it does not *have* meaning. "Meaning" is the Christian alternative to the metaphysical substance of immanence philosophy. "Meaning" becomes almost a synonym for "reality". Note the many compounds formed from it: meaning-nucleus, meaning-side, meaning-moment, meaning-fullness.

* **Meaning-nucleus** – The indefinable core meaning of a **Modality**.

Modality (See **Modal Structure** and **Law-sphere**) – One of the fifteen fundamental ways of being distinguished by Dooyeweerd. As modes of being, they are sharply distinguished from the concrete things which function within them. Initially Dooyeweerd distinguished fourteen aspects only, but since 1950 he introduced the kinematical aspect of *uniform movement* between the spatial and the physical aspects. Modalities are also known as "modal functions", "modal aspects", or as "facets" of created reality.

Modal Structure (see **Modality** and **Law-sphere**) – The peculiar constellation, in any given modality, of its meaning-moments (anticipatory, retrocipatory, nuclear). Contrast with **Individuality-structure**.

* **Naive experience** – Human experience insofar as it is not "theoretical" in Dooyeweerd's precise sense. "Naive" does not mean unsophisticated. Sometimes called "ordinary" or "everyday" experience. Dooyeweerd takes pains to emphasise that theory is embedded in this everyday experience and must not violate it.

Norm (normative) – Post-psychical laws, that is, modal laws for the analytical through pistical law-spheres (see **Law-sphere**). These laws are norms because they need to be positivised (see **Positivise**) and can be violated, in distinction from the "natural laws" of the pre-analytical spheres which are obeyed involuntarily (e.g., in a digestive process).

* **Nuclear-moment** – A synonym for **Meaning-nucleus** and **Law-sphere**, used to designate the indefinable core meaning of a **Modality** or aspect of created reality.

* **Object** – Something qualified by an object function and thus correlated to a subject function. A work of art, for instance, is qualified by its correlation to the human subjective function of aesthetic appreciation. Similarly, the elements of a sacrament are pistical objects.

Opening process – The process by which latent modal anticipations are "opened" or actualised. The modal meaning is then said to be "deepened". It is this process which makes possible the cultural development (differentiation) of society from a primitive ("closed", undifferentiated) stage. For example, by the opening or disclosure of the ethical anticipation in the juridical aspect, the modal meaning of the legal aspect is deepened and society can move from the principle of "an eye for an eye" to the consideration of extenuating circumstances in the administration of justice.

* **Philosophy** – In Dooyeweerd's precise systematic terminology, philosophy is the encyclopaedic science, that is, its proper task is the theoretical investigation of the overall systematic integration of the various scientific disciplines and their fields of inquiry. Dooyeweerd also uses the term in a more inclusive sense, especially when he points out that all philosophy is rooted in a pre-theoretical religious commitment and that some philosophical conception, in turn, lies at the root of all scientific scholarship.

Positivise – A word coined to translate the Dutch word *positiveren*, which means to make positive in the sense of being actually valid in a given time or place. For example, positive law is the legislation which is in force in a given country at a particular time; it is contrasted with the *legal principles* which lawmakers must positivise as legislation. In a general sense, it refers to the responsible implementation of all normative principles in human life as embodied, for example, in state legislation, economic policy, ethical guidelines, and so on.

Qualify – The **Guiding-function** of a thing is said to qualify it in the sense of characterising it. In this sense a plant is said to be qualified by the biotic and a state by the juridical [aspects].

* **Radical** – Dooyeweerd frequently uses this term with an implicit reference to the Greek meaning of *radix* = *root*. This usage must not be confused with the political connotation of the term *radical* in English. In other works Dooyeweerd sometimes paraphrases his use of the term radical with the phrase: *penetrating to the root of created reality*.

* **Religion (religious)** – For Dooyeweerd, religion is not an area or sphere of life but the all-encompassing and direction-giving root of it. It is the service of God (or a substitute no-god) in every domain of human endeavour. As such, it is to be sharply distinguished from religious faith, which is but one of the many acts and attitudes of human existence. Religion is an affair of the **Heart** and so directs all human functions. Dooyeweerd says religion is "the innate impulse of the human selfhood to direct itself toward the true or toward a pretended absolute Origin of all temporal diversity of meaning" (*A New Critique of Theoretical Thought*, Vol.I, 1953, p.57).

* **Retrocipation** – A feature in one **Modality** which refers to, is reminiscent of, an earlier one, yet retaining the modal qualification of the aspect in which it is found. The "extension" of a concept, for example, is a kind of logical space: it is a strictly logical affair, and yet it harks back to the spatial modality in its original sense. See **Anticipation**.

* **Science** – Two things are noted about Dooyeweerd's use of the term "science". In the first place, as a translation of the Dutch word *wetenschap* (analogous to the German *Wissenschaft*); it embraces all scholarly study – not only the natural sciences but also the social sciences and the humanities, including theology and philosophy. In the second place, science is always, strictly speaking, a matter of modal abstraction, that is, of analytically lifting an aspect out of the temporal coherence in

which it is found and examining it in the Gegenstand relation. But in this investigation it does not focus its theoretical attention upon the modal structure of such an aspect itself; rather, it focuses on the coherence of the actual phenomena which function within that structure. Modal abstraction as such must be distinguished from **Naive Experience**. In the first sense, therefore, "science" has a wider application in Dooyeweerd than is usual in English-speaking countries, but in the second sense it has a more restricted, technical meaning.

Sphere Sovereignty – A translation of Kuyper's phrase *souvereiniteit in eigen kring*, by which he meant that the various distinct spheres of human authority (such as family, church, school, and business enterprise) each have their own responsibility and decision-making power which may not be usurped by those in authority in another sphere, for example, the state. Dooyeweerd retains this usage but also extends it to mean the **Irreducibility** of the modal aspects. This is the ontical principle on which the societal principle is based since each of the societal "spheres" mentioned is qualified by a different irreducible modality.

★ Subject – Used in two senses by Dooyeweerd: (1) "subject" as distinguished from **Law**, (2) "subject" as distinguished from **Object**. The latter sense is roughly equivalent to common usage; the former is unusual and ambiguous. Since all things are "subject" to **Law**, objects are also subjects in the first sense. Dooyeweerd's matured conception, however, does not show this ambiguity. By distinguishing between the *law-side* and the *factual side* of creation, both subject and object (sense 2) are part of the factual side.

Subject-Side – The correlate of **Law-side**, preferably called the factual side. Another feature of the factual subject-side is that it is only here that individuality is found.

Substratum – The aggregate of modalities *preceding* a given aspect in the modal order. The arithmetic, spatial, kinematic, and physical, for example, together form the substratum for the biotic. They are also the necessary foundation upon which the biotic rests, and without which it cannot exist. See **Super-stratum**.

Superstratum – The aggregate of modalities *following* a given aspect in the modal order. For example, the pistical, ethical, juridical and aesthetic together constitute the superstratum of the economic. See **Substratum**.

* **Synthesis** – The combination, in a single philosophical conception, of characteristic themes from both pagan philosophy and biblical religion. It is this feature of the Christian intellectual tradition, present since patristic times, with which Dooyeweerd wants to make a radical break. Epistemologically seen, the term *synthesis* is used to designate the way in which a multiplicity of features is integrated within the unity of a concept. The re-union of the logical aspect of the theoretical act of thought with its non-logical "Gegenstand" is called an inter-modal meaning-synthesis.

* **Time** – In Dooyeweerd, a general ontological principle of intermodal continuity, with far wider application than our common notion of time, which is equated by him with the physical manifestation of this general cosmic time. It is, therefore, not coordinate with space. All created things, except the human **Heart**, are in time. On the law-side time expresses itself as time-order and on the factual side (including subject-subject and subject-object relations) as time duration.

Transcendental – A technical term from the philosophy of Kant denoting the *apriori* structural conditions which make human experience (specifically human knowledge and theoretical thought) possible. As such it is to be sharply distinguished from the term "transcendent". Furthermore, the basic (transcendental) Idea of a philosophy pre-supposes the transcendent and central sphere of consciousness (the human **Heart**). This constitutes the second meaning in which Dooyeweerd uses the term transcendental: through its transcendental basic-Idea philosophy points beyond itself to its ultimate religious foundation transcending the realm of thought.

Bibliography

1. Herman Dooyeweerd's Works

Particularly important works are indicated by ‡.

1917 — ‡ *De Ministerraad in het Nederlandsche staatsrecht.*
Amsterdam, Wed. G. van Soest.
The Cabinet in Dutch Constitutional Law. (Doctoral dissertation.)

1920 — *Het vraagstuk der gemeentemonopolies in het belang der volks-gezondheid, hoofdzakelijk beschouwd in het licht van de nieuwe opvattingen in zake de bedrijfsvrijheid.*
Thémis 81st year p.126-151.
The problem of public monopolies regarding public health, mainly considered in the light of recent ideas about business freedom.

1923 — *Het Calvinistisch beginsel der souvereiniteit in eigen kring als staatkundig beginsel.*
Nederland en Oranje, 4th year, p.98-99 ; 185-189 ; 5th year, (1924), p.8-15 ; 27-31 ; 71-76.
The Calvinist principle of sphere sovereignty as a political principle.

1924 — ‡*In den strijd om een Christelijke Staatkunde : proeve van een fundering der Calvinistische levens- en wereldbeschouwing in hare wetsidee.*
Antirevolutionaire Staatkunde, 1 (1924-5), p.7-25; 62-79; 104-118; 161-173; 189-200; 228-244; 309-324; 433-460; 489-504; 528-542; 581-598; 617-634; 2 (1926), p.244-265; 425-445; 1 (1927), p.142-195.
In the Struggle for a Christian Politics: An Essay on the Foundation of the Calvinistic Worldview in Its Law-Idea.

— *Inzage van de bedrijfsboekhouding door de arbeiders vertegen-woordigers in de particuliere onderneming* (advies).
Antirevolutionaire Staatkunde, 1 (1924-5), p.291-306.
Inspection of company records by workers representatives in private companies (a recommendation).

1925 — *Calvinisme en Natuurrecht.* (Referaat voor de Calvinistische Juristen Vereeniging)
Amersfoort, Wed. W. van Wijngen.
Calvinism and Natural Law. (Report of the Calvinist Lawyers Association).

— *Leugen en Waarheid over het Calvinisme.*
Nederland en Oranje, 6th year, p.81-90.
Truth and Falsehood regarding Calvinism.

1926 — *Tweeërlei Kritiek.* Om de principieele zijde van het vraagstuk der medezeggenschap.
Antirevolutionaire Staatkunde, 2nd year, p.1-21.
A Twofold Criticism. About the central issue of the problem of participation.

— *Het oude probleem der Christelijke Staatkunde.*
Antirevolutionaire Staatkunde, 2nd year, p.63-84.
The Old Problem of a Christian Politics.

— *De band met het beginsel.* Inzake het vraagstuk der medezeggenschap. (Rede, uitgesproken voor 'Nederland en Oranje VIII' te Amsterdam)
Nederland en Oranje, 7th year, p.2-18 ; 33-40.
Union with Principle: the problem of participation. Lecture delivered to 'Nederland en Oranje VIII' in Amsterdam.

— ‡*Calvinisme contra Neo-Kantianisme.* Naar aanleiding van de vraag betreffende de kenbaarheid der goddelijke rechtsorde.
Tijdschrift voor Wijsbegeerte, 20th year, p.29-74.
Calvinism versus Neo-Kantianism. In response to the question of the knowability of the divine law.

— ‡*De betekenis der Wetsidee voor Rechtswetenschap en Rechtsphilosophie.* (Rede bij de aanvaarding van het hoogleeraarsambt aan de Vrije Universiteit te Amsterdam, 15 oktober 1926, uitgesproken).
Kampen, J. H. Kok.
The Significance of the Law-Idea for Jurisprudence and Philosophy of Law. (Lecture on acceptance of the post of Professor at the Free University in Amsterdam, delivered 15th October 1926).

1927 — ‡*De oorsprong van de anti-these tusschen Christelijke en humanistische wetsidee en hare beteekenis voor de staatkunde.*
Antirevolutionaire Staatkunde, 1st year, p.73-107.
The source of the antithesis between the Christian and humanist law-ideas and its significance for political theory.

– *De universaliteit der rechtsgedachte en de idee van den Kultuur-staat.*
Almanak van het Studentcorps aan de Vrije Universiteit, p.103-121.
The universality of the principle of legality and the idea of a Culture State. (In: Almanac of the Students' Union at the Free University)

– ‡Het juridisch causaliteitsprobleem in 't licht der *wetsidee.*
Antirevolutionaire Staatkunde, 2nd year, p.21-121.
The problem of legal causality in the light of the law-idea.

– *Beginsel of utiliteit ?*
Nederland en Oranje, May 1928, Nos. 56 and 57.
Principle or Utility?

– *De Protestantsch-Christelijke Reclasseeringvereeniging.*
De Standaard for 24th September.
The Protestant-Christian Association for the Care and Resettlement of Offenders.

1928 – ‡*Beroepsmisdaad en strafvergelding in 't licht der wetsidee.* Een bijdrage tot de dogmatiek van de beroepsmisdaad de lege ferenda. Met Naschrift: Inzake het recht der Calvinistische wetenschapsbeschouwing, en het misverstand eener 'neut-raal-wetenschappelijke' kritiek.
Antirevolutionaire Staatkunde, 2nd year, p.233-309 ; 389-436.
Professional Crime and retributive punishment in the light of the law-idea. A contribution to the dogmatics of professional crime with a view to future law. With postscript: Concerning the claim of the Calvinistic view of science, and the misunderstanding of a 'neutral-scientific' criticism.

1929 – *De strijd om de grondslagen van het volkenrecht.*
De Volkenbond, 4th year, p.316-320.
The conflict regarding the principles of international law.

1930 – ‡*De bronnen van het stellig recht in het licht der wetsidee.* Een bijdrage tot opklaring van het probleem inzake de ver-houding van rechtsbeginsel en positief recht.
Antirevolutionaire Staatkunde, (1930) p.1-67; 224-263; 325-362; (1934) p.57-94.
The sources of positive law in the light of the law-idea. A contribution to resolving the problem concerning the relation between positive law and legal principle.

– ‡*De structuur der rechtsbeginselen en de methode der rechts-wetenschap in het licht der wetsidee.*

In: *Wetenschappelijke Bijdragen*, aangeboden door hoogleer-
aren der Vrije Universiteit ter gelegenheid van haar
vijftigjarig bestaan, 20 oktober 1930.
Amsterdam, N. V. Dagblad en Drukkerij, De Standaard,
p.223-266.
*The structure of legal principles and the methodology of jurisprudence in the light
of the law-idea. In: 'Scientific Contributions', offered by the professors of the
University on the occasion of its fiftieth anniversary, 20th October 1930.*

− *De Dietsche cultuurgedachte uit Calvinistisch oogpunt bezien.*
In: Jaarboek van het Dietsch Studentenverbond, 1929-30,
p.44-47.
The German idea of culture from a Calvinistic perspective.

1931 − ‡*De crisis der Humanistische staatsleer in het licht eener Calvinistische kosmologie en kennistheorie.*
Amsterdam, W. ten Have.
*The crisis in the Humanist theory of the State in the light of a Calvinist
cosmology and epistemology.*

− Bespreking : Annalen der critische philosophie. Orgaan
van het Genootschap voor critische philosophie.
Thémis, 92nd year, p.439-444.
*Discussion: Annals of critical philosophy. Organ of the Society for Critical
Philosophy.*

− Mr D. P. D. Fabius.
Weekblad voor het Recht, 31st December.
D. P. D. Fabius: Obituary.

1932 − ‡*De zin der geschiedenis en de 'Leiding Gods' in de historische
ontikkeling.* Referaat 3e Landdag der Reunisten-Organ-
isatie van NDDD op 17 mei 1932 te Leeuwarden.
Publications of the Reunion Organisation of the NDDD,
No. 5.
*The meaning of history and 'God's Guidance' in historical evolution. Report of
the 3rd conference of the Reunion Organisation of the NDDD on May 17, 1932
at Leeuwardn.*

− *Het Amsterdamsche rapport inzake de medezeggenschap van het
personeel in de Gemeentebedrijven en -diensten.*
Antirevolutionaire Staatkunde, 8th year, p.71-86; 121-132;
157-168.
*The Amsterdam Report on the involvement of staff in municipal enterprises and
services.*

– *Norm en Feit*. Een kritische beschouwing naar aanleiding van het geschrift van Mr S. Rozemond over 'Kant en de Volkenbond'.
Thémis 93rd year, p.155-214.
Fact and Norm. A critical consideration in response to the writings of Mr. S. Rozemond on 'Kant and the League of Nations'.

– *Ter nagedachtenis van Prof. Dr. D.P. Fabius.*
In Calvinistsche Juristen Vereeniging, 1931-2, p.37-39.
In memory of Prof. Dr. D.P. Fabius.

1933 – Rede ter overdracht van het Rectoraat der Vrije Universiteit aan Prof. Dr. D. H. Th. Vollenhoven op Woensdag 21 september 1932.
In : Jaarboek der Vrije Universiteit, 1933, p.65-81.
Lecture on the transfer of the Rectorship of the Free University to Prof. Dr. D. H. Th. Vollenhoven on Wednesday, 21st September 1932.

– *De theorie van de bronnen van het stellig recht in het licht der wetsidee*. Prae-advies (met discussie) voor de Vereeniging voor Wijsbegeerte des Rechts. Handelingen van de Vereeniging voor Wijsbegeerte des Rechts XIX, 1932-33.
Mensch en Maatschappij 9 (1933), p.340-396.
The theory of the sources of positive law in the light of the law–idea. Privileged advice for the Association for Philosophy of Law. Proceedings of the Society for Philosophy of Law, XIX, 1932-33.

– *De Grondwet van de nieuwe Duitsche Evangelische Kerk en de positie der Gereformeerden in de 'Landskerken'.*
Antirevolutionaire Staatkunde, 9th year, p.433-446.
The Constitution of the new German Evangelical Church and the position of the Reformed in the 'Country Churches'.

1934 – *Staat en Beroepsmisdaad*. Het principieele vraagstuk van de gerechte bestraffing der beroepsmisdaad en het beveiligingsrecht.
Orgaan ten dienste der Protestants-Christelijke Reclasseringsvereeniging. 2nd year, p.33-36; 41-43.
The State and Professional Crime. The fundamental question of the retributive punishment of professional crime and security law. The organ of the Protestant-Christian Association for the Care and Resettlement of Offenders, 2nd year, p.33-36; 41-43.

1935 – *Het vraagstuk van het organisch kiesrecht in een nieuw stadium.*
Rede Centrale Kiesvereeniging 'Nederland en Oranje' te Amsterdam, op 28 mei 1934 te Amsterdam.
In Almanak van het Studentencorps aan de Vrije Universiteit, p.105-121.

The problem of the organic franchise in a new stage. Lecture at the Central Select Association 'Nederland en Oranje' in Amsterdam, 28th May 1934.

– ‡*De Wijsbegeerte der Wetsidee.* Vol. I: De Wetsidee als grondlegging der wijsbegeerte. Vol. II: De functioneele zin-structuur der tijdelijke werkelijkheid en het probleem der kennis.
Amsterdam, H. J. Paris.
The Philosophy of the Law-Idea. Volume I: The Law-Idea as foundation of philosophy. Volume II: The functional meaning-structure of temporary reality and the problem of knowledge.

– *Het strafrechtcongres te Berlin.*
De Standaard for 31st August, 2nd and 4th September.
Criminal Law Congress in Berlin.

– ‡*De wetsbeschouwing in Brunner's boek 'Das Gebot und die Ordnungen'.* Referaat 18e Calvinistisch Studentencongres te Lunteren.
Antirevolutionaire Staatkunde, 9th year, p.334-374.
The idea of law in Brunner's book 'Das Gebot und die Ordnung'. Report on the 18th Calvinist Student Congress at Lunteren.

1936 – *Het dilemma voor het Christelijk wijsgeerig denken en het critisch karakter van de Wijsbegeerte der Wetsidee.*
Philosophia Reformata, 1st year, p.3-16.
The dilemma for Christian philosophical thought and the critical character of the Philosophy of the Law-Idea.

– ‡*De Wijsbegeerte der Wetsidee.* Vol. III: De individualiteits-structuren der tijdelijke werkelijk-heid. Amsterdam, H. J. Paris.
The Philosophy of the Law-Idea. Volume III: The individuality-structures of temporary reality.

– ‡*Het tijdsprobleem en zijn antinomieën op het immanentiestandpunt.*
Philosophia Reformata, 1 (1936), p.65-83; 4 (1939), p.1-28.
The problem of time and its antinomies from the immanence standpoint.

– *Het strafcongres te Berlin.*
Orgaan ten dienste der Protestants-Christelijke Reclasseringsvereeniging. 4th year, p.41-44; 50-53; 57-60.
Criminal Law Congress in Berlin. The organ of the Protestant-Christian Association for the Care and Resettlement of Offenders.

– *De strijd om het vraagstuk der Christelijke vakorganisatie van werkgevers in het licht van een oude strijdvraag in de Christelijke levens –en wereldbeschouwing.*

Referaat Algemeene Leden-vergadering der Christelijke Werkgeversvereeniging op 9 september 1936 te 's Gravenhage.
The contest regarding the issue of a Christian trade union of employers in the light of an old controversy in the Christian worldview. Report of the General Sectional Meeting of the Christian Employers Association on the 9th September 1936 in The Hague.

— *De Christelijke Staatsidee.* Referaat Toogdag der Anti-Revolutionaire Jongeren Actie op 3 oktober 1936 te Apeldoorn.
Rotterdam-Utrecht, Libertas Drukkerijen.
The Christian Idea of the State. Report on the Annual Research Day of the AntiRevolutionnary Youth Action on 3rd October 1936 in Apeldoorn

— *Geloof en Historie.* Syllabus 1936-37.
Faith and History.

1937 — *De plicht der jongere generatie tegenover Kuyper's geestelijke nalatenschap.* Rede 19e Bondsdag van den Bond van Meisjesvereenigingen op Gereformeerden Grondslag in Nederland, gehouden te Zwolle 1937.
In: Volhardt. Jaarboek van dezen Bond, p.12-21.
The duty of the younger generation with regard to Kuyper's spiritual legacy. Lecture, 19th Assembly of the Confederation of Girls' Societies of Reformed Persuasion in the Netherlands, held in Zwolle, 1937.

— ‡*De gevaren van de geestelijke ontwapening der Christenheid op het gebied van de wetenschap.*
In: Geestelijk weerloos of weerbaar?
Amsterdam, Uitgeversmaatschappij Holland, p.151-212.
The dangers of the spiritual disarmament of Christianity in the domain of science. (In: Spiritually defenceless or armed?).

— *Het vrijwilligersstelsel in den voorlichtingsdienst en de objectiviteit der reclasseeringsrapporten.*
Orgaan ten dienste der Protestants-Christelijke Reclasseeringsvereeniging, 5th year, p.33-38 ; 41-43.
The voluntary system in public relations and the objectivity of probation reports.

— *Naschrift bij Stoker's verhandeling* (Iets oor Kousaliteit).
Philosophia Reformata, 2nd year, p.97-98.
Postscript to Stoker's treatise 'About Causality' (Iets oor Kousaliteit).

— *De beteekenis van de Wijsbegeerte der Wetsidee voor de theorie der menschelijke samenleving.* Referaat Jaarvergadering van de Vereeniging voor Calvinistische Wijsbegeerte op 16e december 1936 te Utrecht.

Philosophia Reformata, 2nd year, p.99-116.
The significance of the Philosophy of the Law-Idea for the theory of human society. Report of the Annual Meeting of the Association for Calvinist Philosophy on 16th December 1936, at Utrecht.

- *Grondprobleemen in der leer der rechts-persoonlijkheid.* Thémis, 98th year, p.199-263; 367-421.
Fundamental problems in the doctrine of legal personality.

- *Wat de Wijsbegeerte der Wetsidee aan Dr. Kuyper te danken heeft.* De Reformatie, 29th October.
What the Philosophy of the Law-Idea owes to Dr Kuyper.

- J. Bohatec, *'Calvin und das Recht'.*
Tijdschrift voor Rechtsgeschiedenis, 15th year, p.243-258.
J. Bohatec, 'Calvin and Law'. (Critical review).

1938 - *De verhouding tusschen individu en gemeenschap in de Romeinische en Germaansche eigen-domsopvatting.* Referaat 9e Landdag der R.-O. van NDDD, op 19 en 20 april 1938 te Den Dolder.
Publications of the Reunion Organisation of the NDDD, No. 10.
The relationship between individual and community in the Roman and Germanic conception of ownership. Report of the 9th conference of the Reunion Organisation of the NDDD on the 19th and 20th April, 1938 at Den Dolder.

- *Pessimistische Cultuurbeschouwing.* Rede voor De Nederlandse Christelijke Radio-Vereniging op 25 april 1938.
Mededeelingen van de Vereeniging voor Calvinistische Wijsbegeerte, 3rd year, p.1-4.
Pessimistic Cultural Perspectives. Lecture for The Dutch Christian Radio Association on 25th April 1938. Proceedings of the Association for Calvinistic Philosophy.

- *Recht en Historie.* Referaat voor de drie-en twintigste Wetenschappelijke Samenkomst der Vrije Universiteit op 13 juli 1938 te Assen.
Assen, C.F. Hummelen.
Law and History. Lecture for the 23rd Scientific Meeting of the Free University on 13th July 1938 at Assen.

- *Geloof en Wetenschap.* Referaat 21ee Calvinistische Studentencongres te Lunteren 1938. In Geloof en Wetenschap. Uitgave van de Calvinistische Studentenbeweging, p.26-28.
Faith and Science. Lecture for the 21st Calvinistic Student Congress at Lunteren 1938.

- *De niet-theoretische voor-oordeelen in de wetenschap.* Critiek op een oncritische critiek.
  Philosophia Reformata, 3rd year, p.193-201.
  Non-theoretical prejudices in science. Criticism of an uncritical criticism.

- *Ten Geleide.*
  In: J.M. Spier, Inleiding in de Wijsbegeerte der Wetsidee. Enschede-Kampen.
  Foreword (to Spier's Introduction to the Philosophy of the Law-Idea).

1939 — *De niet-theoretische voor-oordeelen in de wetenschap.*
  Vox Theologica, 10th year, p.103-109.
  Non-theoretical prejudices in science.

- ‡*Das natürliche Rechtsbewusstsein und die Erkenntnis des geoffenbarten göttlichen Gesetzes.* Vortrag Theologische Konferenz in Zürich am 28 february 1939.
  Antirevolutionaire Staatkunde, 13th year, p.157-182.
  The natural sense of right and knowledge of the revealed divine law. Lecture at Theological Conference in Zurich on 28th February 1939.

- *De wijsgeerige achtergrond van de moderne democratische reactie tegen het individualisme.*
  Mededeelingen van de Vereeniging voor Calvinistische Wijsbegeerte. 4th year, p.7-10.
  The philosophical background of the modern democratic reaction against individualism. Proceedings of the Association for Calvinist Philosophy.

- ‡*Kuyper's Wetenschapsleer.* Referaat Jaarvergadering van de Vereeniging voor Calvinistische Wijsbegeerte op 2nd January 1939 te Amsterdam.
  Philosophia Reformata, 4th year, p.192-232.
  Kuyper's Theory of Science. Report of the Annual Meeting of the Association for Calvinist Philosophy on 2nd January 1939 at Amsterdam.

- ‡*De transcendantale critiek van het wijsgeerig denken.* Een bijdrage tot overwinning van het wetenschappelijk exclusivisme der richtingen.
  Synthese, 4th year, p.314-339.
  The transcendental critique of theoretical thought. A contribution to overcoming the scientific exclusivism of the directions.

1940 — *Strafrechtspraak en reclasseering onder den nieuwen rechtstoestand voor het bezette Nederlandsche gebied.*
  Orgaan ten dienste der Protestants-Christelijke Reclasseringsvereeniging, 8th year, p.130-140.
  Criminal justice and probation under the new legal condition for the occupied Dutch territory.

- *De Wijsbegeerte der Wetsidee en het substantiebegrip.* Voordracht aan de hand van stellingen en discussie in de vergadering van de Christelijke Vereeniging van Natuur- en Geneeskundigen op 9 december 1939 and 6 januari 1940. Orgaan Christlijke Vereening van Natuur- en Geneeskundigen in Nederland, p.41-58.
  The Philosophy of the Law-Idea and the concept of substance. Lecture using propositions and discussion at the meeting of the Christian Association of Physicists and Physicians in the Netherlands, 9th December 1939 and 6th January 1940.

- *Het tijdsprobleem in de Wijsbegeerte der Wetsidee.* Voordracht voor de Gereformeerde Psychologische Studievereeniging in haar Najaarsvergadering van 1940. Loosduinen, Drukkerij Kleywegt.
  The problem of time in the Philosophy of the Law-Idea. Lecture for the Reformed Association for the Study of Psychology in its Autumn Meeting for 1940.

- ‡*Het tijdsprobleem in de Wijsbegeerte der Wetsidee.* Philosophia Reformata, 5th year, p.160-182 ; 193-234.
  The problem of time in the Philosophy of the Law-Idea.

- *Johannes J. Poortman, Drei Vortrage über Philosophie und Parapsychologie.* Philosophia Reformata, 5th year, p.183-192.
  Johannes J. Poortman, 'Three lectures on philosophy and parapsychology'. (Critical review).

- *De 'Théorie de l'Institution' en de staatsleer van Maurice Hauriou.* Antirevolutionaire Staatkunde, 14th year (1940), p.301-347; 15 (1941), p.42-70.
  The 'Théorie de l'Institution (Theory of the Institution)' and Maurice Hauriou's political theory.

- *Saevis tranquillus in undis.* Calvinistisch Studentblad, 4th December 1940.
  Saevis tranquillus in undis (Latin: Calm amidst the raging waves. Motto of William I of Orange)

1941 — *Dr. H. J. Pos, 'Philosophie der wetenschappen'.* Vox Theologica, 12 (1941), p.85-90.
  Dr. H. J. Pos, 'Philosophy of Science'. (Critical review).

- *De transcendantale critiek van het wijsgeerig denken en de grondslagen van de wijsgeerige denkgemeenschap van het Avondland.* Referaat Jaarvergadering van de Vereeniging voor

Calvinistische Wijsbegeerte op 2 januari 1941 te Amsterdam.
Philosophia Reformata, 6th year, p.1-20.
The transcendantal critique of philosophic thought and the foundations of the the philosophical community of thought in the West. Lecture to the Annual Meeting of the Association for Calvinistic Philosophy on 2 January 1941 in Amsterdam.

— Vraagstukken uit de Natuurphilosophie. Verslag van de zevende algemeene vergadering der Vereeniging voor Thomistische Wijsbegeerte. Bijlage van 'Studia Catholica' 1940.
Philosophia Reformata, 6th year, p.57-64.
Problems in natural philosophy. Report of the seventh general assembly of the Association for Thomistic Philosophy. Supplement to 'Studia Catholica' 1940. (Critical review).

— *Een tweegesprek met Prof. Ovink over dogmatische en critische wijsbegeerte.* Naar aanleiding van 'Philosophie und Sophistik' door Prof. Dr. B.J.H. Ovink.
Gereformeerd Theologisch Tijdschrift, 43rd year, p.209-227.
A conversation with Prof. Ovink on dogmatic and critical philosophy. Regarding 'Philosophy and Sophism' by Prof. Dr. B.J.H. Ovink.

— *De vier religieuze grondthema's in den ontwikkelingsgang van het wijsgeerig denken van het Avondland.* Een bijdrage tot bepaling van de verhouding tusschen theoretische en religieuze dialectiek.
Philosophia Reformata, 6th year, p.161-179.
The four religious ground-motives in the course of the development of philosophical thinking in the West. A contribution to determining the relation between theoretical and religious dialectic.

1942 — *De leer de analogie in de Thomistische wijsbegeerte en in de Wijsbegeerte der Wetsidee.* Naar aanleiding van het verslag van de achtste algemeene vergadering der Vereeniging voor Thomistische Wijsbegeerte: 'De Analogie van het Zijn'.
Philosophia Reformata, 7th year, p.45-57.
The idea of analogy in Thomistic philosophy and in the Philosophy of the Law-Idea. Following the report of the eighth general assembly of the Association for Thomistic Philosophy: 'The Analogy of Being'.

— *Wijsbegeerte der Wetsidee.*
In Encyclopaedisch Handboek voor het Moderne Denken, 2nd Ed. 1942, p.814-825 (3rd Ed. 1950).
Arnhem, Van Loghum Slaterus Uigeversmij NV.

Philosophy of the Law-Idea. Article in: Encyclopaedic Manual of Modern Thought.

1943 — ‡De idee de individualiteits-structuur en het Thomistisch substantiebegrip. Een critisch onderzoek naar de grondslagen der Thomistische zijnsleer.
Philosophia Reformata, 8th year (1943), p.65-99; 9 (1944), p.1-41; 10 (1945), p.25-48; 11 (1946), p.22-52.
The idea of individuality-structure and the Thomistic concept of substance. A critical examination of the foundations of the Thomistic idea of being.

— Preface to J.C. Baak, Het Calvinisme Oorsprong en Waarborg onzer constitutioneele Vrijheden.
Amsterdam, W. ten Have.
Preface to J. C. Baak, 'Calvinism: Origin and Guarantee of our constitutional freedoms'.

— De Anti-these.
Series of articles in Nieuw Nederland from 7th September 1945 to 3rd October 1947.
The Antithesis.

1946 — De regeeringsplannen inzake de publiekrechtelijke bedrijfsorganisatie.
Nieuw Nederland, 25th January, 1st, 15th and 22nd February and 1st March.
The government plans for a public regulatory industrial organisation.

— De verhouding van individu en gemeenschap rechtswijsgeerig bezien. Voordracht, uitgesproken in de Sectie voor Philosophie deel uitmakend van het in april 1946 te Amsterdam gehouden 19e Nederlandsche Philologencongres.
Algemeen Nederlandsch Tijdschrift voor Wijsbegeerte en Psychologie. 39th year, p.5-12.
The relation of the individual and the community from a legal-philosophical perspective. Lecture, delivered in the Philosophy Section, being part of the 19th Dutch Philology Conference in April 1946 held in Amsterdam.

— Het wetsbegrip in de economie.
Mededeelingen van de Vereeniging voor Calvinistische Wijsbegeerte, August, p.2-3.
The concept of law in economics.

— Is een bedrijfstak een natuurlijke gemeenschap?
Nieuw Nederland, for 23rd and 30th August, 6th, 13th and 27th September, 11th October and 1st November.
Is a business enterprise a natural community?

1947 – *Groen van Prinsterer en de souvereiniteit in eigen kring.*
Nieuw Nederland, for 10th, 17th, 24th and 31st January.
Groen van Prinsterer and Sphere Sovereignty.

 – *Wat is een natuurlijke gemeenschap?*
Nieuw Nederland, for 7th, 14th and 21st February.
What is a natural community?

 – *Introduction to a transcendental criticism of philosophic thought.* A
lecture delivered to French students in Amsterdam.
The Evangelical Quarterly, 19th year, p.42-51.

 – ‡*Tien voordrachten over Sociologie.* Syllabus 1946-47 van de
Stichting Studium Generale aan de Technische Hoog-
school te Delft.
Delft, Delftsche Uitgeversmaatschappij, p.129-178.
Ten lectures on Sociology.

 – *Opkomst en grondprobleem der moderne sociologie.*
Nieuw Nederland, for 10th, 24th and 31st October; 7th
November 1947; 12th, 19th and 26th March; 8th April and
13th May 1948.
The rise of modern sociology and its basic problem.

1948 – *Een nieuw geschrift over Hariou's leer der 'Institution'.*
Bestuurswetenschappen 2nd year, p.1-15.
A new writing about Hariou's idea of 'Institution'.

 – *Groens 'Ongeloof en Revolutie'.*
Nederlandsche Gedachten, 4th year, p.53-57.
Groen's 'Belief and Revolution'.

 – *Het wijsgeerig tweegesprek tusschen de Thomistische philosophie
en de Wijsbegeerte der Wetsidee.* Naar aanleiding van Prof.
Dr. H. Robbers, 'Het natuur-genade-schema als religieus
grondmotif der Scholastieke wijsbegeerte'.
Studia Catholica 23 (1948), p.69-78. Philosophia Reformata, 13th year, p.26-31; p.49-58.
*The philosophical discussion between Thomistic philosophy and the Philosophy of
the Law-Idea. Following Prof. Dr. H. Robbers, 'The nature-grace scheme as
religious ground-motive of Scholastic philosophy'.*

 – ‡*Transcendantal problems of philosophic thought.* An enquiry
into the transcendantal conditions of philosophy.
Grand Rapids, Michigan, Wm B. Eerdmans.

 – *Introduction à une critique transcendantale de la pensée philosophique.*

In: Mélanges philosophiques. Bibliothèque du Xème Congres international de philosophie, Volume II, p.70-82. Amsterdam, L. J. Veen.

Introduction to a transcendental critique of philosophical thought.

1949 — ‡*De sociologische verhouding tussen recht en economie en het probleem van het zogeheten 'economisch recht'.*
In: Opstellen op het gebied van recht, staat en maatschappij, aangeboden aan Prof. Dr. A. Anema en Prof. P. A. Diepenhorst bij hunafscheid van de Vrije Universiteit door oud-leerlingen.
Amsterdam, S. J. P. Bakker, p.221-265.

The sociological relationship between law and economics and the problem of the so-called 'economic law'. In: 'Essays on Law, State and Society', presented to Prof. Dr. A. Anema and Prof. P. A. Diepenhorst at their retirement from the University, by their former students.

— Ter nagedachtenis van Harry Diemer, (1904-1945).
Philosophia Reformata, 14th year, p.1-5.

In memory of Harry Diemer, (1904-1945).

— ‡*De vooronderstellingen van ons denken over recht en samenleving in de crisis van het moderne Historisme.* Een critische overpeinzing naar aanleiding van Mr. H. W. Scheltema's 'Beschouwingen over de vooronderstellingen van ons denken over recht en staat'.
Rechtsgeleerd Magazijn Thémis, p.193-248.

The presuppositions of our thinking about law and society in the crisis of modern historicism. A critical reflection in response to Mr. H. W. Scheltema's 'Reflections on the presuppositions of our thinking about law and state'.

— *Het historische element in Groen's staatsleer.*
In: Groen's 'Ongeloof en Revolutie'.
Wageningen, N.V. Gebr. Zomer en Keuning, p.118-137.

The historical element in Groen's political theory.

— J. P. A. Mekkes, 'De beteekenis van het subject in de moderne waardephilosophie onder het licht der wetsidee'.
Antirevolutionaire Staatkunde, 19th year, pp.405-406.

Book Review: J. P. A. Mekkes, 'The significance of the subject in modern philosophy of value in the light of the law-idea'.

— *Reformatie en Scholastiek in de wijsbegeerte.* Volume I: Het Grieksche Voorspel.
Franeker, T. Wever.

Reformation and Scholasticism in Philosophy. Volume 1: The Greek Prelude.

1950 – Mr. R. Kranenberg, 'De grondslagen der rechtswetenschap. Juridische kennisleer en methodologie', 2nd edition.
Rechtsgeleerd Magazijn Thémis, pp.89-98.
*Book Review: Mr. R. Kranenberg, 'The foundations of jurisprudence. Legal
epistemology and methodology'.*

– *De modale structuur van het juridisch oorzakelijkheidverband.*[1]
Mededelingen der Koninklijke Nederlandse Akademie van
Wetenschappen, Afd. Letterkunde, Nieuwe reeks, Deel
13, No. 5.
Amsterdam: North Holland Publishing Company.
*The modal structure of juridical causality. Proceedings of the Royal Dutch
Academy of Sciences: Division of Letters, new series, vol. 13, No. 5.*

– *De strijd om het Schriftuurlijk karakter van de Wijsbegeerte der
Wetsidee.*
Mededelingen van de Vereeniging voor Calvinistische
Wijsbegeerte, juli, p.3-6.
*The battle for the Scriptural character of the Philosophy of the Law-Idea.
Proceedings of the Association for Calvinist Philosophy, July.*

– ‡*Het substantiebegrip in de moderne natuurphilosophie en de
theorie van het enkaptisch structuurgeheel.*
Philosophia Reformata, 15th year, p.66-139.
*The concept of substance in modern natural philosophy and the theory of the
enkaptic structural whole.*

– *Wat is rechtswetenschap?*
In: Interfacultaire Colleges aan de Vrije Universiteit te
Amsterdam, Cursus 1949-50.
Amsterdam, Uitgave van de Vrije Universiteit, p.33-53.
*What is Jurisprudence? (Inter Faculty Lectures at the Free University in
Amsterdam, Course for 1949-50.)*

– *De strijd om het souvereiniteitsbegrip in de moderne rechts- en
staatsleer.* Uitgewerkte rede ter gelegenheid van de 70e
herdenking van de stichting der Vrije Universiteit op 20
oktober 1950.
Amsterdam, H. J. Paris.
*The contest regarding the concept of sovereignty in modern jurisprudence and
political science. (Detailed lecture to mark the 70th anniversary of the founding of
the Free University on October 20, 1950.)*

---

[1] [In *A New Critique of Theoretical Thought*, II, 119, footnote 1, Dooyeweerd refers to
this as *De modale structuur van het juridisch causaliteitsverband.*]

1951   –   *De overspanning van het begrip 'natuurlijke gemeenschap' en het sociologisch universalisme.*
Almanak van het Studentencorps aan de Vrije Universiteit, p.216-229.
The over-extending of the concept of 'natural community' and sociological universalism.

1953   –   ‡*La sécularisation de la Science.* Rapport présenté au 6e Congrès International Réformé, Montpelier 1953.
La Revue Réformée, Nos. 17-18, p.138-155.
The Secularisation of Science. Report presented to the 6th International Reformed Congress, Montpelier 1953.

     –   ‡*La problème de la philosophie chrétienne.* Une confrontation de la conception blondélienne et de l'idée nouvelle concernant une reformation de la pensée philosophique en Hollande. Deux leçons publiques prononcées à l'Université d'Aix-en-Provence-Marseille, en Mai 1953.
Philosophia Reformata, 18th year, p.49-76.
The problem of a Christian philosophy. The engagement between Blondel's conception and a new idea regarding a reformation of philosophical thought in Holland. Two public lectures delivered at the University of Aix-en-Provence-Marseille, May 1953.

     –   ‡*A New Critique of Theoretical Thought.*
Volume I: The necessary presuppositions of philosophy.
H. J. Paris, Amsterdam; Presbyterian & Reformed Publishing Co, Philadelphia.

1955   –   ‡*A New Critique of Theoretical Thought.*
Volume II: The general theory of the modal spheres.
H. J. Paris, Amsterdam; Presbyterian & Reformed Publishing Co, Philadelphia.

2. Additions to the above list

1950   –   *Aard en voorwaarden der wetenschap.* In: Geloof en Wetenschap: Levensbeschouwing en levenshouding van de academicus.
Utrecht, N.V. Dekker and Van De Vegt, p.15-32.
The character and terms of science. (In: 'Faith and Science, life-outlook and life-approach for academics').

1952 — De transcendantale critiek van het theoretisch denken en de thomistische theologia naturalis.
Philosophia Reformata, 17th year, p.151-182.
The transcendental critique of theoretical thought and Thomistic natural theology.

1951 — *De wijsbegeerte der wetsidee en de 'Barthanen'.* Een tweegesprek naar aanleiding van Dr. K. H. Miskotte, 'Barth over Sartre'.
Philosophia Reformata, 16th year, p.145-162.
The Philosophy of the Law-Idea and 'Barthianism'. A dialogue based on Dr. K. H. Miskotte's 'Barth via Sartre'.

— *Encyclopaedie der Rechtswetenschap,* 3 volumes.
Various editions, authorised and unauthorised, 1946-67.
To be published as: Encyclopedia of the Science of Law, 5 volumes projected. Edwin Mellen Press, Lewiston, NY. Volume 1: Introduction, 2002.

3. In collaboration with others.

1926 — With J. W. Noteboom: *De Bioscoopwet* (Wet van 14 mei 1926, Stb. 118), toegelicht met toevoeging van verschillende gegevens uit de practijk.
Alphe, a.d. Rijn, N. Samsom.
The Cinema Act (Act of the 14th May 1926, Stb. 118), illustrated by the addition of several instances from experience.

1928 — With Mr. A. J. L. van Beeck Calkoen, Ds C. Lindeboom and Mr. J. Oranje: *De verhouding van de taak van diaconie overheid en philanthropie inzake de sickenverpleging.*
Diaconal Correspondentieblad, 26th year (1928) p.126-138; 27 (1929) p.158-173.
The relationship of the duties of parish government and philanthropy for health care.

1942 — *De zin der geschiedenis.* In: *De zin der geschiedenis,* by J. D. Bierens de Haan, etc.
Assen, van Gorcum, p.17-27.
The Meaning of History.

1948 — With Drs J. Lever: *Rondom het biologisch soortbegrip.*
Philosophia Reformata, 13th year, p.119-138; 14 (1949) p.6-32; 15 (1950) p.1-23.
About the biological concept of species.

4. Various.

Numerous other essays and articles : Cf. *Rechtsgeleerde opstellen*, door zijn leerlingen aangeboden aan Prof. Dr. H. Dooyeweerd, ter gelegenheid van zijn 25-jarig hoogleraarschap aan Vrije Universiteit.
J. H. Kok, Kampen, 1951, p.279-280.
Legal Scholar Essays, presented to Prof. Dr. H. Dooyeweerd by his students on the occasion of his 25-year professorship at the Free University.

5. D. H. Th. Vollenhoven's Main Works.

1946 — *Calvinisme en Ontologie*
      Mededeelingen van de Vereeniging voor Calvinistische Wijsbegeerte, December, p.1-2.
      Calvinism and Ontology.

1933 — ‡*Het Calvinisme en de Reformatie van de Wijsbegeerte.*
      Amsterdam, H. J. Paris.
      Calvinism and the Reformation of Philosophy.

1950 — *Het Geloof. Zijn aard, zijn structuur en zijn waarde voor de wetenschap.*
      In: *Geloof en Wetenschap.* Levensbeschouwing en Levenshouding van de Academicus.
      Utrecht-Nijmegen. p.71-77.
      Belief. Its nature, structure and value for science. (In: 'Faith and Science, life-outlook and life-approach for academics').

      — ‡*Geschiedenis der wijsbegeerte.* Vol. I: Inleiding en geschiedenis der Grieksche wijsbegeerte voor Platoon en Aristoteles.
      Franeker, Wever.
      History of philosophy. I: Introduction and history of Greek philosophy before Plato and Aristotle.

1926 — *Enkele grondlijnen der kentheorie.*
      Stemmen der Tijds, 15th year, p.380-401.
      Some basic features of epistemology.

1935 — *Die Grundlagen der calvinistischen oder schriftgemäßen Philosophie.*
      Theologische Blatter, Karl Ludwig Schmidt, 14th year, p.45-56.
      The Rudiments of a Calvinist or Scriptural Philosophy.

1948 — ‡*Hoofdlijnen der Logica.*
Philosophia Reformata, 13th year, p.59-118.
Outlines of Logic.

1926 — *Logos en ratio. Beider verhouding in de geschiedenis der westersche
kentheorie.* Rede gehouden bij de aanvaarding van het
hoogleeraarsambt in de faculteit der letteren en wijsbegeerte aan de Vrije Universiteit te Amsterdam op Dins-
dag 26 oktober 1926.
Kampen, J. H. Kok.
*Logos and ratio. Their mutual relationship in the history of Western
epistemology. Lecture given at the acceptance of the post of professor in the Faculty
of Arts and Philosophy at the Free University in Amsterdam on Tuesday 26th
October 1926.*

1932 — ‡*De noodzakelijkheid eener Christelijke logica.*
Amsterdam, H. J. Paris.
The Necessity of a Christian Logic.

1951 — *Norm en natuurwet.*
Mededeelingen van de Vereeniging voor Calvinistische
Wijsbegeerte, 1951, July, p.3-6.
Norm and Natural Law.

1942 — *Psychologie en zielenleven.*
Mededeelingen van de Vereeniging voor Calvinistische
Wijsbegeerte, 1942, June, p.4-5.
Psychology and the life of the soul.

1938 — ‡*Realisme en Nominalisme.*
Philosophia Reformata, 3rd year, p.65-83; 150-165.
Realism and Nominalism.

1941 — ‡*Richtlijnen ter oriëntatie in de gangbare wijsbegeerte.*
Philosophia Reformata, 6th year, p.65-86; 7 (1942) p.9-46;
8 (1943) p.1-33.
Guidelines for orientation in contemporary philosophy.

1950 — *De souvereiniteit in eigen kring bij Kuyper en bij ons.*
Mededeelingen van de Vereeniging voor Calvinistische
Wijsbegeerte, 1950, december, p.4-7.
Sphere Sovereignty according to Kuyper and according to us.

1932 — *Taak en plaats der wijsbegeerte aan de Vrije Universiteit.*
Antirevolutionaire Staatkunde, 6th year, p.395-411.
The role and place of philosophy at the Free University.

1952 — *De visie op den Middelaar bij Kuyper en bij ons.*

Mededeelingen van de Vereeniging voor Calvinistische Wijsbegeerte, 1952, september, p.3-9; december, p.3-4.
The view of the Mediator according to Kuyper and according to us.

1929 — *De eerste vragen der psychologie.* Referaat gehouden op 9e november 1929 voor de gereformeerde psychologische studivereeniging, Loosduinen.
The primary questions of psychology. Lecture held on November 9th 1929 for the Reformed Association for the Study of Psychology.

1940 — *Wijsbegeerte en Theologie.*
Mededeelingen van de Vereeniging voor Calvinistische Wijsbegeerte, 1940, July, p.3-5.
Philosophy and Theology.

6. Critiques, Studies and Works relating to Herman Dooyeweerd's Philosophy.

M. de Mullewie, O.P., (Überschau: *Philosophie en Tijdgeest*): H. Dooyeweerd, *Reformatie en Scholastiek in de wijsbegeerte*, I; J. M. Spier, *Wat is Calvinistische Wijsbegeerte?* Ders., *Calvinisme en Existentie-Philosophie.*
Tijdschrift voor Philosophie 14 (1952), p.714-717.
(Overview: Philosophy and Zeitgeist): H. Dooyeweerd, Reformation and Scholasticism in Philosophy, I; J. M. Spier, What is Calvinist Philosophy? idem, Calvinism and Existential Philosophy.

J. D. Dengerink, *Critisch-Historisch onderzoek naar de sociologische ontwikkeling van het beginsel der 'souvereiniteit in eigen kring' in de 19e en 20e eeuw.*
Kampen, J. H. Kok, 1948.
Historical-critical study of the sociological development of the principle of sphere-sovereignty in the 19th and 20th century.

J. P. A. Mekkes, *Proeve eener critische beschouwing van de ontwikkeling der Humanistische Rechtsstaatstheorieën.*
Rotterdam, Libertas, 1940.
Examination of a critical review of the development of Humanistic Theories of the Rule of Law.

J. P. A. Mekkes, *De Wijsbegeerte en het staatsleven.*
In: *Wijsbegeerte en Levenspractijk,* J. M. Spier (Ed).
Kampen, J. H. Kok, 1948, p.76-96.
Philosophy and Political Life.

F. H. von Meyenfeldt, Het Hart (leb, lebab) in het Oude Testament.
Leiden, Brill, 1950.
Heart in the Old Testament.

K. J. Popma, *Achtergrond der Wijsbegeerte.* Rede gehouden bij de aanvaarding van het ambt van bijzonder hoogleeraar namens de stichting bijzondere leerstoelen Calvinistische Wijsbegeerte aan openbare Universiteiten en Hoogescholen, aan de Rijksuniversiteit te Groningen op 16 oktober 1948.
Antirevolutionaire Staatkunde, 19 (1949), p.188-189.
Background of Philosophy. Lecture given at the acceptance of the post of special professor, on behalf of the foundation of special chairs of Calvinistic Philosophy in Public High Schools and Universities, at the University of Groningen on 16th October 1948.

K. J. Popma, *Calvinistische Geschiedenisbeschouwing.*
Franeker, T. Wever, 1945.
Calvinistic Philosophy of History.

K. J. Popma, *Eerst de Jood, maar ook de Griek.*
Franeker, T. Wever, 1950.
First the Jew, then also the Greek.

K. J. Popma, *Historicale methode en historische continuïteit.*
Philosophia Reformata, 17th year (1952), p.97-145.
Historical method and historical continuity.

K. J. Popma, *De Oudheid en wij.*
Kampen, J. H. Kok, 1948.
Antiquity and us.

K. J. Popma, *De Plaats der Theologie.*
Franeker, T. Wever, 1946.
The Place of Theology.

H. Robbers, S.J., Book Review of H. Dooyeweerd, *Wijsbegeerte der Wetsidee II.*
Studiën 125 (1936), p.152-153.

H. Robbers, S.J., *Hoe is philosophie mogelijk?*
Algemeen Nederlands Tijdschrift voor Wijsbegeerte en Psychologie, 40 (1948), p.159-170.
How is philosophy possible?

H. Robbers, S.J., *Het natuur-genade-schema als religieus grond-motief der scholastieke wijsbegeerte.*
Studia Catholica 23 (1948), p.69-86.
The nature-grace framework as religious ground-motive of scholastic philosophy.

H. Robbers, S.J., *Neo-Thomisme en moderne wijsbegeerte.*
Utrecht-Brussel, 1951. Bibliotheek van Thomistische Wijsbegeerte.
Neo-Thomism and modern philosophy.

H. Robbers, S.J., *Christelijke philosophie in Katholieke en Calvinistische opvatting.*
Studiën 124 (1935), p.85-99.
Christian philosophy in Catholic and Calvinist opinion.

H. Robbers, S.J., *Wijsbegeerte en Openbaring.*
Utrecht-Brussel, 1948. Bibliotheek van Thomistische Wijsbegeerte.
Philosophy and Revelation.

H. Robbers, S.J., *Calvinistische Wijsbegeerte.*
Studiën 127 (1937), p.324-331.
Calvinistic Philosophy.

Sassen, Ferdinand, *Katholicisme en Wijsgeerig denken.*
Amsterdam, North-Holland Publishing, 1946.
Catholicism and philosophical thought.

J. M. Spier, *Calvinisme en Existentie-philosophie.*
Kampen, J. H. Kok, 1951.
Calvinism and existential philosophy.

J. M. Spier, *Inleiding in de Wijsbegeerte der Wetsidee.*
Kampen, J. H. Kok, 4th ed. 1950.
Introduction to the Philosophy of the Law-Idea.

J. M. Spier, *De norm voor ons geloven.*
In: Wetenschappelijke Bijdragen door leerlingen van D. H. Th. Vollenhoven aangeboden ter gelegenheid van zijn 25-jarig hoogleraarschap aan de Vrije Universiteit 1951, p.72-89.
The standard for our belief. (In: Scientific Contributions, by students of D. H. Th. Vollenhoven, presented on the occasion of his 25-year professorship at the Free University).

J. M. Spier, *De strijd om het substantiebegrip.*
Pro Ecclesia, 1941-42.
The debate over the concept of substance.

J. M. Spier, *Het substantieprobleem met name binnen het Gereformeerde denken.*
The problem of substance, particularly within Reformed thinking

J. M. Spier, *Het veld van onderzoek voor de theologie.*

Philosophia Reformata, 15th year (1950), p.169-178; 16 (1951), p.1-15.
The field of enquiry for theology.

J. M. Spier, *Wat is Calvinistische Wijsbegeerte?*
Kampen, J. H. Kok, 1950.
What is Calvinist Philosophy?

H. G. Stoker, *Die Calvinisme en di leer van die wetskringe.*
In: C P Boodt (ed.), *De Reformatie van het Calvinistisch denken*, 1939, p.38-81.
Guido de Bres Publishers, The Hague.
Calvinism and the doctrine of law-spheres. (In C. P. Boodt (ed.), The Reformation of Calvinist Thought.)

H. G. Stoker, *Teologiese, wysgerige en vakwetenskaplike etiek.* In: Wetenschappelijke Bijdragen door leerlingen van D. H. Th. Vollenhoven aangeboden ter gelegenheid van zijn 25-jarig hoogleraarschap aan de Vrije Universiteit 1951, p.44-51.
Theological, philosophical and scholarly ethics. (In: Scientific Contributions, by students of D. H. Th. Vollenhoven, presented on the occasion of his 25-year professorship at the Free University).

H. G. Stoker, *Iets oor Kousaliteit.*
Philosophia Reformata, 2nd year (1937), p.65-96.
Something about Causality.

H. G. Stoker, *Iets oor Kousaliteitskennis.*
Philosophia Reformata, 3rd year (1938), p.1-24.
Something about the Science of Causality.

H. G. Stoker, *Die wysbegeerte van die skeppingsidee; of, grond-beginsels van 'n Kalvinistiese Wysbegeerte.*
Pretoria, J. H. de Bussy, 1933.
The Philosophy of the Idea of Creation; or, Fundamental Principles of a Calvinist Philosophy.

H. G. Stoker, *Die Nuwere Wysbegeerte aan die Vrye Universiteit.* Pretoria, J. H. de Bussy, 1933.
The New Philosophy at the Free University.

H. L. van Breda, O.F.M., *Une philosophie calviniste. La 'Philosophie de l'idée de la loi'.*
Revue philosophique de Louvain 47 (1949), p.279-283.
A Calvinist Philosophy. The Philosophy of the Law-Idea.

C. van Til, *Prof. Vollenhoven's Significance for Reformed Apologetics.* In: Wetenschappelijke Bijdragen door leerlingen van D. H. Th.

Vollenhoven aangeboden ter gelegenheid van zijn 25-jarig hoogleraarschap aan de Vrije Universiteit 1951, p.68-71.
(In: Scientific Contributions, by students of D. H. Th. Vollenhoven, presented on the occasion of his 25-year professorship at the Free University).

C. Veenhof, *In Kuyper's Lijn.* Enkele opmerkingen over den invloed van Dr. A. Kuyper op de 'Wijsbegeerte der Wetsidee'.
Goes, Oosterbaan & Le Cointre, 1939.
In Kuyper's footsteps. Some observations on the influence of Dr A. Kuyper on the 'Philosophy of the Law-Idea'.

J. M. Spier (Ed), *Wijsbegeerte en Levenspractijk.* De betekenis van de wijsbegeerte der wetsidee voor velerlei levensgebied.
Kampen, J. H. Kok, 1948.
Philosophy and Practical Life. The significance of the Philosophy of Law-Idea for many areas of life.

W. Young, *Towards a Reformed Philosophy. The Development of a Protestant Philosophy in Dutch Calvinistic Thought since the time of Abraham Kuyper.*
Franeker, T. Wever and Grand Rapids, Piet Hein, 1952.

S. U. Zuidema, *Karakter van de moderne Existentie-Philosophie.*
Publications of the Reünisten Organisatie van NDDD, 1947, 18.
The character of modern existentialist philosophy.

S. U. Zuidema, *De mensch als historie.* Rede gehouden bij de aanvaarding van het ambt van buitengewoon hoogleeraar in de Facultieit der letteren en wijsbegeerte aan de Vrije Universiteit te Amsterdam op Woensdag 9 juni 1948.
Franeker, T. Wever, 1948.
Man as History. Lecture given on accepting the post of special professor in the Faculty of Arts and Philosophy at the Free University of Amsterdam on Wednesday, 9th June 1948.

S. U. Zuidema, *Nacht zonder dageraad.* Naar aanleiding van het atheïstische en nihilistisch existentialisme van Jean-Paul Sartre.
Anti-revolutionaire Staatkunde 18 (1948), p.345.
Night without dawn. On the atheistic and nihilistic existentialism of Jean-Paul Sartre

S. U. Zuidema, *Heidegger's Wijsbegeerte van het zijn.*
In: Wetenschappelijke Bijdragen door leerlingen van D. H. Th. Vollenhoven aangeboden ter gelegenheid van zijn 25-jarig hoogleraarschap aan de Vrije Universiteit 1951, p.222-243.

Heidegger's Philosophy of Existence. (In: Scientific Contributions, by students of D. H. Th. Vollenhoven, presented on the occasion of his 25-year professorship at the Free University).

Dr. Michael Fr. J. Marlet, S.J., *Grundlinien der kalvinistischen 'Philosophie der Gezetsesidee' als christlicher Transzendental- philosophie.* (Münchener theologische Studien im Auftrag der Theologischen Fakultät München; II. Systematische Abteil- ung, 8 band.)
München, Karl Zink Verlag, 1954.
Elements of the Calvinist 'Philosophy of the Law-Idea' as Christian transcendental philosophy. (Munich theological studies for the Theological Faculty of Munich; II. Systematic Section, volume 8.)

General Index

(Page numbers referring to footnotes, and book titles, are in italics.)

Index of Greek terms

Index of Latin terms

Index of Dutch terms

Index of German terms

Printed in the USA
CPSIA information can be obtained
at www.ICGtesting.com
CBHW031140060724
11231CB00010B/31